STANDARD GRADE **MODERN STUDIES**

BRITAIN

Second Edition

Jim Bryden, Kenny Elder, Brian McGovern, Duncan Murray

Series Editor: **Frank Healy**

Hodder Gibson

A MEMBER OF THE HODDER HEADLINE GROUP

The Publishers would like to thank the following for permission to reproduce copyright material:

Photo credits

Foundation/General Photographs
01.01 Molly Cooper/Photofusion; 01.02 © 2005 Scottish Parliamentary Corporate Body; 01.03 Scottish Labour Party, Scottish Liberal Democrats, Scottish Conservative Party, Scottish National Party; 01.05 PA/Empics; 01.07 © Peter Aprahamian/Corbis; 01.08 PA/Empics; 01.11 Don Gray/Photofusion; 01.14 Alex Segre/Rex Features; 01.15 PA/Empics; 01.17 © 2005 Scottish Parliamentary Corporate Body; 01.18 Michael Crabtree/PA/Empics; 01.19 Alisdair Macdonald/Rex Features; 01.20 Simon Walker/Rex Features; 01.21 PA/Empics; 01.22 PA/Empics; 01.24 Jonathan Player/Rex Features; 01.25 David Jones/ PA/Empics; 01.26 PA/Empics; 01.39 Popperfoto/Alamy; 01.40 © 2005 Scottish Parliamentary Corporate Body; 01.42 © 2005 Scottish Parliamentary Corporate Body; 01.43 © 2005 Scottish Parliamentary Corporate Body; 01.44 © 2005 Scottish Parliamentary Corporate Body; 01.45 © 2005 Scottish Parliamentary Corporate Body; 01.47 Scottish National Party; 01.51 Renfrewshire Council; 01.55 Philippe Hays/Rex Features; 01.56 Greenpeace UK; 03.05 Stan Gamester/Photofusion; 03.08 © Kim Kulish/Corbis; 03.09 Paula Solloway/Photofusion; 03.11 © Ed Kashi/Corbis; 03.15 Alex Segre/Rex Features; 03.18 Equal Opportunities Commission (EOC) Scotland; 03.22 BSIP, Tremelet/Science Photo Library; 03.25 JobCentre Plus; 03.26 Department for Work and Pensions; 03.27 Scottish Enterprise; 03.28 Scottish Enterprise; 04.08 Paula Solloway/Photofusion; 05.02 SHOUT/Alamy; 05.03 Rex Features; 05.10 David Tothill/Photofusion; 05.11 Richard Young/Rex Features; 05.13 Jim West/Alamy; 05.14 Help the Aged; 05.15 Stock Connection Distribution/Alamy.

General/Credit Photographs
01.01 PA/Empics; 01.07 Alisdair Macdonald/Rex Features; 01.08 Flying Colours/Getty Images; 01.09 David Mansell/Alamy; 01.10 David Mansell/Alamy; 01.14 © Peter Aprahamian/Corbis; 01.18 Photograph © 2005 Scottish Parliamentary Corporate Body; 01.19 David Cheskin/PA/Empics; 01.20 Photograph © 2005 Scottish Parliamentary Corporate Body; 01.21 Photograph © 2005 Scottish Parliamentary Corporate Body; 01.22 Photograph © 2005 Scottish Parliamentary Corporate Body; 01.23 Rex Features; 01.44 Shelter; 01.45 Ash Scotland; 01.46 Pete Addis/Photofusion; 01.47 Molly Cooper/Photofusion; 01.48 Photofusion Picture Library/Alamy; 01.49 Friends of the Earth; 02.01 James Fraser/Rex Features; 03.04 Fresh Talent/Scottish Executive; 03.17 David Cheskin/PA/Empics; 03.18 David Cheskin /PA/Empics; 03.35 Scottish Enterprise; 03.36 Scottish Enterprise; 05.09 Jim West/Alamy; 05.10 Rex Features; 05.11 Help the Aged; 05.12 AllOver photography/Alamy.

Acknowledgements
Artworks by Jeff Edwards and Fakenham Photosetting Ltd.

Every effort has been made to trace all copyright holders, but if any have been inadvertently overlooked the Publishers will be pleased to make the necessary arrangements at the first opportunity.

Although every effort has been made to ensure that website addresses are correct at time of going to press, Hodder Gibson cannot be held responsible for the content of any website mentioned in this book. It is sometimes possible to find a relocated web page by typing in the address of the home page for a website in the URL window of your browser.

Orders: please contact Bookpoint Ltd, 130 Milton Park, Abingdon, Oxon OX14 4SB. Telephone: (44) 01235 827720. Fax: (44) 01235 400454. Lines are open from 9.00 – 6.00, Monday to Saturday, with a 24-hour message answering service. Visit our website at www.hoddereducation.co.uk. Hodder Gibson can be contacted direct on: Tel: 0141 848 1609; Fax: 0141 889 6315; email: hoddergibson@hodder.co.uk

© Frank Healy, Jim Bryden, Kenny Elder, Brian McGovern and Duncan Murray 2006
First edition published 1997
(0340 655577)
This edition published in 2006 by
Hodder Gibson, a member of the Hodder Headline Group
2a Christie Street
Paisley PA1 1NB

Impression number   10 9 8 7 6 5 4 3 2 1
Year   2010 2009 2008 2007 2006

Cover photos from Photodisk, Getty Images and Still Digital
Typeset in 11 point Galliard by Fakenham Photosetting Limited, Fakenham, Norfolk
Printed and bound in Dubai
A catalogue record for this title is available from the British Library

ISBN-10: 0 340-81435-7
ISBN-13: 978-0-340-814352

Contents Foundation/General

1 Representation and Participation at National and Local Level   **1**

Democracy   1
Constitutional Monarchy   2
Structure of British Government   3
Making a Law – Legislation   7
The Work of Parliament   9
How Equal is Parliament?   10
Inside the House of Commons   13
Pressures on our Representatives   16
Political Parties   18
The House of Lords   20
The British Electoral System   21
How Fair is the British Electoral System?   23
The Scottish Parliament   27
Local Government   33
Pressure Groups   40

2 Participation at Work: Trade Unions   **85**

Types of Union   87
Trade Union Negotiations and Industrial Action   88
How are Individual Trade Unions Organised?   89
The Trade Union Congress   89
Changes in Union Membership   90
Conservatives and Trade Unions   92
The Labour Party and Trade Unions   92
Trade Unions and Europe   94

3 Employment/Unemployment   **112**

The Labour Force   112
Who are the Unemployed?   112
Changing Patterns of Employment   114
The North–South Divide   115
New Technology   117
Unemployment in Europe   121
Employment by Industry   123
Inequality in the Workplace   124
Age and Employment   128
Disability and Employment   130
Low Pay   131
Helping the Unemployed   133

4 Families with Dependent Children   **166**

The Family   166
Income   169
Childcare and Employment   170
Benefits   171
The Child Support Agency   173
Pressure Groups   173

5 The Elderly   **183**

Population Changes   183
The Elderly in Scotland   184
Problems Facing the Elderly – the Needs of the Elderly   186
Meeting the Health Care Needs of the Elderly   189
Meeting the Elderly's Financial Needs   193
Fight for the 'Grey Vote'   195
Voluntary Organisations/ Pressure Groups   195
Inequality in Retirement   196
Ageing Europe   197

FOUNDATION/GENERAL

Contents General/Credit

1 Representation and Participation at National and Local Level 43

Democracy	43
Constitutional Monarchy	43
Structure of British Government	44
Making a Law – Legislation	47
The Work of Parliament	48
How Equal is Parliament?	50
Inside the House of Commons	51
Pressures on our Representatives	53
Political Parties	57
The House of Lords	58
The British Electoral System	61
How Fair is the British Electoral System?	62
The Scottish Parliament	66
Local Government	73
Pressure Groups	80

2 Representation in the Workplace 95

Types of Union	95
Trade Union Negotiations and Industrial Action	96
How are Individual Trade Unions organised?	99
The Trade Union Congress	102
Changes in Union Membership	103
Conservatives and Trade Unions	106
The Labour Party and Trade Unions	107
Trade Unions and Europe	109

3 Employment and Unemployment 138

The Labour Force	138
Who are the Unemployed?	138
Changing Patterns of Employment	139
The North–South Divide	140
New Technology	142
Unemployment in Europe	145
Employment by Industry	147
Inequality in the Workplace	148
Age and Employment	155
Disability and Employment	156
Low Pay	158
Helping the Unemployed	159

4 Families with Dependent Children 175

The Family	175
Income	178
Childcare and Employment	178
Benefits	179
The Child Support Agency	180
Pressure Groups	182

5 The Elderly 199

Population Changes	199
The Elderly in Scotland	200
Problems Facing the Elderly – the Needs of the Elderly	202
Meeting the Health Care Needs of the Elderly	205
Meeting the Elderly's Financial Needs	210
Fight For the Grey Vote	213
Voluntary Organisations/Pressure Groups	214
Inequality in Retirement	215
Ageing Europe	216

Investigating on the Web	219
Index	221

Representation and Participation at National and Local Level

Democracy

The word democracy means 'rule by the people'. Britain is a democracy because the voting public (electorate) have a say in how the country is run. They do this by voting for people to represent them in political assemblies such as the European Parliament, the UK Parliament in London, the Scottish Parliament in Edinburgh and in our local councils. Of course, not everyone in the country has a say in how Britain is run, but we will look at this question later within this section.

Members of the public in the UK may also be involved with a trade union or a pressure group and take part in protests over issues they feel strongly about. These issues may be local, national or international, for example, the closure of a school or hospital or protests against the Iraq War.

Representative Democracy

Britain is a **representative democracy** which means that the voters – people 18 years of age and older – choose a representative to speak on their behalf at one of the political assemblies. In this way they have a say in how the country is run.

Some people are not allowed to vote:

◆ people in prison
◆ members of the House of Lords
◆ people in mental institutions
◆ people who have not registered to vote.

Representatives normally, but not always, belong to a **political party**. Some representatives are independent, like the MSP shown in Figure 1.2.

Figure 1.1 Protest against Iraq War

Figure 1.2 Dennis Canavan, Independent MSP for Falkirk West

The major parties are shown in Figure 1.3.

Figure 1.3 The major political parties

Some smaller parties in Scotland include the Scottish Socialist Party and the Green Party.

Each political party tries to appeal to the voters in a **manifesto**. The party uses its manifesto to try and gain support of the necessary number of voters to win the **election** (general election or by-election). Nevertheless, since 1945 no British political party has gained more than 50 per cent of the votes in a general election. In 2005, the Labour Party gained only 35 per cent of the vote, but got more seats than the other parties and became the government.

Elections occur quite often in Britain and Figure 1.4 gives a good idea of the main types of elections. The political party that wins the general election becomes the government and it runs Britain for a maximum of five years. Our present Government is run by the Labour Party, who have been in power since 1997. Labour won the general election in June 2001, which meant that the next election had to be called by May 2006. The Prime Minister can call the election early, and he did this time, it happened on May 5th 2005.

By-elections are only held if an MP resigns their seat or dies.

Type of election	Area covered	Title of representative
European elections	European Union	Member of European Parliament (MEP)
General Elections	United Kingdom	Member of Parliament (MP)
Scottish Parliament	Scotland	Member of Scottish Parliament (MSP)
Council elections	Local area	Councillor

Figure 1.4 Types of elections in the UK

Voter Apathy

A recent concern in British elections, whether it be at a council level or at national level, is the voter **turnout** – the difference between the number of people who are eligible to vote and the number of people who actually vote.

In 2005, only 61.3 per cent of the people eligible to vote did so, in 1997 it was 71.4 per cent and in 2001 it was 59.4 per cent. This voter **apathy** is a worry in a democratic system. One suggestion to ensure a bigger turnout is to fine those people who do not vote in the elections. Other suggestions include the use of online ballot papers and increased use of postal voting.

Constitutional Monarchy

Britain is also a **constitutional monarchy** but this does not have an effect on our representative democracy. All that this means is that Britain has a Head of State, the Queen, but she does not have anything to do with running the country. The government does that.

The Queen has a small number of roles to play in the political system. The main one is to sign all of the new laws that have passed, this is known as giving the **Royal Assent**, in other words giving approval by the Head of State.

Figure 1.5 State opening of parliament

Activities

1   What does the word 'democracy' mean? *(1 mark)*

2   How can the UK be seen as a democracy? *(2 marks)*

3   List three ways that UK citizens can participate in politics?   *(3 marks)*

4   Why is the electorate smaller than the UK population?   *(2 marks)*

5   How do voters choose their representatives? *(2 marks)*

6   What are the conditions that must be met before a person is allowed to vote? *(2 marks)*

7   Using the information from Figure 1.4, answer the following questions:
    a) What is an MSP? *(1 mark)*
    b) What do the initials MEP stand for? *(1 mark)*

8   Who is the head of state in the UK? *(1 mark)*

9   Explain what is meant by the term Royal Assent. *(2 marks)*

Structure of British Government

Separation of Powers

The government is divided into three separate parts, each has a different role to play in running the country.

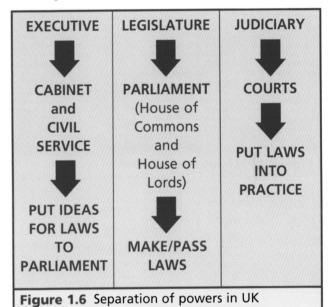

Figure 1.6 Separation of powers in UK government

1 – Parliament – the Legislature

The legislature is that part of government which looks at ideas and suggestions for a new law and decides whether or not they should become a law. The ideas for a new law are called **bills**.

Bills usually come from the **manifesto** of the political party in power but can also come from other groups who want to change the law for one reason or another, for example, pressure groups like Help the Aged, or professional groups like the Law Society. In Scotland, the Scottish Parliament also makes laws in the same way as the Westminster Parliament, but with no House of Lords.

House of Commons

The House of Commons is made of Members of Parliament – the political representatives who have been elected by the voting public. At present there are 646 MPs, each representing a **constituency** which is also known as a 'seat'.

FOUNDATION/GENERAL

3

House of Lords

The members of the Lords are not elected. To become a member of the Lords you need to have a 'title' such as Baroness or Duke. The name given to a person who holds a title is a **peer**.

Figure 1.7 The House of Lords

In 2002, there were about 750 peers in the Lords, down from 1200 in the late 1990s. In November 2001, the government produced a White Paper recommending the reform of the House of Lords. Recommendations included the following:

- reduced membership of the Lords to about 600 peers
- the 92 hereditary peers to be removed
- number of bishops to be reduced to 16
- direct elections of 20 per cent of the members (120 Peers)
- another 20 per cent of members to be appointed by the new Appointments Commission.
- remaining 60 per cent (360 Peers) to be selected by political parties based on their share of the votes at the 2001 general election.

In December 2002, the House of Lords was made up of:

- 550 Life peers – usually made a member of the House of Lords by a government for their 'lifetime'
- 91 hereditary peers – a member of the House of Lords because he/she has inherited the title from a relative who has died
- 28 Law Lords (top judges) and
- 24 archbishops and bishops of the Church of England.

2 – The Monarch

The monarch's role is to open parliament, read the King or Queen's Speech, which sets out the government's bills for the session, and finally to give Royal Assent to bills to allow them to become laws.

The Executive

The government runs the country and makes important decisions about how our taxes are spent.

The government's ideas for laws are proposed as bills which are put before Parliament in the hope of becoming a law.

There are over 1000 members of the two Houses of Parliament but only about 100 of these are in the government, known as the Executive. The most senior members of the government are in the **Cabinet**.

Members of the Cabinet are chosen by the Prime Minister. Most come from the House of Commons but a small number are from the House of Lords. All are members of the Labour Party, the political party in power since 1997.

Since the Cabinet re-shuffle after the 2005 general election, there are 23 members of the Cabinet. However the Cabinet can have a larger or smaller number of members. The Prime Minister, who is also the leader of the Cabinet, decides on who is going to be in the Cabinet.

The Civil Service supports the executive by carrying out the administrative duties, offering advice and information to Ministers, and carrying out research for departments.

Senior member of the government run a department and are called **Ministers**. There are also some Ministers without Portfolio who do not have a specific department to run. The shaded box below shows the composition of the 2005 Cabinet and the government departments run by Ministers.

The Judiciary

The Judiciary is made up of the judges and the courts. The House of Lords has a very important role to play because it is the highest court of appeal in the UK, except for criminal cases in Scotland. The Lord Chancellor, shown in the House of Lords in Figure 1.8, has a similar job to the Speaker in the House of Commons.

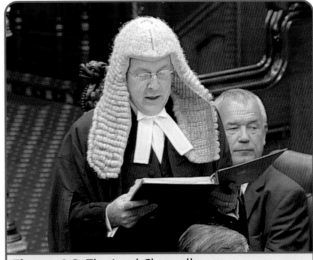

Figure 1.8 The Lord Chancellor

Tony Blair – Prime Minister, First Lord of the Treasury and Minister for the Civil Service

John Prescott – Deputy Prime Minister and First Secretary of State

Gordon Brown – Chancellor of the Exchequer

Geoff Hoon – Leader of the House of Commons and Lord Privy Seal

Lord Falconer of Thoroton QC – Secretary of State for Constitutional Affairs and Lord Chancellor

Jack Straw – Secretary of State for Foreign and Commonwealth Affairs

Charles Clarke – Secretary of State for the Home Department

Margaret Beckett – Secretary of State for Environment, Food and Rural Affairs

Hilary Benn – Secretary of State for International Development

David Blunkett – Secretary of State for Work and Pensions

Alistair Darling – Secretary of State for Transport and Secretary of State for Scotland

Patricia Hewitt – Secretary of State for Health

Peter Hain – Secretary of State for Northern Ireland and Secretary of State for Wales

John Reid – Secretary of State for Defence

Baroness Amos – Leader of the House of Lords and Lord President of the Council

Alan Johnson – Secretary of State for Trade and Industry

Ruth Kelly – Secretary of State for Education and Skills

Tessa Jowell – Secretary of State for Culture, Media and Sport

Hilary Armstrong – Parliamentary Secretary to the Treasury (Chief Whip)

Ian McCartney – Minister without Portfolio

John Hutton – Chancellor of the Duchy of Lancaster (Minister for the Cabinet Office)

Des Brown – Chief Secretary to the Treasury

David Miliband – Minister of Communities and Local Government

Also attending Cabinet:

Lord Goldsmith – Attorney General

Douglas Alexander – Minister of State for Europe in the Foreign and Commonwealth Office

Lord Grocott – Lords Chief Whip and Captain of the Gentleman at Arms

The judiciary is separate from Parliament and it is responsible for interpreting British and European law.

Sometimes the judiciary and the executive can come into conflict when a member of the Government acts illegally and the courts rule against them. An example of this type of disagreement occurred quite recently when the former Home Secretary, David Blunkett, was judged to be acting illegally by deporting asylum seekers before they could put their case for asylum in the UK properly to the courts.

Although we talk about the executive and the judiciary being separate, some members of the judiciary are appointed by the leader of the Executive, the Prime Minister (PM). Examples of PM appointments to the judiciary are the Attorney-General and the Solicitor-General.

Activities

1 Name the three parts of the British government. *(3 marks)*

2 Which part of the government is responsible for:
a) interpreting the laws of the UK and the European Union? *(1 mark)*
b) putting bills forward to parliament? *(1 mark)*
c) making the laws? *(1 mark)*

3 Which two bodies make up parliament? *(2 marks)*

4 What are members of the House of Lords called? *(1 mark)*

5 In what way has the Lords changed? *(2 marks)*

6 List four government departments. *(2 marks)*

7 Who is the leader of the cabinet and what is his name? *(2 marks)*

8 What does the civil service do? *(3 marks)*

9 What role does the House of Lords have in the justice system? *(2 marks)*

10 Who is the leader of the Lords? *(1 mark)*

11 What evidence is there to show that the executive and the judiciary are not separate? *(2 marks)*

How Does a Political Party Become the Government?

After a general election, the political party which wins most of the seats (constituencies) in the House of Commons is asked to form the government. At present there are 646 constituencies in the UK and a political party has to win 324 of these to form the government.

If a party had 324 seats it would have an overall majority of one seat. An overall majority means that the political party which has formed the government has more seats than all of the other political parties' added together. Figure 1.9 shows the results from the 2001 and 2005 general elections.

Political party	2001 General Election Number of Seats won	2005 General Election Number of Seats won
Conservative	166	197
Labour	412	356
Liberal Democrats	52	62
SNP	5	6
Others	24	24

Figure 1.9 General election results: 2001 and 2005

The political party with the second largest number of seats becomes Her Majesty's Official Opposition. Their job is to scrutinise and 'keep tabs' on the work of the government.

The job of government is to run the country for the next five years (this is the maximum amount of time between general elections). The government will introduce new laws and these will mainly come from the party's election promises made in their **manifesto**.

Each political party has its own manifesto which outlines what the party's policies are and what it would do if elected. The voters will look at the party's policies before deciding who to vote for. In 1997, 2001 and 2005 the electorate must have felt that Labour's manifesto promises were more appealing than other parties.

Figure 1.10 General election results: percentage of votes cast for each party in 2005

Activities

1 What is the other name for a 'seat'? *(1 mark)*

2 How many MPs are there in the UK? *(2 marks)*

3 How does a political party become the government? *(2 marks)*

4 How many seats are required for a political party to have an 'overall majority'? *(2 marks)*

5 From Figure 1.9 answer the following questions:
   a) which political parties lost seats in 2005? *(3 marks)*
   b) which political parties gained seats in 2005? *(2 marks)*
   c) which political party became the government? *(2 marks)*
   d) what was the majority of the winning party? *(2 marks)*

6 What is the maximum amount of time between general elections? *(1 mark)*

7 Explain what a manifesto is. *(2 marks)*

8 From Figure 1.10 what were the percentages of votes won by the three major political parties in 2005? *(3 marks)*

Making a Law – Legislation

Most laws are made by parliament – this happens in the House of Commons and House of Lords. Parliament is also known as the **legislature**. This means that parliament is the law-making body.

Before a new law receives the Royal Assent it is known as a **bill**. Most of the bills that go to parliament are the ones that the ruling government want and they are likely to come from the manifesto. There are three main types of bills:

1 Government Bills

Ideas for a new law which the government puts forward. Most bills come from the government. For example, in 1997, the Labour Government passed a new law which allowed the establishment of a Scottish Parliament.

2 Private Members Bills:

Ideas for a new law which are put forward by individual MPs. Not all MPs can put forward this type of bill. Each year all MPs names are put into a hat and a number are drawn out. The names which are drawn out of the hat have the opportunity to put forward their own bill, they are responsible for writing it out and getting support from other MPs for the bill.

Private Members bills which don't have the government's backing usually fail to become a law. Government and Private Members bills usually affect most people in the country.

Some bills become laws because of emergencies. For example, in 2001 the spread of Foot and Mouth disease in sheep led to emergency legislation in an attempt to stop the spread in Britain. Emergency legislation was also passed to cope with terrorism, especially after the September 11th attacks on the USA.

Figure 1.11 The Foot and Mouth outbreak in 2001

3 Private Bills:

These bills usually deal with by-laws and local council legislation. For example, a recent by-law in Renfrewshire banned drinking alcohol in public places unless on licensed premises.

Government bills and Private Members bills are known as **public bills** because the resulting law (when passed) would affect the whole of British society – the general public. Figure 1.12 shows the number of public bills introduced and those which became law.

How a Bill Becomes Law – Legislative Process

The original idea for a new law may be put forward in a **Green Paper** and all the people involved or affected by the idea are asked to give their opinion on it, such as MPs and interested groups. A proposed new law becomes a document called a **White Paper** which is presented to parliament at the First Reading.

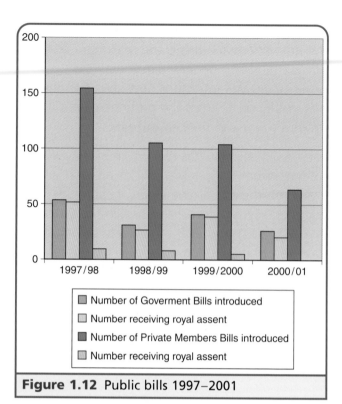

Legend:
- ■ Number of Goverment Bills introduced
- □ Number receiving royal assent
- ■ Number of Private Members Bills introduced
- □ Number receiving royal assent

Figure 1.12 Public bills 1997–2001

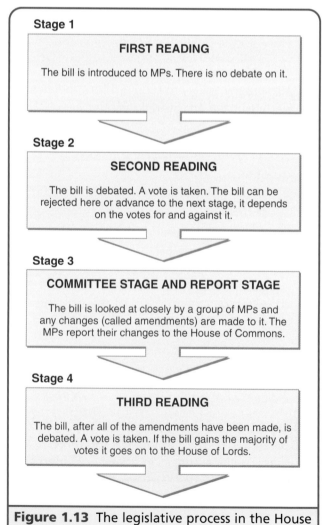

Stage 1

FIRST READING

The bill is introduced to MPs. There is no debate on it.

Stage 2

SECOND READING

The bill is debated. A vote is taken. The bill can be rejected here or advance to the next stage, it depends on the votes for and against it.

Stage 3

COMMITTEE STAGE AND REPORT STAGE

The bill is looked at closely by a group of MPs and any changes (called amendments) are made to it. The MPs report their changes to the House of Commons.

Stage 4

THIRD READING

The bill, after all of the amendments have been made, is debated. A vote is taken. If the bill gains the majority of votes it goes on to the House of Lords.

Figure 1.13 The legislative process in the House of Commons

In the House of Lords the whole process is repeated again. Any amendments made to the bill in the House of Lords are looked at when the bill goes back to the House of Commons and these are discussed. If there are no amendments the bill will go from the House of Lords to the Queen for the Royal Assent.

Once a bill has Royal Assent it becomes a law and goes to the **Statute Book** where all laws are written.

Figure 1.14 The Palace of Westminster

Activities

1 Where are laws made? *(2 marks)*

2 What is another name for laws? *(1 mark)*

3 How important is the manifesto of the political party that wins the general election in the making of new laws? *(2 marks)*

4 What are the main types of bills? *(3 marks)*

5 Explain the difference between a Public and a Private bill. *(2 marks)*

6 From Figure 1.12 answer the following questions:
   a) Which type of public bill has least success in becoming law? *(2 marks)*
   b) Which type of public bill has most success in becoming law? *(2 marks)*

7 Why do Private Members bills have difficulty becoming law? *(2 marks)*

8 Not all new legislation comes from the manifesto – why? *(3 marks)*

9 What is a white paper? *(2 marks)*

10 List the main stages that a bill must go through. *(4 marks)*

The Work of Parliament

Parliament has a number of duties to perform and these can be listed under a number of key areas.

Making laws – the Queen, the Lords and the Commons all have to agree to any new law that is passed.

Examining the work of the government – the Lords and the Commons examine the work of the government on behalf of the British public. They ask questions, take part in debates and are members of committees which look closely at the work of the government.

Parliament challenges the government and asks it to explain its policies. This role is known as **scrutiny**, an example of this is 'Question Time' where MPs have the opportunity to question government ministers about their department's activities. For example, in 2003 and 2004 Jack Straw, the Foreign Secretary was regularly questioned about the British army's role in Iraq.

'Prime Minister's Question Time' is held once a week, giving MPs the chance to ask questions of the leader of the government. On January 28th 2004 there was a very challenging 'Question Time' for Tony Blair when he was asked about the report following the Hutton Inquiry into claims by a BBC reporter that the government had exaggerated the threat posed by Iraq.

Control of finance – only the Commons can give permission to collect taxes and decide how the money is spent.

Protecting the public – the interests of the public are protected by MPs when they examine

Figure 1.15 Tony Blair answering questions at the 'dispatch box' during Prime Minister's Question Time

6 Name the following politicians: Prime Minister, Leader of the Opposition and the Foreign Secretary. *(3 marks)*

7 Which of the two Houses of Parliament has no say in the collection of taxes? *(1 mark)*

8 Why does parliament have to examine European Union proposals? *(2 marks)*

9 What is the highest court of appeal in Britain? *(1 mark)*

10 Which cases are not looked at by the court of appeal at the House of Lords? *(2 marks)*

the work of the government. Complaints made to MPs can be investigated by parliament.

Following European Union Proposals – the Commons and Lords also have committees which look at the proposals for new European laws. Sometimes UK laws have to be changed in light of new European law.

Debating Current Affairs – parliament debates on national and international issues. Since the invasion of Iraq in 2003 there have been a number of debates on this international issue. A national issue that has been debated is the introduction of top-up fees for students in England and Wales.

Hearing Appeals – the House of Lords is the highest appeal court in the UK. It hears appeals on all cases except Scottish criminal cases.

Activities

1 List the duties of parliament. *(3 marks)*

2 Explain the term scrutiny. *(3 marks)*

3 What is Prime Minister's Question Time? *(2 marks)*

4 Give two examples of issues that have been raised at Question Time. *(2 marks)*

5 Why was January 28th 2004 important for the Prime Minister? *(3 marks)*

How Equal is Parliament?

Figure 1.16 lists political parties and seats won after the 2005 general election. The table does not show that only 19 per cent of all MPs are women and under 2% are from ethnic minority backgrounds. Is this fair?

Party	Seats won
Labour	356
Conservative	197
Liberal Democrats	63
Democratic Unionists	9
SNP	6
Sinn Fein	5
Plaid Cymru	3
SDLP	3
Ulster Unionists	1
Others	3

Figure 1.16 Parties and seats in the House of Commons, 2005
Source www.open.gov.uk

FOUNDATION/GENERAL

The total number of MPs includes 125 women and 15 from ethnic minorities. The British population is about 51 per cent female and 49 per cent male. In the House of Commons these are just under 19 per cent women and about 81 per cent men. Is this fair?

At the general election of 2005 the number of female MPs rose from 118 to 125. In Scotland the number of female MPs fell from 11 to 9 – 8 Labour and 1 Liberal Democrat.

In almost every other European country, except Ireland and France, parliaments have a large percentage of MPs who are female. In Sweden 43 per cent of MPs are female. In the Scottish Parliament 37 per cent of MSPs are female.

Why Are There So Few Women MPs?

Women face the same difficulties in politics as they would in any other job. Some of the reasons for this include:

◆ bringing up a family

◆ running the home

◆ lack of contacts to help them get into politics

◆ amount of time required to be a politician means less time with their family

◆ the centre of British politics is London and this is too far away for most women to continue family commitments

◆ women tend to be less well paid than men and politics can be expensive

◆ selection – committees tend to be male dominated.

The Labour Party wants to increase the number of women in politics and has introduced **positive action** to try to improve the chances for women in politics.

Positive Action

Methods used in Britain and elsewhere in Europe include:

◆ all-women shortlists – selection committees select only female candidates

◆ twinning – two constituencies located close together choose two candidates – one male and one female

◆ clustering – a number of constituency selection committees choose a number of female candidates.

All of these methods relate to the 'First Past the Post' voting system (FPP).

Zipping is another possible method. It is used under Proportional Representation (PR) and the candidates selected on the list are alternately male then female.

Positive action was needed because women were discriminated against in the **selection process** so were not given the chance to show how good an MP they could be. If parliament is to be truly representative of the British population then **positive action** is necessary.

From a Scottish perspective women appear to be progressing towards greater equality at the Scottish Parliament.

Figure 1.17 Rosie Kane, Scottish Socialist Party List MSP

Scottish Women: Fact File

- 37 per cent of MSPs are female
- over 50 per cent of the Scottish population are female
- 41 per cent of hospital consultants under 35 are female
- for every pound earned by a man in Scotland a women only earns 80 pence
- over 50 per cent of secondary school teachers are female but only 10 per cent are headteachers.
- 33 per cent of all new police officers are female
- 90 per cent of single parents are female.

Activities

1   What was the government majority in the 2005 election?   *(1 mark)*

2   What percentage of MPs are women or from ethnic minorities?   *(2 marks)*

3   Did the number of women MPs increase or decrease in the 2005 general election? *(2 marks)*

4   How are Britain, France and Ireland different from most other European countries? *(2 marks)*

5   In terms of women representatives, how does the Scottish Parliament differ from the British one?   *(2 marks)*

6   Give three reasons why women find it difficult to become MPs?   *(3 marks)*

7   What does 'positive action' for women mean?   *(2 marks)*

8   Give two methods of 'positive action'. *(2 marks)*

Ethnic Minorities

At the 2005 general election only fifteen MPs from ethnic minority backgrounds were elected. In 1992 there were only six. Thirteen of these MPs came from the Labour Party – two from the Conservative Party. In terms of their share in the British population there should be 44 Black and Asian MPs.

Why do candidates from an ethnic minority background find it so difficult to be chosen as candidates or representatives in the British political system? One person who has an opinion on this is Neelam Bakshi who was a local government councillor in the 1990s:

If the political system represented the numbers of the ethnic minorities in the British population they would have 30 MPs.

Political parties do not select ethnic minority candidates because of institutionalised racist practices.

There has to be a way to increase the number of ethnic minority MPs to allow them to become fully involved in all political parties so that they can play a bigger part in society.

Source: Abridged – *The Herald* 11 November 1995

2 per cent of Scotland's population are from ethnic minorities. There is only 1 ethnic minority MP, Mohammed Sarwar, Labour MP for the Central constituency in Glasgow. Mr Sarwar became the first Scottish Asian MP.

The Scottish Nationalist Party (SNP) have also tried to bring the ethnic minorities into the political system. As well as selecting Asian candidates for election they set up 'Scots Asians for Independence' in the 1990s but as yet there are no MSPs from ethnic minority backgrounds.

Disabled Representatives

Another group in society which has not yet gained equality in the political arena are the disabled.

Figure 1.18 Anne Begg MP

At present there are two very high profile MPs who have a disability. One is Anne Begg (shown in Figure 1.18) Labour MP for Aberdeen South who is in a wheel chair.

Figure 1.19 David Blunkett MP

Another high profile MP is David Blunkett, the former Home Secretary, who is blind. He was

appointed Secretary of State for Works and Pensions after the 2005 General Election (Figure 1.19).

Activities

1 How many ethnic minority MPs would there be if their share of seats reflected their share of the British population? *(2 marks)*

2 What has the SNP done to increase the number of Asians in Scottish politics? *(2 marks)*

3 Name two high profile disabled MPs. *(2 marks)*

Inside the House of Commons

Figure 1.20 The chamber of the House of Commons

The House of Commons is the chamber where the elected representatives (MPs) sit. The Government and its MPs sit on one side of the chamber with all the opposition parties sitting across from them (see Figure 1.20). The main opposition party sits directly opposite with the other opposition parties to the side.

The House of Commons is a debating chamber and usually a vote is taken at the end of a debate. The MPs vote by going though one of two lobbies. This type of voting is called a division and the Aye (in favour) and the No (against) lobbies are called **division lobbies**.

As MPs file out into the division lobbies, they are counted by tellers who inform the **Speaker** who announces the result of the vote.

Front Benches

Figure 1.21 Labour's front benches

The MPs who sit on the front benches are usually the promoted MPs who may be in the Cabinet. They are usually in control of a government department (Ministers) and they speak on matters connected to that department. For example, the Foreign Minister will speak on the situation in Iraq.

The Opposition also have promoted MPs on their front benches and they may be in the **Shadow Cabinet**. Just like the government's Foreign Minister, the Shadow Foreign Minister will question or give his or her views on the situation in Iraq.

Backbenchers

Backbenchers are unpromoted MPs and they sit on the same side as their political party, behind those in the front-benches. The majority of MPs sit on the 'back-benches' in the House of Commons, behind the leaders of their party. This explains why they are called **backbenchers**.

Figure 1.22 Backbench MPs

The Whip System

The ordinary MP can normally be expected to follow the **party line**, meaning that they vote in the way that the leader of their party wants. But to make sure that MPs vote as expected, there are the **Chief Whips** and **Whips** of each party to make sure this happens.

Along with the party's Chief Whip, who is a member of the Cabinet or Shadow Cabinet, there are a number of Whips to help keep the MPs in line. One of the jobs of the Whips is to keep the backbench MPs informed of important debates in the House of Commons. To do this each MP receives a written notice of the debates that will soon occur in the House of Commons. These notices are also called Whips.

One-line whip:
lets MPs know that a vote will take place.

Two-line whip:
lets MPs know that they should attend unless they have made an arrangement with an 'opposite' MP not to attend. This is called a pair. The Whip's office must approve this.

Three-line whip:
MPs must attend.

There are times when MPs do not want to vote with their party, and if they are determined to do so may vote with the opposition. Some may **abstain** (not vote). The recent situation with regard to student top-up fees may have lead to some Labour MPs abstaining rather than voting against the Government.

Labour whip is 'like a bouncer'

The man charged with ensuring Tony Blair is not defeated over university top-up fees was last night accused of behaving like a 'nightclub bouncer'.

As the Prime Minister's allies launched a last-minute drive to avoid defeat in Tuesday's Commons vote, rebels claimed the Government was using dirty tricks to buy off dissidents.

Deputy Chief Whip Bob Ainsworth has been given the job of prowling the Commons corridors on Tuesday, using his hardman reputation to cow rebel MPs. The ex-sheet metal worker has already faced claims of bullying.

Ex-Labour MP and Independent MSP Dennis Canavan claimed Mr Ainsworth once stood in his way in front of a voting lobby. 'He used his bulk to block my way in an intimidatory fashion when I went towards the division lobby,' Mr Canavan said. 'He said to me: "You must vote in our lobby". I said to him: 'Don't you dare stand in my way and tell me how to vote, get out of my bloody way before I haul you before the Speaker".

'He behaved more like a Soho nightclub bouncer than an MP. I only hope he doesn't try to do the same thing on Tuesday.'

Figure 1.23 A newspaper article from 25th January 2004
Source: *Mail on Sunday*

MPs also have another choice – they can rebel against their own party line. Figure 1.23 shows just how far Whips will go to make sure that party discipline is achieved.

The actual voting on top-up fees for students saw a rebellion of 72 Labour MPs voting against their own party – Labour. The Government won the vote on the second reading of the Higher Education Bill by just 5 votes – 316 to 311 votes.

Rebel MPs may be disciplined if they vote against the party. They may 'lose the Whip' which means that they will receive no information about events in the House of Commons, get no secretarial support or, in extreme circumstances, they may be de-selected by the constituency party, that is, not put forward by the party to stand as an MP in the next election.

In November 2003, 62 Labour MPs voted against the Government during the vote on NHS foundation hospitals. The largest rebellion against Mr Blair's Government was in March 2003 in a vote about the Iraq War. The *Evening Times* stated that 133 Labour MPs voted against the Government. The vote was won only because the Conservative Party backed the Government.

Her Majesty's Opposition

The political party which receives the second largest number of seats at a general election is known as the Her Majesty's Opposition. The Conservative Party won 197 seats at the 2005 General Election and became Her Majesty's Opposition.

Michael Howard was the leader of the Conservative Party at the 2005 General Election. He replaced Iain Duncan Smith in November 2003. Mr Howard is the Leader of the Shadow Cabinet, also known as 'the alternative government in waiting'.

The aims of the opposition and other parties such as the Liberal Democrats are to:

◆ criticise and scrutinise government policy

◆ seek amendments (changes) to government bills

◆ put forward its own ideas to improve their chances of winning the next general election.

The leader of the opposition has only a few official duties but he can work with the government in arranging business in the House of Commons.

Activities

1 Where in the Commons do promoted MPs sit? *(1 mark)*

2 What is the Shadow Cabinet? *(2 marks)*

3 Who sits on the 'backbenches' in the Commons? *(1 mark)*

4 What is meant by the 'party line'? *(2 marks)*

5 What is the job of the party Whips (the people not the notices)? *(2 marks)*

6 List the three types of Whip notices and state which one is most important. *(4 marks)*

7 What choices are open to an MP who does not agree with their party's policy? *(2 marks)*

8 From Figure 1.23, how did the Deputy Chief Whip try to prevent a rebel MP from voting? *(4 marks)*

9 What happened in the vote on the second reading of the Higher Education Bill? *(2 marks)*

10 Name the other two examples of rebellions by Labour MPs which have occurred recently. *(2 marks)*

11 Who is the Opposition party? *(2 marks)*

12 Who is the Leader of the Opposition? *(1 mark)*

13 What is the Shadow Cabinet? *(2 marks)*

14 Name two other opposition parties apart from the Conservatives. *(2 marks)*

Pressures on our Representatives

At each level of political activity there are pressures placed on our representatives:

◆ councillors represent a ward with a few thousand constituents

◆ MSPs represent about 67,000 constituents

◆ MPs also represent about 67,000 constituents

◆ MEPs represent about 500,000 constituents (7 MEPs for the whole of Scotland).

The successful **candidate** at any election therefore has a lot of responsibilities to his or her constituents. This means:

◆ voting at council/parliament level in a way the constituents would want

◆ attending regular debates and participating in votes

◆ supporting their political party in debates and votes

◆ attending local constituency events.

We can divide the work of an MP into two parts:

◆ working in the constituency

◆ working in Parliament.

Working in the Constituency

Constituency work is mainly carried out at the weekend or holidays. The average number of

Figure 1.24 An MP working in his constituency

16

people in a constituency is about 65,000 although constituencies held by a Conservative MP tend to be more rural (and so cover a larger area) and the number is then 72,000. Representing such a large number can be difficult. To do this, MPs:

◆ hold surgeries
◆ attend group meetings
◆ attend local events
◆ listen to pressure groups
◆ undertake administrative duties.

Speaking out at meetings (debates)

Voting in Parliament

Constituents

Party Whips

Pressure Groups

Conscience

Figure 1.25 Pressures on an MP

Working in Parliament

Most MPs spend Monday to Friday in London. The House of Commons is **anachronistic**, meaning out of date. For example, the main business takes place between 3 pm and 10.30 pm. The Scottish Parliament has normal working hours of 9 am to 5 pm.

Figure 1.26 The late Robin Cook making a speech in the Commons

There is talk about reforming the House of Commons with the following suggestions:

◆ family-friendly hours
◆ breaks at school holidays
◆ fewer late sittings
◆ earlier start time for Question Time (12 noon instead of 3 pm)
◆ fewer Commons sittings on Fridays.

Until reforms take place, MPs face demanding hours. Figure 1.27 shows a typical day in the life of an MP in Parliament.

11.30 am Prayers then the Speaker takes their chair
Preliminary Business motions for by-elections
Unopposed Private Bills (no debate on these)
11.35 am Questions to Ministers
12.00 pm Questions to Prime Minister (Wednesday only)
12.30 pm Urgent questions (important unscheduled questions taken)
Business statement (Thursday only)
Business taken after Questions
Ministerial Statements – explaining government response to a current political issue
Requests for Emergency Debates – if approved these will usually happen the next day
Public Business
Introduction of Public Bills – First Readings
Government Business Motions – e.g. to allow the House to work late that day
Motions for leave to introduce Bills (Tuesday and Wednesday only) – known as a 'Ten Minute Rule Bill'
Other Public Business – later stages of bills, general debates etc.
7.00 pm   Public Business ends (6.30 on Thursday)
Presentation of Public Petitions – motion for the House to adjourn held
10.30 pm House adjourns

Figure 1.27 Daily schedule for the House of Commons
Source House of Commons Information Office

MPs duties involve the following:

◆ attending/participating in debates
◆ voting
◆ attending committee meetings (Standing or Select Committees)
◆ meeting lobbyists
◆ asking questions at Question Time and Adjournment Debates
◆ putting forward Private Member's bills.

Not all MPs attend all of the events in Parliament as Figure 1.28 shows.

FOUNDATION/GENERAL

Galloway has worst Commons vote record

Labour reject George Galloway was named and shamed yesterday as the MP with the worst voting record in Westminster.

The Glasgow Kelvin rebel, expelled from the party last year over the war on Iraq, voter fewer times in the Commons in the last parliamentary session than any other backbencher.

Galloway, with just a 14 per cent showing, was one of several Scottish MPs in the bottom 20 listed by website thepublicwhip.org.uk.

Ex-Scottish Office Minister Brian Wilson MP came 12th from the bottom, voting in just 29 per cent, while SNP Commons leader Alex Salmond came 17th from bottom, with only 31.8 per cent.

Even Father of the House Tam Dalyell only appeared for 45 per cent of divisions, partly because of his refusal to vote on English-only issues.

Mr Galloway also attended fewer debates than every other backbencher, except for the Sinn Fein members, who are barred from the House for refusing to take the oath of allegiance.

But last night he was unrepentant. In the past 16 months I have spoken at more than 500 public meetings,' he said. 'I have taken my politics on to the road. I think that is more productive than voting in the Commons.'

Mr Dalyell said that he would vote more often if the Government did not have such a massive majority.

He added: 'Some of the other work MPs do is more important than whether the Government gets a minority of 163 or 164.'

Figure 1.28 A newspaper article from 3rd January 2004

Source *Daily Mail*

Activities

1 What is the average number of constituents that an MP represents? *(2 marks)*

2 What are the responsibilities an MP has to their constituents? *(2 marks)*

3 What are the two aspects of an MP's job? *(2 marks)*

4 How can the House of Commons be seen as being out-dated? *(2 marks)*

5 List the possible reforms to the House of Commons. *(3 marks)*

6 What are the duties of MPs at the House of Commons? *(3 marks)*

7 Which MP has the worst voting record in the House of Commons? *(1 mark)*

8 How does he defend himself? *(2 marks)*

9 Why is it important for MPs to vote in the House of Commons? *(2 marks)*

10 Look at Figure 1.27 and answer the following:
   a) when is Prime Minister's Question Time? *(1 mark)*
   b) at what time does public business end? *(1 mark)*
   c) when does the House of Common's business end? *(1 mark)*

Political Parties

Figure 1.29 lists the political parties and the number of seats won in the 2005 general election. The numbers in the table may differ from other tables because the Speaker and the three Deputy Speakers are counted separately.

Party	Seats won
Labour	356
Conservative	197
Liberal Democrats	63
Democratic Unionists	9
SNP	6
Sinn Fein	5
Plaid Cymru (Welsh Nationalists)	3
SDLP	3
Ulster Unionists	1
Others	3

Figure 1.29 Parties and Seats in the House of Commons, 2005

There are other parties who are not listed in the table because they did not win any seats in the general election, such as the Green Party. Also the number of political parties might change, as the following article from the *Evening Times* shows.

Galloway Launches New Party

George Galloway has launched his new political coalition party at a rally in London. The Glasgow Kelvin MP was kicked out of the Labour Party for his remarks about the war in Iraq and describing Tony Blair and George Bush as 'wolves'.

But yesterday, he was joined by 1000 anti-war activists on what he described as an historic day for his new party – Respect: The Unity Coalition. It aims to be an alternative to New Labour.

George Galloway's party, Respect, won the Bethnal Green and Bow seat at the 2005 General Election.

The three main political parties in Britain are:

◆ Conservatives – leader Michael Howard
◆ Labour Party – leader Tony Blair
◆ Liberal Democrats – leader Charles Kennedy.

These major political parties have the most seats in the House of Commons. The Conservative and the Labour Parties are the most influential – they are called the 'big two'.

Since 1945 no other political party has been in government apart from Labour and Conservative. More recently (over the last 25 years) the Conservatives were in government from 1979 until 1997 and the Labour Party since 1997.

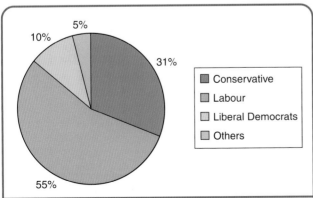

Figure 1.30 2005 General Election results: percentage of seats won per party
Source House of Commons Information Office

At the 2005 General Election, Labour and Conservative seats amounted to 553 out of a total of 646. The Labour Party won 55 per cent of the seats and the Conservatives won 31 per cent as can be seen in Figure 1.30.

Political Change in Britain

Traditional views of the policies of British political parties place them into three political categories. There used to be clear division between the parties but not now. Figure 1.31 gives us a simple explanation of the differences between the political parties in the past.

LEFT WING	CENTRE	RIGHT WING
LABOUR	**LIBERAL DEMOCRATS**	**CONSERVATIVES**
Socialism	Social Democracy	Capitalism
Supports traditional industries	Mixed economy	Low taxes
Higher welfare spending with higher taxes to pay for this	Higher taxes than Conservatives	Small welfare state
Comprehensive education	Spending on health and education by government	Law and order
Support for unions	Personal freedoms (for individuals to decide about their own future)	Strong army
		Private education
		Reduce union power

Figure 1.31 Traditional principles of the political parties

Since the 1990s, the Labour Party has moved closer to the centre of the political spectrum. The Labour Government under Tony Blair has introduced a number of policies that could be claimed to be closer to Conservative policy than 'traditional Labour.'

New Labour policies include:

FOUNDATION/GENERAL

◆ lower taxes

◆ low inflation

◆ no return to the old-style comprehensive education

◆ no re-nationalisation because it would cost too much

◆ no major changes to Conservative anti-union laws.

Many 'Old Labour' MPs have left parliament. New Labour MPs tend to follow the party line but this may be changing. Three recent major rebellions by Labour MPs on issues such as the war in Iraq, NHS foundation hospitals and student top-up fees have shown that many Labour MPs believe Tony Blair has gone too far to the right. Tony Blair's reduced majority in the 2005 General Election may lead to more successful rebellions.

Activities

1 What is another name for the Welsh Nationalist Party? *(1 mark)*

2 Why are some British political parties not mentioned on the table? *(2 marks)*

3 Which new political party has recently been set up? *(1 mark)*

4 Who was this party set up by? *(1 mark)*

5 Name the leaders of the three main political parties. *(3 marks)*

6 Explain what is meant by the 'big two'. *(2 marks)*

7 Which political parties have been in power over the last twenty-five years? *(2 marks)*

8 From Figure 1.31, name the three different types of policies. *(2 marks)*

9 How do New Labour policies differ from those of Old Labour? *(3 marks)*

10 List three policies of New Labour. *(3 marks)*

11 What evidence is there that not all Labour MPs support New Labour? *(2 marks)*

The House of Lords

All bills go through both Houses of Parliament before receiving the Royal Assent and becoming law. The Lords is very important in the law-making process. Figure 1.32 shows how the members of the Lords spend their time.

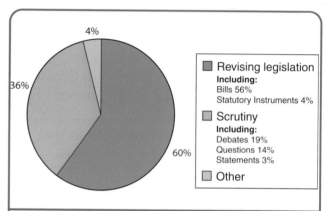

4%

36%

60%

■ Revising legislation
Including:
Bills 56%
Statutory Instruments 4%

■ Scrutiny
Including:
Debates 19%
Questions 14%
Statements 3%

□ Other

Figure 1.32 How the House of Lords spends its time

Source House of Lords Information Office

The following list shows the role of the Lords in British politics:

◆ it makes laws – bills can be started here or can be changed except those dealing with government finance

◆ it monitors the government by scrutinising the bills under debate and it has more time to do this than the Commons.

◆ it provides expertise – many important people are given a peerage and they have expertise in a range of areas such as education, industry and the law

◆ it is a court of appeal – the Lords is the highest appeal court in the UK.

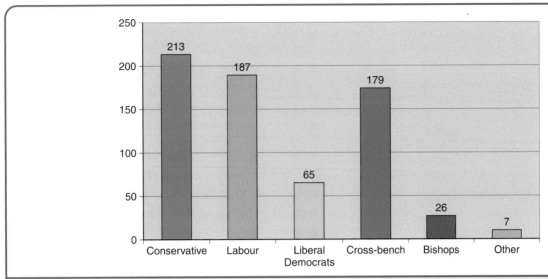

Figure 1.33 Party representation in the House of Lords in 2003

Political Parties in the House of Lords

Many members of the Lords were originally in the House of Commons and still have strong political party ties. Traditionally the Lords was dominated by Conservative peers and this was still the case in March 2003, as Figure 1.33 shows.

In recent years, the Labour Government has stated that the Lords must be changed because it is not democratic. Members of the Lords are not elected. In 1999, the Government passed the Lords Act which aimed to reduce the number of peers. In May 2002, the Government gave the job of reforming the House of Lords to a Joint Committee of both Houses of Parliament.

This Committee reported in December 2002 and suggested options ranging from members being fully appointed to being fully elected. MPs could not make up their mind between a fully appointed House of Lords – which seemed undemocratic – to a fully elected House which would be democratic but might challenge the House of Commons. Nor could they make their minds up on any options in between. The situation to date is that not much progress has been made.

Activities

1 What role does the House of Lords play in the law-making process?   *(2 marks)*

2 What three important duties are carried out by the Lords?   *(3 marks)*

3 Which political party dominates the Lords?   *(1 mark)*

4 Why does the Labour Government want to reform the House of Lords?   *(2 marks)*

5 What happened in 1999 that will have an affect on the Lords?   *(1 mark)*

6 Why has reform of the House of Lords not been successful so far?   *(1 mark)*

The British Electoral System

The Westminster electoral system is quite simple: a candidate in an election who receives more votes than any of the other candidates is the winner of the constituency and then represents it as an MP.

The political party that wins most seats in the whole of Britain in a general election becomes the government until the next general election. The name given to the British voting method is 'First Past the Post' or FPP.

Advantages of First Past the Post:

◆ quick and easy to understand

◆ link with MP and Constituency

◆ produces a clear winner, there are no coalitions

◆ extremist parties do not succeed in getting MPs elected (for example the BNP or NF).

Disadvantages of First Past the Post:

◆ two parties dominate

◆ small parties have few representatives

◆ lots of people do not bother to vote

◆ Labour or the Conservatives always win.

At present there are 646 constituencies in Britain and if one political party wins more than 324 of these it will have more seats than **all of the other parties** together. In this case the party will form a **majority** government.

Name	Party	Number of votes
George Young	SNP	20,578
Margaret Auld	SSP	18,706
Mary Lamb	Liberal Democrats	11,632
George Bull	Labour	8004

Figure 1.34 Fictitious election results using FPP (turnout = 65 per cent)

If a political party wins more seats than any other single party, but less than 324, it will form a **minority** government. This means that if all the other parties seats are added together they would have more seats in parliament than the government.

Figure 1.34 shows a result from a fictitious election using First Past the Post. The winner is George Young who has a majority of under 2000. If we count up all the votes against George Young you will see that about 38,000 people **do not** want him as their MP.

This is called a **marginal seat** because the margin between the winner and the loser is very narrow. Other political parties will target this seat at the next election. If George Young had received many more votes than the competing party's candidate, for example 30,578, then this would have made it a safe seat.

In a marginal seat the political parties will aim to win support from the voters who have not made up their minds who to vote for. This type of voter is called a '**floating voter**' because they swing from one party to another.

To win a general election the political parties hope to do two things:

1 win over the floating voter to their party

2 win the marginal seats.

Activities

1 Why is the British electoral system seen as being simple? *(2 marks)*

2 Name the electoral system used in Britain. *(2 marks)*

3 List three advantages and three disadvantages of the present electoral system. *(6 marks)*

4 How many seats does a political party need to form a majority government? *(2 marks)*

5 What is a minority government? *(2 marks)*

6 From Figure 1.34 answer the following questions:
   a) who won the seat? *(1 mark)*
   b) what was the turnout? *(2 marks)*
   c) explain why this is a marginal seat. *(2 marks)*

7 What is a safe seat? *(2 marks)*

8 Who or what is a floating voter? *(2 marks)*

9 What two things must a political party do to win a general election? *(2 marks)*

The Timing of General Elections

The governing party wants to be re-elected and the opposition parties also want to be elected to run the country. It is therefore important that the government picks the right time to call a general election – a time when their standing is good in the eyes of the voters. The following list shows factors that are important in calling the general election:

◆ the **feel good factor** – if people believe they are better-off under the government this will affect how they vote

◆ the **economy** – if unemployment is low or falling this could affect **'working class'** voters

◆ taxes – voters do not like increases in tax or increases in mortgage rates

◆ how well the government is doing. For example, are they carrying out the promises they made in the **manifesto** and how well they are doing this.

One way in which people express their views about how well the government is doing is through **opinion polls**.

Opinion polls before the 2005 General Election showed that Tony Blair (the Labour leader) was not doing very well. Recent criticisms of Tony Blair from within his own party over Iraq, top-up fees and foundation hospitals have helped to reduce the lead that Labour had over the Conservatives in the polls. The reason for this is the public do not like to see splits within political parties.

Activities

1 List the factors that are important in the timing of a general election. *(3 marks)*

2 Why are opinion polls important? *(2 marks)*

3 Why is the Prime Minister not doing well in recent opinion polls? *(2 marks)*

How Fair is the British Electoral System?

The results from the 2005 general election shows that the Labour and Conservative parties do better from the First Past the Post System than other parties (see Figure 1.35).

This shows that the winning Labour Party only received 35 per cent of the votes, which means that 65 per cent of the voters did not vote for them, and yet the Labour party became the government.

Political party	Percentage of votes	Percentage of seats
Conservatives	32	31
Labour	35	55
Liberal Democrats	22	10
Others	10	5

Figure 1.35 Percentage of votes versus seats won, 2005 election

The reasons for this situation are:

◆ constituencies are of different sizes and have different numbers of voters. Labour constituencies have an average of 67,000 voters. Conservative constituencies have around 72,000 voters because these constituencies are usually larger, rural areas.

◆ the Conservative and Labour parties are better organised and have more money. So they contest most constituencies

◆ Liberal Democrat supporters are spread throughout Britain whereas Labour and Conservative supporters are concentrated in certain areas of the country; Labour in the cities and the Conservatives in rural areas and the South East of England.

Figure 1.36 gives an idea of how many votes it took to elect an MP from the different major parties in 2001. This is based on the number of actual votes divided by the number of MPs each party has in Parliament.

Political party	Votes required (to elect an MP)
Conservatives	50, 347
Labour	26, 031
Liberal Democrats	92, 583
Others	98, 819

Figure 1.36 Votes needed to elect an MP

In Scotland the SNP require 92,862 votes to elect an MP to Westminster.

Change in the British Electoral System?

The First Past the Post system (FPP) has been criticised as being unfair. For example, the Labour Party only received 35 per cent of the total vote but became the government which means the majority of the country did not vote for them. Critics say that they electoral system should be changed.

Another electoral system is the Alternative Voting System. This would require only a small change to our present system, but it would mean that the **electorate** (the voters) would get more than one vote.

Voters would list candidates in order of preference, for example, by ranking them 1, 2, 3, 4 and so on. A candidate then needs to get 50 per cent of the 'first preference votes' to get elected. In other words, more than 50 per cent of the voters would have to mark him/her down as their number one choice on their ballot paper.

In the second count the voting papers from the candidate with the least votes are looked at to see the second preference of these voters. The votes are divided up between the remaining candidates according to the number of '2's that they received and in this way the seat for parliament is filled.

A fairer system of elections is based on **Proportional Representation** (PR). Under PR a political party would receive the same proportion of seats in parliament as they had received votes in an election. For example, a party receiving one third of the votes would gain one third of the seats.

Many other countries use PR. For example, the Scottish Parliament uses the Additional Members System (AMS) alongside FPP.

Other forms of PR are:

◆ Single Transferable Vote (STV)
◆ the National Party List (NPL).

Under STV Britain would have:

◆ larger constituencies
◆ multi-member constituencies – political parties would put forward more than one candidate for each constituency
◆ votes would list candidates in order of preference.

STV is a very complicated form of PR and it uses a **quota formula** to work out which candidates are to be elected:

$$\frac{\text{NUMBER OF VOTES CAST}}{\text{NUMBER OF SEATS} +1} +1$$

It would also include the **re-distribution of votes** until the required number of candidate quotas were reached. They do this by allocating the votes of the candidate who has already achieved the 'quota' to other candidates. This practice would be continued until all the seats of that constituency were filled.

Advantages and Disadvantages of PR

As with our present FPP system, there are reasons why PR would be good for Britain, but it may also cause some problems.

Advantages of FPP:

◆ cheap to organise and run
◆ simple, so easily understood by the electorate

- results are known quickly – by early morning/next day
- British people are accustomed to it.

PR has been criticised because, among other things, it is very complicated and voters might have difficulty understanding how it works. In addition, coalitions between parties to gain power might mean that manifesto promises are broken.

Advantages of PR:

- all votes would count – no wasted votes
- fairer allocation of seats
- no big swings in policy when there is a change in government
- need to produce change by reducing the power of Labour and Conservatives.

In 1997 the Jenkins Commission recommended that Britain should use a PR system called the Alternative Top Up. Five years later there has been no introduction of this form of PR. It has been suggested that a **referendum** on electoral reform should be undertaken. A referendum is when all of the electorate are asked their opinion on a single issue.

Political party	First Past the Post	Proportional Representation
Conservatives	197	209
Labour	356	239
Liberal Democrats	63	142
SNP	6	11
Plaid Cymru	3	6
Greens	0	3
UKIP	0	14
BNP	0	4
Others	4	0

Figure 1.37 Theoretical comparison of seats for some political parties under FPP and PR – 2005 general election

Activities

1 What percentage of the electorate did not vote for the Labour party at the 2005 general election? *(2 marks)*

2 How did the Labour party manage to become the government with less than 50 per cent of the total vote? *(3 marks)*

3 How many votes are required to elect an MP for the following political parties:
   a) Labour
   b) Liberal Democrats
   c) SNP?

4 What is Proportional Representation? *(2 marks)*

5 How does PR work? *(2 marks)*

6 List three types of PR. *(3 marks)*

7 What are the advantages of the First Past the Post electoral system? *(4 marks)*

8 List four advantages of Proportional Representation. *(4 marks)*

9 What did the Jenkins Commission recommend? *(2 marks)*

10 From Figure 1.37 which political party would more than double the number of seats it has under PR? *(2 marks)*

11 How many seats would Labour win under PR? How many more seats would the Liberal Democrats have under PR? *(2 marks)*

Getting Involved in Politics

Many people in Britain are involved in politics in one way or another and this is called **political participation**.

The most common method for people who are **eligible** to vote in an area, who are over 18 year olds, and are listed in the **electoral register** is to vote in elections.

Participation in Elections

The following people are eligible to vote:

- people over 18 years of age
- people registered to vote

- people who stay in Britain – that is:
  - British citizens
  - members of the commonwealth
  - nationals of EIRE who reside in Britain
  - British citizens who have resided abroad for less than 20 years.

Some people are **not** allowed to vote at elections, including the following:

- prisoners who have been sentenced
- members of the House of Lords
- people in mental institutions
- people who have not registered in their electoral constituency
- people who have been convicted of illegal electoral offences in the last five years.

Who won't vote?

And the winner is: The Stay at Home Party

The Apathy Factor

From a total electorate of 44 million, 25,960,000 people voted, 18,040,000 (41%) didn't bother.

Figure 1.38 Newspaper article on voter apathy in the 2001 General Election
Source *Daily Mail*

Figure 1.38 shows that at the 2001 general election over 18 million people did not vote. Some suggestions for this include:

- a general lack of interest in politics
- the feeling that their vote will not affect the outcome of the election
- a protest against British elections
- more interest in single issue campaigns
- increased homelessness
- difficulty in attending polling stations for reasons such as illness, holiday or involvement in another activity

- no one political party appeals to the voter because policies are very similar, therefore choice is limited
- some commentators suggest there are too many elections in Britain and the voters are fed-up with going along to vote at regular intervals.

The British government is so concerned about the numbers of people not voting that it is considering introducing penalties (such as fines) for non-voters, similar to the system in Australia.

Why it is Important to Vote

In the past there has been a lot of conflict between groups fighting for the right to vote and those who are already able to vote. In some cases, people died while protesting to gain the right to vote or took extreme measures like chaining themselves to fences at parliament or throwing themselves under moving horse-drawn carriages.

Voting is an important democratic right in Britain and it is the individual's responsibility to vote. If a person does not vote then they have no right to criticise the government's actions or voice an opinion on new legislation. In other words, non-voters lose their political voice.

Figure 1.39 Emmeline Pankhurst addressing a Suffragette meeting

Activities

1   Who can vote in British elections?
    (4 marks)

2 What is voter apathy? *(2 marks)*

3 What percentage of voters did not vote at the general election in 2001? *(2 marks)*

4 Give four reasons why people did not bother to vote? *(4 marks)*

5 Why is it important to vote? *(2 marks)*

Election Day and Voting

Polling stations stay open from 7.00 am to 10.00 pm. Voters bring **polling cards** and their name is ticked-off the election register. Each voter is given a **ballot paper** which they take into a **polling booth**. They mark a cross (X) against the candidate of their choice. (In Scottish Elections, voters choose a List MSP as well as an FPP MSP. The voter then folds their ballot paper and puts it into the sealed **ballot box**.

After 10.00 pm all ballot boxes are taken to a central location where they are counted. Once all of the ballot papers have been counted, the winner is announced.

Activities

1 How long are polling stations open for on election day? *(1 mark)*

2 Describe the voting process. *(4 marks)*

3 What happens to the ballot papers after voting is over? *(2 marks)*

Figure 1.40 The new Scottish parliament building

The Scottish Parliament

In 1998 the Scotland Act created the first Scottish Parliament for 300 years. It is a **devolved** (or 'home rule') parliament, which means that the powers that it has have been given to it by the British Parliament – it is not independent. Assemblies for Wales, Northern Ireland, and London were all devolved at the same time.

Scotland held a **referendum** in 1979 which failed to show public support for a Scottish Parliament. However, on September 11th 1997 a second referendum gave overwhelming backing for a Scottish Parliament with tax raising powers. This led to the Labour government introducing a Bill in parliament which began the process towards the Scotland Act 1998.

Important parts of the Scotland Act included:

◆ elections to the Scottish Parliament involving FPP linked with a system of PR in recognition that Scotland had four major political parties

◆ limited tax powers

◆ the aim to provide more equality of gender in the Scottish Parliament

◆ power over education, law, health and tourism amongst other things.

Elections to the Scottish Parliament

The most recent elections to the Scottish Parliament took place in May 2003. The important aspects of the Scottish Parliament elections can be summarised as follows:

◆ a total of 129 MSPs are elected

◆ 73 MSPs are elected by FPP according to Westminster Constituencies plus one MSP for Orkney and one for Shetland

◆ 56 MSPs are elected by the Additional Member System of PR using regional lists

Representation and Participation at National and Local Level

◆ 56 MSPs on Regional Lists – 7 MSPs each for the following 8 areas: Glasgow, west of Scotland, central Scotland, Lothians, north east Scotland, south of Scotland, mid Scotland and Fife, Highlands and Islands

Two Votes

Each elector has two votes – one for FPP and the other for AMS.

Electors vote for constituency MSPs. The candidate who wins the highest number of votes is elected. Electors also vote for a party in the regional list vote. Parties get additional MSPs based on the proportion of votes cast in the election, for instance. If a party gets eight Constituency MSPs but the proportion of votes cast means that they should have got ten, they will get an additional two regional list MSPs. If a party gets no constituency MSPs, but the proportion of votes cast means they should have got four, they will get an additional four regional list MSPs.

The parties themselves draw up a list of candidates with their most important candidates at the top (number one, number two etc.). Those at the top of the list are most likely to be elected.

Activities

1 When was the current Scottish Parliament set up? *(1 mark)*

2 What are the two types of electoral systems used in the Scottish Parliament? *(2 marks)*

3 Explain how the Additional Member System works. *(4 marks)*

4 Look at Figure 1.41 and answer the following questions.
   a) Which party would have won if the election was only by First Past the Post? *(1 mark)*
   b) Which parties would have no MSPs if the election was only by First Past the Post? *(4 marks)*
   c) How many Conservative MSPs are there? *(1 mark)*
   d) List the political parties that each have one MSP? *(2marks)*
   e) How many seats are required for a majority in the Scottish Parliament? *(1 mark)*
   f) How many seats do Labour and the Liberal Democrats have between them at the Scottish Parliament? *(2 marks)*

2003 Scottish Parliament Election Results

Political party	FPP MSPs	List MSPs	Total MSPs
Labour	46	4	50
Conservative	3	15	18
SNP	9	18	27
Liberal Democrats	13	4	17
Green Party	0	7	7
SSP	0	6	6
Save Stobhill Hospital	1	0	1
Senior Citizens Unity Party	0	1	1
Dennis Canavan	1	0	1
Margo MacDonald	0	1	1
Totals	73	56	129

Figure 1.41 2003 Scottish Parliament election results

What Does the Scottish Parliament Do?

The Scottish Parliament makes laws and decisions about issues that affect the lives of the Scottish people. The areas which they have the power to make important decisions about are called **devolved matters**, this means that they affect only Scotland.

Devolved matters include:

◆ agriculture, forestry and fisheries

◆ education

◆ environment

◆ health

◆ law and home affairs

◆ local government, social work and housing

◆ sport and the arts

◆ transport and economic development.

MSPs have been able to pass many more bills in these areas than would have been possible before devolution. This is because there was very little time at Westminster to discuss purely Scottish matters.

Areas which affect all of the UK are called **reserved matters** and these are dealt with by the Westminster Parliament. These include defence, immigration, pensions and social security.

Activities

1 What are devolved matters? *(2 marks)*

2 Make a list of six devolved matters. *(6 marks)*

3 What are reserved matters?   *(2 marks)*

4 List four reserved matters.   *(2 marks)*

The Scottish Parliament: Developments to Date

The Scottish Parliament is barely six years old and it has already had three **First Ministers** (like a Prime Minister) since May 1999:

◆ Donald Dewar unfortunately died

◆ Henry McLeish was forced to resign over money matters

◆ Jack McConnell – the present First Minister.

Figure 1.42 Jack McConnell

Unlike Westminster where one party usually forms the government, a Labour–Liberal Democrat coalition runs the government of Scotland, the Scottish Executive.

Labour and the Liberal Democrats have a **partnership agreement** which means that:

◆ together they have a majority of MSPs (67) in the Scottish Parliament

◆ Nicol Stephen (a Liberal Democrat MSP) is Deputy First Minister and other Liberal Democrats are also members of the Scottish Executive along with Labour MSPs

◆ both parties support one another and the Scottish Executive in the Scottish Parliament

◆ some Liberal Democrat policies, such as abolition of student tuition fees, free personal care for the elderly and proportional representation for local council elections become Scottish Executive policies and have become law

◆ the Scottish Parliament has the fourth highest proportion of women in parliament in the world (39.3 per cent)

Labour–Liberal Democrat Coalition

Figure 1.43 Nicol Stephen, Deputy First Minister
Source www.scottish.parliament.uk

The electoral system used for the Scottish Parliament makes it less likely that one party will win an overall majority of seats. Therefore parties have to agree to work together in order to get a majority of MSPs (65 out of 129) to form the government of Scotland and to get laws passed.

The Labour Party needed to link up with any party which has more than 15 seats. The Liberal Democrats have 17 seats giving the Labour–Liberal Democrats coalition a total of 67 seats. The leaders of both parties signed a partnership agreement promising to support

each other and work together in the Scottish Parliament and Scottish Executive.

Activities

1 In which ways does the Scottish Parliament differ to the Westminster one? *(4 marks)*

2 Who is the First Minister? *(2 marks)*

3 Who are the coalition partners in the Scottish Parliament? *(2 marks)*

4 Why did Labour have to look for another political party to set up a coalition? *(2 marks)*

5 What did Labour and the Liberal Democrats promise in the Partnership Agreement? *(2marks)*

Legislation in the Scottish Parliament

The Scottish Executive (government) has three basic jobs:

1 to put ideas for new laws forward to the Scottish Parliament

2 to be responsible for the work of Scottish departments – for **devolved matters**

3 to take charge of Scottish Executive spending.

Proposals for a new law are called a Bill. The Scottish Executive, MSPs or committees concerned with specific issues can put forward proposals for a new law. Private individuals or groups can also put forward Bills. A Bill must go through certain stages before it becomes a law, these are given below.

Stage 1
A committee looks at the Bill and asks for interested parties to comment. The Bill is then debated by the whole of parliament, they decide if it should go to Stage 2.

FOUNDATION/GENERAL

Stage 2

The Bill goes back to the committee who may suggest amendments after looking at it in detail.

Stage 3

Parliament looks at the Bill after these changes have been made and may suggest further changes before it is debated by all of the MSPs.

If the majority of MSPs agree (more than 65) then the Bill goes to the Queen for Royal Assent and becomes law in Scotland.

Committees in the Scottish Parliament

Committees have an important role in the Scottish Parliament. They hold inquiries into Scottish issues such as the cost of the new Scottish Parliament building. They look at Scottish Bills and can put forward Bills themselves.

Most MSPs are members of committees. At present there are seventeen committees made up of between seven and eleven MSPs from different political parties.

There are two types of committees. They first type are **subject committees** which deal with education or health, for example. The second type are **mandatory committees** which deal with such things as finance and European issues that affect Scotland.

Over the past four years committees have looked into 118 different issues that affect Scottish people. Some examples are community care, the fishing industry and drug misuse and deprived communites.

Activities

1   What is a Bill?   *(2 marks)*

2   Who can introduce a Bill to the Scottish Parliament?   *(2 marks)*

3   What are the stages a Bill must go through to become a Scottish Law?   *(2 marks)*

4   Name a recent issue that has been looked at by a committee of the Scottish Parliament? *(2 marks)*

5   What is the average size of a committee? *(1 mark)*

6   What are the two types of committees at the Scottish Parliament?   *(2 mark)*

The Role of the MSP

Figure 1.44 Pauline McNeil Constituency MSP for Glasgow Kelvin

Source www.scottish.parliament.uk

There are 129 MSPs for Scotland, 73 constituency MSPs and 56 regional list MSPs.

Each person in Scotland has one constituency and seven regional List MSPs representing them. Even if you did not vote for any of these eight MSPs, they will still represent you in the Scottish Parliament.

The people of Scotland have an alternative way

FOUNDATION/GENERAL

to seek help from a member of the Scottish parliament in comparison to voters in Westminster elections. Constituents can either seek the help of a constituency MSP or regional list MSP, or both.

Out of 129 MSPs, 51 are women, so Scottish people could seek the support of a female MSP if they specifically wanted to. Unfortunately, there are no ethnic minority MSPs as yet.

An MSP can help in the following ways:

◆ speaking in debates
◆ introducing a bill to change the law
◆ asking for a debate on an issue or problem
◆ seeking answers from the Scottish Executive, for example, during Question Time
◆ asking for changes to bills
◆ referring you to another person or organisation.

You can arrange to meet your MSP at the Scottish Parliament, visit his/her surgery or email them.

The Presiding Officer

Figure 1.45 George Reid, Presiding Officer of the Scottish Parliament

The Presiding Officer is George Reid, MSP. He had two Deputy Presiding Officers and he is elected by all of the MSPs.

The presiding officer has to be politically impartial which means that he can have no link to any political party at the Scottish Parliament. Their job is to undertake the following duties:

◆ keep order during debates and other business in the Chamber
◆ agree to business for the Chamber
◆ decide on what the Scottish Parliament can discuss.

Activities

1 How many MSPs could you approach about a local issue? *(1 mark)*

2 Which options do Scottish electors have which voters for the Westminster parliament do not have? *(2 marks)*

3 How many women MSPs are there? *(2 marks)*

4 In what ways can an MSP help a constituent with a problem? *(3 marks)*

5 What is the name of the current presiding officer? *(1 mark)*

6 Who elects the presiding officer? *(1 mark)*

7 What does political impartiality mean? *(2 marks)*

8 What are the main duties of the presiding officer? *(3 marks)*

Investigation

Visit the Scottish Parliament website at: www.scottish.parliament.uk

Find the names of your constituency and regional list MSPs by clicking onto the MSP button and then using the map to help you.

Write down the names of your constituency MSP and your regional list MSPs and any committees they serve on.

Find out more about the work of the Scottish Parliament by clicking on 'education' then 'exploring the parliament'.

Local Government

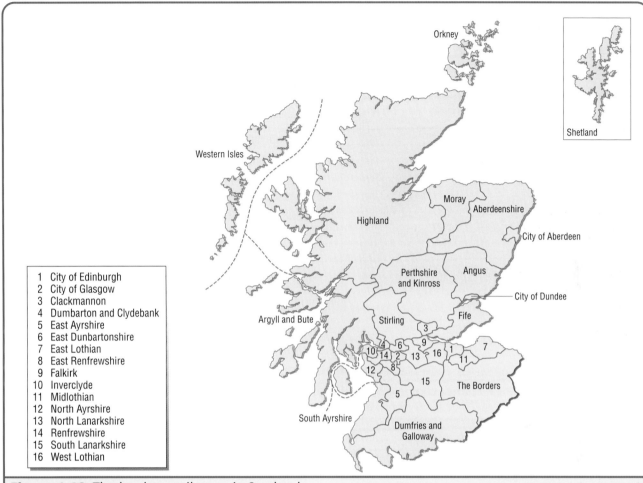

Orkney

Shetland

Western Isles

Moray

Aberdeenshire

Highland

City of Aberdeen

Perthshire
and Kinross

Angus

City of Dundee

Argyll and Bute

Stirling

Fife

3

9

10

4

6

14

2

13

16

1

7

12

8

11

15

5

The Borders

South Ayrshire

Dumfries and
Galloway

1 City of Edinburgh
2 City of Glasgow
3 Clackmannon
4 Dumbarton and Clydebank
5 East Ayrshire
6 East Dunbartonshire
7 East Lothian
8 East Renfrewshire
9 Falkirk
10 Inverclyde
11 Midlothian
12 North Ayrshire
13 North Lanarkshire
14 Renfrewshire
15 South Lanarkshire
16 West Lothian

Figure 1.46 The local council areas in Scotland

The local council is that part of the British political system where the representative at local level is closest to the people who voted for them.

The present system of local government was set up in 1996 with 32 councils instead of the old system which had a total of 65 councils (regional and district). The councils provide local services. Most of the money for this comes from **central government** via the Scottish Executive.

Councils also charge **council tax** based on the value of houses in the council area. Council tax payments represent only between 15 per cent to 25 per cent of the total amount councils need to run services. Other finance comes from charging for local services such as libraries, rental accommodation and leisure centres.

Some services provided by the local government include the following:

- ◆ environmental services such as cleansing
- ◆ recreation and leisure
- ◆ housing
- ◆ education
- ◆ social work
- ◆ fire brigade
- ◆ police
- ◆ roads.

These services are best provided at a local level because issues can be more easily identified and solutions found at that level.

Councillors are elected by the local people to decide how these services are provided. Once they are elected to the local council, the area they represent is called a **ward**. It is likely that a councillor lives locally and knows some of the people personally. The problems facing the

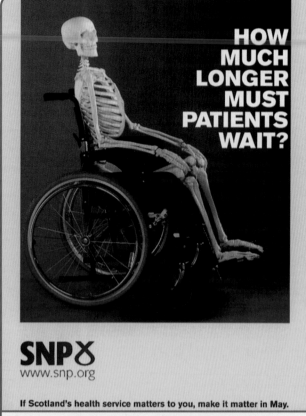

SNP
www.snp.org

If Scotland's health service matters to you, make it matter in May.

Figure 1.47 An SNP local council campaign leaflet

Activities

1. How many councils are there in Scotland? *(1 mark)*

2. Where does most of the money for council services come from? *(1 mark)*

3. What other sources of funding do councils have to pay for local services? *(4 marks)*

4. Describe the services that councils provide. *(4 marks)*

5. What is the area a councillor represents called? *(1 mark)*

6. Why might councillors be in close contact with the feelings of local people? *(2 marks)*

7. What are the people who are involved in the day to day running of services called? *(1 mark)*

8. Look at Figure 1.47 used in the council elections in Renfrewshire in 2003. How does this SNP leaflet show that political parties campaign on wider issues at local level? *(1 mark)*

ward's constituents would also be well-known to the councillors.

Councils employ Officers, such as the director of education, who are in charge of the day to day running of council services.

Electing Councillors

Councillors are currently elected using First Past the Post. At local council elections candidates from the major political parties try to get elected on issues that come from the **manifesto** of the local party.

However, as can be seen from Figure 1.47, many parties campaign in local elections on issues which councils do not have control over, such as pensions, the health service, defence and national taxes.

Some councils also have a large number of independent candidates who are not members of any political party. Independent candidates stand as individuals who feel that they can represent constituents better by not belonging to a political party.

In most councils, the political party which wins most wards becomes the ruling or administration group. The leader of that party becomes the **leader** of the **council**.

The ruling groups in Figure 1.48 are in bold. In some cases the ruling groups did not win a majority of wards but run the council as a minority administration. This means they have to get the support of members of other parties or groups to win votes at council meetings.

In some councils, the ruling group got the same number of wards as the other parties combined. In East Dunbartonshire, for instance, the Liberal Democrats became the ruling group after cards were cut at the first council meeting to decide who would become **provost**. In South Ayrshire, the Labour party also won on a cut of cards.

At council meetings the provost chairs the meeting. He or she can vote with his or her political party and, if the votes are tied, the

FOUNDATION/GENERAL

provost has a second vote and can vote again. This is called a **casting vote**. This means that even if the parties have the same number of councillors, the party which the provost belongs to will have an extra vote.

Council	Labour	SNP	Liberal democrats	Conservative	Independent/ other	Total	Ruling party or coalition
Aberdeen City	14	6	**20**	**3**	0	43	Liberal Democrats/ Conservative
Aberdeenshire	0	15	**28**	11	**14**	68	Liberal Democrats/ Independents
Angus	1	**17**	3	2	6	29	SNP
Argyll and Bute	0	3	8	2	**23**	36	Independent
Clackmannanshire	**10**	6	0	1	1	18	Labour
Dumfries and Galloway	14	**5**	5	**11**	12	47	Independent/ Liberal Democrats/ SNP
Dundee	**10**	11	**2**	5	1	29	Labour/ Liberal Democrats
East Ayrshire	**23**	8	0	1	0	32	Labour
East Dunbartonshire	9	0	**12**	3	0	24	Liberal Democrats
East Lothian	**17**	1	1	4	0	23	Labour
East Renfrewshire	**8**	0	3	7	2	20	Labour
Edinburgh	**30**	0	15	13	0	58	Labour
Eilean Sair	4	3	0	0	**24**	31	Independent
Falkirk	14	**9**	0	2	**7**	32	SNP/ Independent
Fife	**36**	11	23	2	6	78	Labour
Glasgow	**71**	3	3	1	1	79	Labour
Highland	8	6	9	0	**57**	80	Independent
Inverclyde	6	0	**13**	0	1	20	Liberal Democrats
Midlothian	**15**	0	2	0	1	18	Labour
Moray	5	3	1	1	**16**	26	Independent
North Ayrshire	**21**	3	0	4	2	30	Labour
Orkney Islands	0	0	0	0	21	21	Independent
Perth and Kinross	5	15	**9**	**10**	2	41	Conservative/ Liberal Democrats/ Labour/ Independent
Renfrewshire	**21**	15	3	1	0	40	Labour

Figure 1.48 2003 Scottish council election results – **continued overleaf**
Source CoSLA

Council	Labour	SNP	Liberal democrats	Conservative	Independent/ other	Total	Ruling party or coalition
Scottish Borders	0	1	8	10	15	34	Independent/ Conservative
Shetland Islands	0	0	4	0	18	22	Independent
South Ayrshire	15	0	0	15	0	30	Labour
South Lanarkshire	51	9	2	2	3	67	Labour
Stirling	12	0	0	10	0	22	Labour
West Dunbartonshire	17	3	0	0	2	22	Labour
West Lothian	18	12	0	1	1	32	Labour
Totals	509	176	174	122	241	1222	

Figure 1.48 *continued*

Source CoSLA

Activities

1 What method of voting is currently used to elect councillors? *(2 marks)*

2 What is the party that wins the council elections called? *(2 marks)*

3 What is the leader of that party called? *(2 marks)*

4 Which political party or group controls the council you live in? *(1 mark)*

5 How many councils are run by:
   a) Labour
   b) SNP
   c) Liberal Democrats
   d) Conservatives
   e) Independents
   f) Coalitions of parties? *(6 marks)*

6 Which political party has the largest number of councillors in Scotland? *(4 marks)*

7 How many councillors are there in Scotland overall? *(2 marks)*

8 How were the results in East Dunbartonshire and South Ayrshire decided? *(2 marks)*

9 What is the provost's second vote called? *(2 marks)*

What Do Councillors Do?

Councillors represent constituents from their wards and they run local government services on their behalf. The councillors have a lot of responsibility for providing a good level of service in education, the local environment and other services.

In addition to the Officers who are in charge of the day to day running of services, the local council also employs different types of workers to deliver the services, for example, teachers in schools or joiners in the housing repairs service.

Councillors attend meetings where they debate on local issues. A vote will be taken at the end of a debate. Councillors are paid an allowance for attending local council meetings.

The work of a councillor is usually done in committees, where decisions are taken for all services, for example, the education committee discusses and makes decisions on educational matters.

There are also meetings involving the councillors of the individual political parties, called **group meetings**, where **policy decisions** are made in line with the national party's view on the running of local government. As in the House of Commons, councillors vote with their political party.

Figure 1.49 shows the number of councillors of the different political parties in Renfrewshire Council in 2003.

Composition of Renfrewshire Council	
Party	**Councillors**
Labour	21
SNP	15
Liberal Democrats	3
Conservative	1

Figure 1.49 Composition of Renfrewshire Council in 2003

Councillors hold **surgeries** where local constituents who have a problem with a local service can go along to ask for help. The times of the surgeries, names and addresses of councillors are usually published in the local newspaper, as the extract from the *Paisley Daily Express* below shows.

Renfrewshire Council Surgeries 2004

David Mylet
Ward 30 – Moorpark
Cherrie Centre
Saturday 7th February
10am-11am
Tuesday 17th February
6.30pm-7.30pm

Sam Mullin
Ward 37 – Parkmains
Old Farmhouse Centre
Tuesday 10th February
10am-11am
Bridgewater Community Centre

Iain Langlands
Ward 40 – Bishopton
Bishopton Community Centre
Saturday 7th February
10am-11am
Bishopton Community Centre
Wednesday 10th February
6.30pm-7.30pm

Public Notice
Annabel M Goldie MSP
List Member for the West of Scotland is holding a Surgery in Asda, Linwood, on Monday 9th February 12pm-2pm

Figure 1.50 Surgery notices advertised in a local paper
Source *Paisley Daily Express*

By living in the area which they represent, the councillors are also likely to have more dealings with their constituents as they go about their daily activities, like meeting at the shops or in the park.

Often councillors hold 'unofficial surgeries' by listening to the local people talk about their problems or complain about local services. This is an important part of the local councillor's job as they are only involved part-time in their official duties.

Councillor Profile

Renfrewshire Council is a typical Scottish local government area. The headquarters are in the council buildings in the centre of Paisley. There are 40 wards in Renfrewshire Council and it is a mixture of wealthy rural areas and suburbs and other urban areas where people are not so well off. Labour is the ruling group and the SNP is the main opposition party.

Mr Brian Lawson is an SNP councillor on Renfrewshire Council and he has represented the ward of Gallowhill, Greenlaw and Whitehaugh since 1992.

Councillor Lawson also has a job – he is a computer systems consultant. He is also the SNP spokesperson on roads and transport. He represents Renfrewshire Council on the Strathclyde Passenger Transport Authority (SPTA) and is a member of the Renfrewshire Valuation Board.

One Saturday morning in September 2002, Councillor Lawson went around his ward leafleting his constituents with information on

FOUNDATION/GENERAL

the new free travel initiative for pensioners in the Strathclyde Passenger Transport area.

Figure 1.51 Brian Lawson, SNP Councillor, Renfrewshire Council

The free travel scheme is good news for many of Councillor Lawson's constituents as many will be able to enjoy free travel on buses and trains.

It was passed by the Scottish Parliament (which is controlled by Labour and the Liberal Democrats) and is administered in Councillor Lawson's area by SPTA. Councillors who are on the SPTA come from all political parties.

Councillor Lawson regards it as important to inform his constituents of the benefits the scheme will give them. The story of Councillor Lawson and his Saturday morning activities gives a flavour of the work of a councillor. Councillor Lawson also seeks to keep in contact with his constituents by a variety of means, as the following notice shows:

To contact Councillor Lawson:
- write to him at 24 Brabloch Crescent, Gallowhill, Paisley, PA3 4RG
- email him at brian@paisleysouthsnp.org
- telephone him on 842 3525
- (9 am – 5 pm, Monday – Friday)

Meet Councillor Lawson at his surgery on the first Thursday of every month at Williamsburgh Primary School or at Gallowhill Community Centre on the third Thursday (from 6.30 pm – 7 pm).

When people contact Councillor Lawson he can represent their views in a number of ways, such as:

- voting at council meetings
- trying to ensure council services improve
- writing to others on behalf of constituents
- speaking on their behalf at committee or full council meetings.

Like many councillors, Mr Lawson has a good idea of the issues affecting his constituents because he stays locally. They use the same services as everyone else in the local area and know the good and bad aspects of services such as roads, leisure, education and social services. Councillors try to represent their constituents well and of course hope to get re-elected at the next council elections.

Activities

1 What duties does Councillor Lawson carry out at the local council? *(2 marks)*

2 What did Councillor Lawson do to pass on the good news about free travel for pensioners? *(2 marks)*

3 How might Councillor Lawson benefit from passing on the good news? *(2 marks)*

4 How can his constituents contact him? *(4 marks)*

5 List four ways that a councillor can represent their constituents at the local council? *(4 marks)*

6 What do councillors hope will happen at the next council elections? *(2 marks)*

Should Councillors Work Full Time?

Arguments for:
- MPs, MSPs and MEPs get a salary
- councillors work long hours for their constituents

- full time councillors work harder
- it is difficult to do two jobs well at the same time
- better candidates might stand for election if a wage is paid
- councillors give up a lot for their constituents and don't even get a pension when they retire.

Arguments against:

- paying 1222 councillors will cost a lot of money
- the most important councillors already get larger allowances
- there is not enough work for all councillors to work full time
- many councillors do not want to give up their jobs.

A little over half of all councillors have jobs. A quarter are full time councillors and just over a fifth are retired, as Figure 1.52 shows.

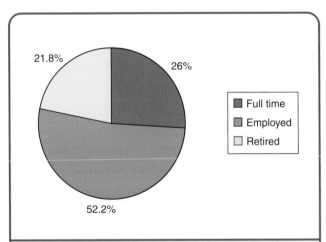

21.8%

26%

52.2%

Full time
Employed
Retired

Figure 1.52 Employment status of councillors
Source www.cosla.gov.uk

Full time councillors spend an average of 43 hours per week on council business. Part-time councillors typically work 27 hours per week.

Being a part-time councillor can have a negative effect on the full-time job that the councillor does. An article in the *Evening Times* (Figure 1.53) shows the risk that one Glasgow City councillor faced because of her absences from her job because of council business.

Councillor's duties cost Kirsteen her city job

Miss Mosson says council work is a full-time job.

Figure 1.53 Newspaper article from a Glasgow paper
Source *Evening Times*

Activities

1 What are the main arguments for councillors to work full time? *(6 marks)*

2 What are the main arguments against councillors working full time? *(4 marks)*

3 What evidence is there that full time and part-time councillors work long hours for their constituents *(4 marks)*

4 Why did Councillor Kirsteen Mosson lose her job? *(2 marks)*

The Scottish Parliament and Local Government Elections

Council elections are held every four years. Councillors are elected by First Past the Post – the same way as MPs. MSPs and MEPs are elected by forms of Proportional Representation.

In some council areas, one political party runs the council, although they did not get the majority of the vote. For example, in Glasgow Labour won 71 out of 79 wards even though only 48 per cent of those voting voted Labour. The SNP won 20 per cent of the vote but only three Councillors were elected. Only 40 per cent of the electorate in Glasgow used their vote.

In 2003, the Labour Party did not win enough seats in the Scottish Parliament to run the Scottish Executive on their own. Labour and the Liberal Democrats made a partnership agreement which meant that both parties would work together as a coalition government for Scotland.

Both parties also agreed that:

FOUNDATION/GENERAL

'for the next local government elections the proportional Single Transferable Vote system of election. The multi-member wards would have either three or four members, depending on local circumstances'.

Source Partnership Agreement 2003

The Local Governance (Scotland) 2003 Bill introduced a new remuneration package for councillors (pay and pensions and severance payments for councillors) and reduced the age at which people can stand for election in a local authority to 18.

The Convention of Scottish Local Authorities (CoSLA) and many councils are opposed to changing the voting system as they feel that the direct link between the councillor and his/her ward will be broken. (instead of one councillor per ward there will be three, four or even five).

Glasgow City Council is to take on the Scottish Executive over plans to reform the voting system for local government elections.

Ministers are looking at plans to introduce proportional representation in time for the next council elections in four years.

Labour MSPs signed a coalition deal with the Liberal Democrats which included the promise of PR voting by single transferable vote for 2007.

It means the first-past-the-post system will be scrapped with the likely result that Labour will lose its stronghold on councils across Scotland.

The party holds 71 of the 79 seats on the Glasgow council and is now fighting to maintain the status quo.

Council leader Charles Gordon said after a meeting of senior Labour councillors: "We are making it clear we are against the single transferable vote because it destroys the link between a ward and its elected member.

"It could give a tremendous influence to parties which only represent a small percentage of the electorate and will not necessarily result in concession politics.

"That can lead to lack of initiative and lack of a clear strategy."

In May the Convention of Scottish Local Authorities warned it was to stage a four-year war against the voting proposals from the Scottish Executive.

An Executive spokesman said plans to reform the voting system would be considered by MSPs before the end of the year.

The spokesman said: "A significant number of people who responded to an earlier consultation document supported the introduction of the single transferable system of vote."

Figure 1.54 Newspaper article from 25th September 2003
Source *Evening Times*

However, councillors do support:

◆ **payment of councillors**

◆ **severance payments if a councillor is defeated at an election or decides not to stand again**

◆ **pensions for retiring councillors**

◆ **reducing the age of councillors.**

The Scottish Parliament will have the final say on how councillors will be elected in 2007 when they pass the Local Governance Bill.

Activities

1 Using the Glasgow results, what criticisms can be made of First Past the Post? *(4 marks)*

2 What is CoSLA's main criticism of the Scottish Executive's proposals? *(2 marks)*

3 What does Figure 1.54 say will happen in those councils controlled by Labour? *(2 marks)*

4 Why are severance payments important, particularly if STV is introduced? *(2 marks)*

5 Who will have the final say on how councils are elected? *(2 marks)*

Pressure Groups

In a democracy people have both **rights** and **responsibilities**. An important right is the **freedom of speech** to put your views forward. One way of doing this is to join with others in a **pressure group**.

Pressure groups are groups of people who try to influence the government or other public bodies by taking action, including contacting MPs or other important people to put forward their views at Westminster. There are two types of pressure group:

1 The sectional pressure groups
These are normally professional bodies or interest groups like the British Medical

Association. Their aims are to protect their members' interests and future development. One important pressure group is the Confederation of British Industry (CBI) which represents 150,000 separate businesses in Britain.

2 Promotional Pressure Groups:

These type of pressure groups are interested mainly in a social cause and gain publicity for it. Environmental protection groups have been active in recent years, such as Greenpeace, Friends of the Earth, and various animal rights groups.

Figure 1.55 Greenpeace protesters occupy Sizewell B nuclear power station – January 2003

Membership of Pressure Groups

In recent years the membership of pressure groups has increased quite quickly, especially for environmental groups like Friends of the Earth.

A particularly successful pressure group with a very low membership is the Save The Stobhill Hospital Group. With only a few hundred members they managed to elect their leader (Jean Turner) to the Scottish Parliament in the 2003 elections.

Mrs Turner stood as an Independent candidate and beat her Labour opponent into second place. Mrs Turner is now in a better position to put pressure upon our representatives. It shows what can be done if a group feels strongly enough about an issue.

Putting on the Pressure

In order to get their message across to people, pressure groups use a variety of methods:

Speaking out at meetings	Letters to newspapers
Petitions **GREENPEACE**	Advertising
Media coverage	Direct Action

Figure 1.56 Methods used by pressure groups

How Governments Use Pressure Groups

Governments are often in contact with pressure groups to find out their views. Pressure groups are able to provide the government with up to date information and helpful feedback on policies and this can be very useful. The British Medical Association was consulted by the Conservative Government before the government reformed the National Health Service. This did not stop the medical profession from criticising the reforms of the NHS.

Pressure Groups and Parliament

The name given to the activity carried out by pressure groups in parliament is called **lobbying**. This means speaking to MPs in the lobby of parliament or by any other means to try to get them to put forward their ideas on a particular topic.

There are a number of ways that a MP might be able to influence parliament – by the introduction of a **private member's bill** or by asking questions at **question time**. In addition, some pressure groups **sponsor** MPs, for example, Tony Blair is sponsored by the Transport and General Workers' Union. MPs are expected to put forward the interests of the group which sponsored them in the House of Commons.

Pressure Groups – Good or Bad for Democracy?

Some people see pressure groups as being good for democracy but others see them as a threat. The following lists show both sides of the argument:

Advantages of pressure groups:

◆ make governments more efficient
◆ encourage freedom of speech
◆ allow political participation
◆ bring attention to social problems
◆ help social progress
◆ provide information that politicians might not have.

Disadvantages of pressure groups:

◆ pressure groups are not elected
◆ demonstrations can lead to violence
◆ can slow down change
◆ control of demonstrations cost money
◆ can be biased
◆ can corrupt politicians by offering bribes.

Activities

1 What are pressure groups? *(2 marks)*

2 What did Jean Turner do to bring attention to her pressure group? *(2 marks)*

3 What is another name for a sectional pressure group? *(1 mark)*

4 Why were sectional pressure groups set up? *(2 marks)*

5 What are promotional pressure groups? *(2 marks)*

6 Give three examples of cause groups. *(3 marks)*

7 How does Greenpeace attract attention to it's cause? *(5 marks)*

8 Why would the government consult with the Law Society or the BMA? *(3 marks)*

9 Why are pressure groups sometimes seen as being bad for democracy? *(3 marks)*

Representation and Participation at National and Local Level

Democracy

Britain is known as a **representative democracy**. This means that power lies in the hands of the people.

Britain has a population of some 60 million people who express their political desires by voting for political parties whose role is to represent them. These political parties compete with each other to win the support of the people at any particular point in time.

Elections are the mechanisms used to translate the wishes of the electorate into political power. In the United Kingdom the **electorate** (those over 18 years old and registered to vote) can vote for:

1 their Member of Parliament (MP)

2 their local councillor

3 their Member of the European Parliament (MEP)

4 in Scotland, Wales and Northern Ireland, people can also vote for regional parliaments or assemblies.

The electoral system is the method used to determine which candidates and political parties will represent us.

Areas of the country are divided into 646 constituencies which elect one MP each. The candidate who wins more votes than any other becomes the MP. This is called, 'First Past the Post.'

One might get the impression that British people are well represented. However, since 1945 no British government has enjoyed the support of more than 50 per cent of the electorate.

Constitutional Monarchy

Figure 1.1 The Queen at the state opening of parliament

Britain is a representative democracy, but it is also a **constitutional monarchy**. This means that Britain is governed by ministers in the name of the Queen who is the head of state. The Queen's function in the political or legislative process is purely ceremonial.

However the Queen does play an important part in the legislative process. All Bills passed by parliament can only become law if they receive the **Royal Assent** (the Royal seal of approval). In theory the Queen could block legislation by refusing to give the Royal Assent. This could lead to a constitutional crisis.

If any attempt was made to abolish the monarchy in Britain, any such attempt would have to be by Act of Parliament. This means the Queen would have to give it the Royal Assent for it to become law.

Activities

1   What does the term 'representative democracy' mean?

2   What is the role of political parties?

3   Who are the main representatives the British people can vote for?

4   What evidence that people in England are not as well represented as people in other parts of the UK?

5   Why might any government since 1945 find it difficult to state it enjoyed the support of the majority of the British people?

6   What part does the Queen play in the political process?

Structure of British Government

The government is usually formed by the political party with the most seats in the House of Commons. There are 646 seats in the House of Commons. If a political party wishes to form a government with an overall majority then the figure of 324 seats or more is desirable.

In the 2005 General Election Labour won 356 seats. The political party which comes second in the general election is granted the title of Her Majesty's Official Opposition.

The Role of Government

The job of any government is to govern but also to put into practice those promises made to the electorate in the run up to the general election. Political parties publish **manifestos** (an outline of their intended policies and legislation) before a general election.

When a political party is elected it seeks to put its manifesto promises into action by passing bills in parliament which then become the law of the land.

The Labour Party's 2005 manifesto lays out its vision for the UK in nine main areas:

◆   **rising prosperity in an opportunity society**

◆   **education – more children making the grade**

◆   **crime and society – safe communities, secure borders**

◆   **NHS – free for all, personal to each**

◆   **elderly people – secure today, prepared for the future**

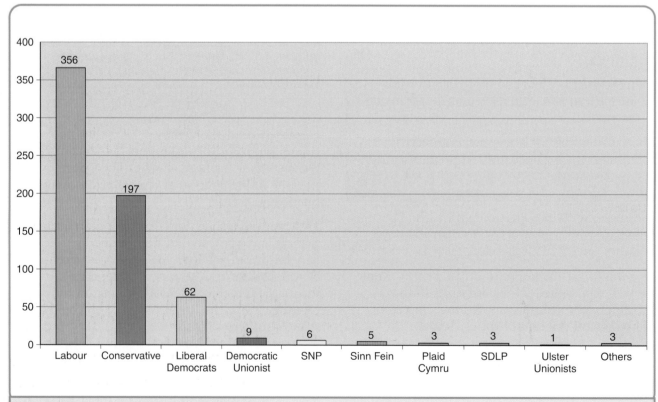

Figure 1.2 General election results 2005

- families – choice and support at work and at home
- international – a stronger country in a secure, sustainable and just world
- quality of life – excellence for all
- democracy – power devolved, citizens empowered.

When the Labour Party was re-elected in 2005, its aim was to put the above manifesto promises or commitments into action by spending money in a certain way and by passing laws.

Spending Our Money

The government pays for its policies through taxes and borrowing. In November of each year the chancellor announces how much he needs to raise in taxes and how the government intends to spend the money.

In Spring, the following year he announces the details in the budget. The budget must get the support of the House of Commons if his plans are to become law.

The chancellor announced taxes of £423 billion and expenditure of £460 billion. This expenditure amounts to £7,800 for every man, woman and child in the United Kingdom. The Government would have to borrow £37 billion to balance the books.

Activities

1 What does a party's manifesto set out?

2 What does a party seek to do if they become the government?

3 Look at Figures 1.3 and 1.4. What are the three biggest items of expenditure and the three biggest sources of government income?

4 What sources of income could you raise if you wanted to cut borrowing?

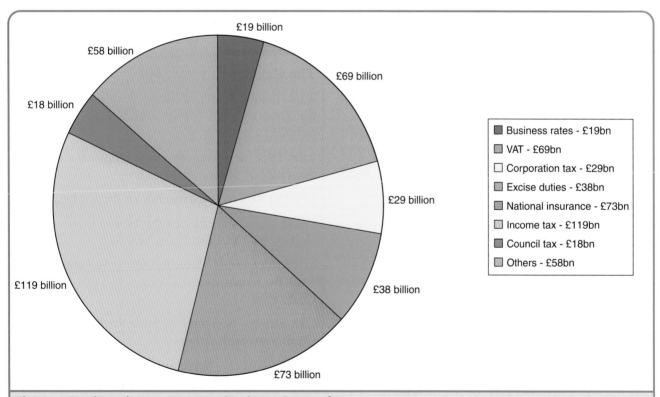

£19 billion
£58 billion
£18 billion
£69 billion
£29 billion
£38 billion
£73 billion
£119 billion

- Business rates - £19bn
- VAT - £69bn
- Corporation tax - £29bn
- Excise duties - £38bn
- National insurance - £73bn
- Income tax - £119bn
- Council tax - £18bn
- Others - £58bn

Figure 1.3 Where the government raises its tax income from
Source www.hm-treasury.gov.uk

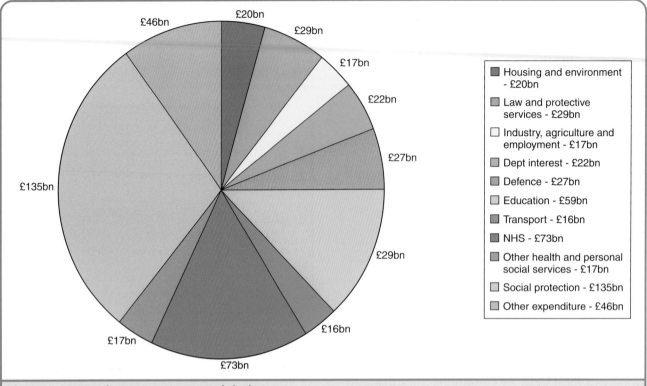

Figure 1.4 How the government spends its income
Source www.hm-treasury.gov.uk

The Executive

The government is the body of ministers responsible for running the country, chosen from the party which wins the most seats in a general election.

Of the Labour MPs elected in the 2005 General Election, 90 are members of the government. The most senior of these government ministers are known as the **Cabinet**. The leader of the Cabinet, and therefore of the government, is the Prime Minister, Tony Blair.

In addition to 23 members of the Cabinet, the government also includes Ministers of State and Under-Secretaries of State for each of the government departments.

For instance in the 2001–2004 Cabinet Charles Clarke, the former Secretary of State for Education and Skills had three Ministers of State responsible for Children, Lifelong Learning and School Standards and three Under-Secretaries of State for Skills, Early Years and Schools.

At the time there were 111 members of the government, including 90 MPs and 21 Peers.

The Cabinet in June 2005

Tony Blair – Prime Minister, First Lord of the Treasury and Minister for the Civil Service

John Prescott – Deputy Prime Minister and First Secretary of State

Gordon Brown – Chancellor of the Exchequer

Geoff Hoon – Leader of the House of Commons and Lord Privy Seal

Lord Falconer of Thoroton QC – Secretary of State for Constitutional Affairs and Lord Chancellor

Jack Straw – Secretary of State for Foreign and Commonwealth Affairs

Charles Clarke – Secretary of State for the Home Department

Margaret Beckett – Secretary of State for Environment, Food and Rural Affairs

Hilary Benn – Secretary of State for International Development

The Cabinet in June 2005 continued

David Blunkett – Secretary of State for Work and Pensions

Alistair Darling – Secretary of State for Transport and Secretary of State for Scotland

Patricia Hewitt – Secretary of State for Health

Peter Hain – Secretary of State for Northern Ireland and Secretary of State for Wales

John Reid – Secretary of State for Defence

Baroness Amos – Leader of the House of Lords and Lord President of the Council

Alan Johnson – Secretary of State for Trade and Industry

Ruth Kelly – Secretary of State for Education and Skills

Tessa Jowell – Secretary of State for Culture, Media and Sport

Hilary Armstrong – Parliamentary Secretary to the Treasury (Chief Whip)

Ian McCartney – Minister without Portfolio

John Hutton – Chancellor of the Duchy of Lancaster (Minister for the Cabinet Office)

Des Brown – Chief Secretary to the Treasury

David Miliband – Minister of Communities and Local Government

Also attending Cabinet:

Lord Goldsmith – Attorney General

Douglas Alexander – Minister of State for Europe in the Foreign and Commonwealth Office

Lord Grocott – Lords Chief Whip and Captain of the Gentleman at Arms

All members of the government are paid an additional allowance on top of their MP's salary. They are expected to support government policies or Cabinet decisions in the House of Commons or in any public statements. They must resign from the government if they disagree and wish to speak in parliament or publicly against government policies or Cabinet decisions.

In the 2001–2005 Government, Robin Cook resigned as Foreign Secretary and Clare Short resigned as Secretary of State for International Development because they disagreed with the Cabinet's decision to go to war against Iraq.

Activities

1   What do we mean by the term the executive?

2   What are the more senior members of the government known as?

3   What are members of the government expected to do if they disagree and speak against the government's policies or Cabinet decisions?

The Parliamentary System

The British Parliament is said to be **bicameral**, which means it is made up of two chambers. These are the House of Commons and the House of Lords. The House of Commons is made up of 646 MPs who represent 646 constituencies. These MPs are elected.

The House of Lords is an unelected chamber of peers. Their number has been greatly reduced in recent years as part of the Labour Government's reforms. In December 2002 there were 550 life Peers; 28 Law Lords, 91 hereditary Peers and 24 bishops.

Laws, except financial bills, require the support of both Houses of Parliament.

Activities

1   What does the term 'bicameral' mean?

2   Explain the difference between those who sit in the House of Commons and those who sit in the Lords.

3   Why might the Lords be said to be undemocratic?

Making a Law – Legislation

The idea for a new piece of legislation may come from a variety of places:

◆ **the party manifesto**
◆ **pressure groups such as Child Poverty Action Group, Help the Aged**
◆ **professional bodies, for example, the Law Society, the British Medical Association**
◆ **government departments.**

Most legislation (bills) which go through parliament are the results of the government's manifesto commitments.

There are basically three types of bill.

Public Bills – Government Bills and Private Members Bills are both Public Bills, in that they relate to matters of general concern, and must be introduced by a Member of Parliament (MP) or Peer (member of the House of Lords).
An example of a Government Bill (also known as a Public Bill) would be the Criminal Justice Bill.

Private Member's Bills – Individual MPs are given the opportunity to get legislation passed. A good example of this was the Voting Age (reduction to 16) which failed to go through parliament because it lacked government support. PMBs have very little chance of success without government backing.

Private Bills – Those which deal with by-laws etc and local authority legislation.

Passage of a Bill

Consultation

Before a Bill reaches parliament, the government sets out its general ideas for the Bill. This is outlined in a Green Paper. There can then be an input from focus groups and policy forums and those with a specific interest in the proposed legislation. They may be asked by the government to comment, or may themselves put forward views to the government on the issues outlined in the Green Paper.

Inside Parliament

First reading: Here the Bill is introduced to let MPs know the text of the Bill. No debate takes place.

Second Reading

The main principle of the Bill is debated by MPs and a vote or division takes place. MPs file through the two main division lobbies. If there are more ayes than no's then the Bill proceeds to the next stage. Because of the whipped majority, a government defeat at this stage is almost unknown.

Committee Stage

A clause by clause scrutiny takes place by the Standing Committee. The government has an in-built majority and amendments can take place.

Report Stage

Any amendments are considered by MPs who wish to contribute to the debate. Occasional changes to the wording of the Bill can take place.

Third Reading

The final version is debated and voted on. Once a Bill has passed its third reading in the Commons, it goes to the House of Lords. (It passes through the same stages there as it does in the Commons.)

The Lords vote on amendments and these amendments are incorporated into the Bill. The Bill then passes back to the Commons to discuss changes by the Lords.

Royal Assent

The Royal Assent is given by the Lord Commissioners on behalf of the monarch.

The Bill then becomes law and goes into the Statute Book.

Activities

1   How is the government usually formed?

2   What are the main types of Bills?

3   Explain the difference between a Public Bill and a Private Members Bill.

4   From what sources can proposals for a Bill come from?

5   Explain what happens in the following stages
    a) Second Reading
    b) Committee Stage
    c) Third Reading.

6   What in-built safety device does the government have at the Committee Stage?

The Work of Parliament

Legitimisation

A government acquires its authority to rule from its party's support in the House of Commons. If it loses that support it must resign.

If the ruling party loses a general election it must accept that result and hand over power to the winning party. This happened in 1997 when the ruling Conservative party was defeated and handed over power to Labour who had won a resounding victory at the general election.

Representation

Parliament is like a market place in which MPs let the government know our views. The political party provides a crude link between the people and the government.

MPs can also take up pressure group causes and try to introduce a Private Member's Bill.

However it cannot be said that parliament is a true reflection of society because it is predominantly male, white, middle class, middle aged and better educated than the average citizen.

Legislation

Government translates its manifesto commitments into policy in the form of Public Bills for parliamentary approval. If the government has a majority it can usually make its manifesto commitments into law.

A manifesto commitment can sometimes be sidelined to a committee (for example, electoral reform was passed to Jenkins) or to a backbencher (this was done regarding banning hunting with dogs).

Scrutiny

Calling the government (the executive) to account is one of the most important powers of parliament. In terms of finance this is one of most historic checks over government spending.

The Public Accounts Committee (PAC) checks that £460 billion a year of public money has been properly spent. The National Audit Office claims to save £7 of public money for every £1 it costs.

However, it is also argued that the PAC holds few public hearings and parliament pays little attention to its annual debate. Another example of the scrutinising function of parliament is the fact that the opposition party is given 20 days a year to table motions opposing government policy.

At Question Time the government is also held to account. Backbench MPs can ask questions of government ministers responsible for particular government departments. The Foreign Secretary, Jack Straw, was asked questions about Britain's involvement in Iraq in the immediate aftermath of the invasion in March 2003.

The Prime Minister, Tony Blair, is also held to account. During Prime Minister's Question Time, which is held once a week, the leader of the opposition, will ask questions which are designed to hold the PM to account for government policy.

Ian Duncan Smith, a former Conservative leader, was not regarded as effective at Question Time.

Michael Howard, who replaced him, is regarded by some in the media as being better at putting Tony Blair on the spot.

Questions can be either oral or written. Again, however, there are major criticisms of Question Time.

Government ministers are given the questions in advance and so have time to prepare an answer, saving them from the embarrassment which might arise from an impromptu question (this is when the minister is unaware of the question to be asked).

The opposition further lack the information and civil service back-up which the government has at its disposal.

Another criticism is the fact that Prime Minister's Question Time now only takes place once a week instead of twice a week. There is, however, evidence that the government does not always get its own way.

Each government department has a corresponding Select Committee which looks at its work. Governments are usually wary of these Select Committees which publish reports and can question government ministers. The Select Committee on Intelligence and Security was able to question Geoff Hoon, the Defence Secretary over the Kelly affair after the top government scientist tragically took his own life in July 2003.

Debates

The government is forced to explain and defend its policies in public. On 4th December 2003 there was a backbench debate on compensation for nuclear test veterans. It is argued that debates are insignificant in that they very rarely change government policy.

Although the executive has been accused of arrogance in recent years over its readiness to ignore the Commons, a parliamentary row sustained by the media can force a government reaction.

A good example was Liberal Democrat MP Norman Baker's campaign over the Hinduja passport affair in 2001. Peter Mandelson, a government minister, was forced to resign after extensive coverage in newspapers and other media.

Activities

1 What are the five main functions of parliament?

2 How can it be said that parliament is not truly representative of society as a whole?

3 How can the ordinary MP take up the cause of pressure or interest groups?

4 Give examples of the scrutinising functions of the House of Commons.

5 What evidence is there that the government has all the advantages?

  You must answer in depth with reference to specific examples.

6 What are Select Committees and give a recent example of one at work?

7 What evidence is there that the media are an effective check on government?

How Equal is Parliament?

Occupational Background

Among MPs returned after the 2001 General Election, the most common occupations across the three main parties were teachers (117 MPs) and company executives or directors (77 MPs).

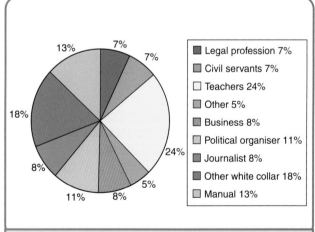

Figure 1.5 Labour MPs by occupation in 2001

Legend:
- Legal profession 7%
- Civil servants 7%
- Teachers 24%
- Other 5%
- Business 8%
- Political organiser 11%
- Journalist 8%
- Other white collar 18%
- Manual 13%

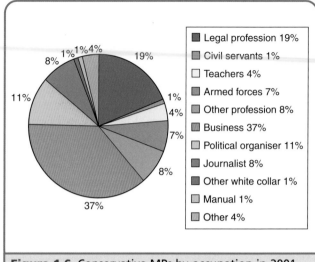

Figure 1.6 Conservative MPs by occupation in 2001

Legend:
- Legal profession 19%
- Civil servants 1%
- Teachers 4%
- Armed forces 7%
- Other profession 8%
- Business 37%
- Political organiser 11%
- Journalist 8%
- Other white collar 1%
- Manual 1%
- Other 4%

In 2001, company executives and directors comprised 30 per cent of the Conservative parliamentary party. The most common occupations among Labour MPs were teachers (24 per cent). 25 per cent of Liberal Democrat MPs were company executives or directors.

(Source: House of Commons Research Paper.)

Gender

Although female representation doubled at the 1997 election to 120 MPs it fell back slightly to 118 MPs at the 2001 election. The Labour Party has the largest number of female representatives by far with 95 female MPs. There were 14 Conservative women, five Liberal Democrats and four from other parties (2001 election). The number of female MPs increased to 125 after the 2005 General Election.

Gender and Representation

In terms of gender, only 19 per cent of MPs are women but at local council level the figure is 28 per cent. However, in terms of voting, women's votes are crucial to any election result. The majority of voters are women simply because they are the majority of the population.

Nevertheless, voter turnout amongst women is falling faster than that of men. In the 2001 General Election only 58 per cent of women voted. In 2005, 38 per cent of women voted Labour compared to 34 per cent of men.

Ethnic Minorities

There were 57 ethnic minority candidates from the Labour, Liberal Democrat and Conservative parties who stood in the 2001 general election.

12 ethnic minority MPs were elected. They were all Labour MPs. In 2005, the number of ethnic minority candidates from the three main parties increased to 113. Fifteen were elected – thirteen for Labour and two for the Conservatives.

A group known as Operation Black Vote was set up to campaign for greater black political representation.

It appears that few black or Asian candidates are ever selected for safe seats. This is especially the case for the Conservative and Liberal Democrat parties.

In terms of proportion to population size there should be 44 black and Asian MPs.

Figure 1.7 Mohammed Sarwar, Scotland's only ethnic minority MP.

Activities

1 Why could it be said that MPs are not truly representative of the general population in terms of their social class/occupational background?

2 What evidence is there to suggest that there is disproportionate under-representation in terms of gender?

3 Give reasons why ethnic minority voters might feel that Operation Black Vote was unsuccessful and that they might be under-represented.

Inside the House of Commons

The Whip System

MPs traditionally vote along party lines. This is because they are elected to represent their political party in parliament. If an MP belongs to the party of government then he/she is under tremendous pressure to 'tow the party line'.

Each political party has a Chief Whip whose job it is to make sure that MPs in that party vote the way the leadership want them to. The Chief Whip has other party Whips to help him.

Prior to the 2005 General Election, Labour had 412 MPs, and of these approximately 320 were ordinary backbench MPs who had to be controlled.

Whips issue notices to the MPs when there is an important division (vote) in the House of Commons. There are basically three types of command or Whip an MP can receive:

One line Whip

This lets MPs know that a vote will take place. Attendance is not compulsory but would be appreciated.

Two line Whip

This lets MPs know they should attend unless they have made an arrangement with another 'opposite' MP not to attend. This is known as 'pairing off' or 'having a pair'. The party Whips must approve this.

Three line Whip

MPs must attend at all costs.

However there are occasions when MPs disobey the party line. This usually happens when their conscience dictates that the party line is very different from what they as individuals believe.

This is particularly difficult for Tony Blair. His 'New Labour' policies are regarded by many Labour MPs as being too close to the Conservative's policies.

A study in late 2003 revealed that since the 2001 general election, a total of 197 Labour MPs have rebelled against the leadership on 141 separate votes.

A hard core of 30 Labour MPs regularly vote against the government.

Sick MPs are to be ferried in for vote as Whips pull out all the stops

There will be no rest this weekend for Hilary Armstrong, the government Chief Whip, and her troops as they pull every trick to bring in the votes.

One Labour MP, who has a broken ankle, will be brought by car from Bradford. Another Labour MP will get no help because the Whips are not sure how he will vote.

Seven Opposition MPs are having their flights paid to come back from a meeting in Strasbourg.

Seventeen Labour MPs who are at the same meeting are having to pay their own fares.

Paul Flynn, a Labour MP, will have to pay £600. He said, 'I will be coming back and I will vote against the Government.'

Source: *Independent* 25th January 2004 (abridged)

Activities

1 What is the role of the Chief Whip?

2 Explain the significance of the three types of 'Whip'

3 What evidence is there that the present government is facing much opposition from its own MPs?

4 Look at the abridged article from the *Independent*. What tactics did the Chief Whip employ to help the government win the vote?

5 What did the Opposition do to increase their vote?

6 What actions can the Whips or the party take if the MP fails to support the party line in the House of Commons?

In January 2004, Mr Blair faced one of his most difficult parliamentary sessions. Many Labour MPs opposed his policy to introduce university top-up fees.

When MPs came to vote in the House of Commons, 72 Labour MPs voted against the Government. Labour's Commons majority of 161 was reduced to only five. Despite the reduced majority the Government had won the vote.

Whips can also put pressure on the MP by contacting the MP's constituency party. If their constituency party turns against the MP, they can decide to adopt another candidate at the next election and the MP will be out of a job.

In very extreme cases the party can 'remove the Whip' from the MPs who rebel. This means that even if they attend the Commons they are not representing the party they were elected for.

In May 2003 George Galloway, Labour MP for Glasgow Hillhead, was suspended from the party after allegedly urging Iraqis to kill British troops as they were legitimate targets. He was subsequently expelled from the Labour Party in October 2003. He formed a new anti-war party (Respect) and won the Bethnal Green and Bow seat from Labour at the 2005 election.

What is the role of the Opposition?

The term 'opposition' applies to the political party which has the second biggest number of seats at the general election.

In 2001 the Conservative Party was led by William Hague. As the leader of the opposition, he took on the task of choosing a Shadow Cabinet. The job of the Shadow Cabinet is to 'shadow' their opposite number in the Cabinet. The shadow cabinet acts as an alternative government in waiting.

Ian Duncan Smith succeeded William Hague to become the leader of the opposition. He lasted in this role until November 2003, when Michael Howard took over.

The new Shadow Cabinet under Michael Howard was more streamlined. It only had 12 members including Howard himself. In some cases, Members of the Conservative Shadow Cabinet have to 'shadow' more than one government Minister.

The Conservatives lost the 2005 General Election and Michael Howard announced he would resign. The new Conservative leader will have to choose a new Shadow Cabinet.

Michael Howard's Streamlined Shadow Cabinet (pre-2005 Election)

Michael Howard – Leader of the Opposition

Michael Ancram – Foreign Affairs, International Development and Deputy Leader

Lord Strathclyde – Opposition Leader in the House of Lords

Oliver Letwin – Exchequer and Economic Affairs

David Davis – Home, Constitutional and Legal Affairs

Tim Yeo – Public Services, Health and Education

Theresa May – Environment and Transport

David Curry – Local and Devolved Government

Liam Fox and Lord Saatchi – Joint Chairmen of the Conservative Party

David MacLean – Chief Whip (Commons)

David Willets – Policy Co-ordination, Work and Pensions

Shadow Cabinet Ministers also have Shadow Secretaries of State and Parliamentary Private Secretaries. Nevertheless, these are much fewer in number than the 111 members of the government.

Unlike the government, opposition parties also do not have support from the Civil Service. This means that they have to get advice from outside organisations or pay for political researchers and advisors. Opposition parties receive an allowance to help them pay for these services.

When Tony Blair stands at the despatch box answering questions at PM's Question Time, his opposite number, the leader of the opposition, will try to 'catch him out' over the government's policies. The job of the leader of the opposition is to offer the country an alternative leader if that party were to win the general election.

The role of Shadow Cabinet Ministers is similar. Their job is to challenge their opposite number in the government. This is made more difficult as a Shadow Minister may have to challenge one or more ministers.

A major criticism of this system of **adversarial politics** is that real debate is stifled, leading to a 'slanging' match between the government and the opposition.

Charles Clark, Labour Education Minister criticised the Conservatives for voting against university top-up fees, although many of them supported the proposals. His view was that Conservatives only voted against them because they wanted to defeat Tony Blair's government. The Conservative view was that their job was to oppose, not support, the government.

Activities

1 Which party becomes Her Majesty's Opposition?

2 What disadvantages do the opposition face compared with the Government?

3 What is the leader of the opposition's main role?

4 Why might a Shadow Cabinet member have an especially difficult job?

5 What is the major criticism of 'adversarial politics'?

6 How would the Conservatives respond to Charles Clark's criticisms?

Pressures on our Representatives

The Work of the MP

Figure 1.8 Barbara Follet, MP for Stevenage

The following is the abridged version of a pamphlet from Barbara Follett detailing her work as MP for Stevenage.

My role as an MP is to represent all the people in my constituency, not just those who voted for me. My job as MP is to help you with all matters for which parliament or central government is responsible.

Many people think that as an MP I can solve all their problems. Unfortunately, this is not the case. MPs can only help with those matters for which parliament or central government is responsible.

Such problems might be tax problems involving the Inland Revenue (but not council tax which is paid to your local authority); problems involving the NHS; problems involving the DSS such as benefits, pensions; issues dealt with by the Home Office such as immigration; issues such as school closures dealt with by the Department of Education and Employment.

How I deal with constituents problems

If a constituent has a problem involving central government I can use a number of methods available to help resolve the matter.

I can write a letter to the relevant department or official. If that does not work I can write a letter to the Minister involved or by even making an appointment to see the Minister personally.

In the case of administrative incompetence I can refer the case to the Ombudsman. This person can only be approached by an MP.

What can I do inside the House?

If I have not received satisfactory answers, after having used the above methods, I can raise the issue in the House in front of the press and the public. The most popular method is for me to put the Minister on the spot by asking a question at Question Time one afternoon.

Another way to raise an issue is the half hour Adjournment Debate which takes place at the end of the day. To be successful I have to have by name chosen by ballot.

The Early Day Motion is another way to get matters resolved. If I use this method I place on record my opinion.

It may be that the problem is a common one involving a lot of people. I may try to introduce a Private Member's Bill. This type of action is only seldom successful but publicity is drawn to the matter and the Minister may be persuaded to make changes in the future.

Activity

Explain in detail how an MP can help someone in his constituency who has a problem with the NHS.

You must write your answer in essay form.

Figure 1.9 Nigel Griffiths, MP for Edinburgh

'It is a great privilege to serve you as the first Labour MP in history for this constituency. My job is to represent all my constituents, irrespective of how they vote. I am the first MP to live in this constituency so I know the local issues and the problems.'

Diary Extracts by Nigel Griffiths MP

Monday 2nd December 2002
Constituency meeting

Friday 29th November 2002
Constituency Advice Meeting

Friday 29th November 2002
Royal Blind School Assembly, present prize to Christmas card design winner

Thursday 28th November 2002
Asian Pacific Business Association – promoting UK Manufacturers

Wednesday 27th November 2002
Commons pre-budget speech by Chancellor

Wednesday 27th November 2002
Questions to PM

Wednesday 27th November 2002
Meet Chairman of US Business Incubators

Wednesday 27th November 2002
Meet party from George Watson School for tour of Parliament

Weekly News and Notice Board
Nigel is helping 220 staff made redundant by Telesens KSCL on 28th June. None of the 220 employees have received their salary for June.

Constituents have accused the US buyer, Convergys and the receivers Deloitte and Touche of trying to avoid paying the wages to sell the company as a going concern.

Questions are being asked whether this is an attempt to bypass UK employment law. Nigel has contacted the Department of Trade and Industry to investigate the matter.

Activities

1 What does Nigel Griffiths say is special about himself?

2 'Nigel Griffiths works hard for his constituency.' What evidence is there in the sources to support this view?

3 What evidence is there that Nigel Griffiths plays a wider role than just being a constituency MP?

Opposition MPs

Opposition MPs work very much like MPs from the party of government. However, they do not enjoy the same type of access to government Ministers, who are less likely to help someone whose job it is to try to defeat the government and to be re-elected by his/her constituents at the next election.

Opposition MPs, like all MPs, seek to keep a high profile in the local press in order to convince electors that they are doing a good job – and should be re-elected.

Peter Duncan was Scotland's only Conservative MP after the 2001 election. He was MP for Galloway and Upper Nithsdale. His constituency was a largely farming community, but also included the area around Stranraer. The reduction in the number of Scottish MPs from 72 to 59 led to his seat being merged with a nearby Labour seat. He failed to win this seat in 2005.

Figure 1.10 Peter Duncan, Scotland's only Conservative MP from 2001 to 2005

The following titles of press releases (in italics) were directed at the local press and are from the MP's website.

22nd December 2003 – Health Service Discrimination by postcode exposed by MP.
The MP complained about NHS patients in his rural constituency having to pay travel costs to hospital when NHS patients in the Highlands do not.

22nd December 2003 – Duncan blasts Cairnryan speeding problem.
The MP presented a petition to the police about speeding in part of his constituency.

6th January 2004 – Duncan's fury at Scottish MPs abuse of Westminster.
The MP criticises Scots (Labour) MPs voting on matters which only affects England and Wales.

This was in the run up to the vote in the House of Commons on university tuition fees on 27th January 2004. The government's majority of 161 was reduced to five. Many Scottish Labour MPs voted for a bill which would only directly affect students at English and Welsh universities. The government would have lost the vote if Scots Labour MPs had abstained.

9th January 2004 – Local MP calls for port police to be relocated.

Peter Duncan urged that the port police be moved from Stranraer to Cairnryan when Stena Sealink moves its services.

15th January 2004 – Duncan demands answers from Scottish Power.
The MP raised issues regarding problems with blackouts and power supply which affected his rural constituents.

15th January 2004 – Local MP welcomes development at Carlisle Airport.
News that Peter Duncan had tabled an Early Day Motion in the House of Commons, saying this will help business and tourism and blaming the government if there is any delay.

Activities

1 List the main issues covered in the press releases.

2 What evidence is there that Peter Duncan MP regards regular press contacts as important?

3 State which of the issues:
   a) were direct or indirect criticisms of the government or the Labour Party.
   b) were purely local issues to show he was taking up constituents problems.

4 Explain, in your own words, which issues Peter Duncan was addressing and for each say what you think he was trying to achieve.

5 What happened to Peter Duncan in the 2005 election?

The role of MPs: should this be their only job?

The *BBC News Talking Point* programme asked listeners for their views.

Background: William Hague, former Tory party leader, has added two new roles to his current job as a backbench MP. He has taken up the post as political and economic adviser to JCB, one of Britain's biggest companies. He also became non-executive director of an engineering firm in the town where he grew up.

Many other politicians have taken up lucrative business links. Kenneth Clarke, former Tory Chancellor, earns £100,000 a year as vice chairman of BAT industries.

But should our politicians be free to work outside parliament as a way of 'keeping in touch with reality', or should they just dedicate their energies to being an MP?

Here are some of the listeners' comments

'. . . they're moonlighting on the job. That's why they didn't want parliament televised. People would see the place is usually empty. They say they are away doing constituency work. More like lining their own pockets.'

'Let's have them on a flexitime system and pay them for the time they are actually in the House.'

'Why shouldn't MPs have more than one job? I see nothing wrong with having directorships as long as the time spent on this does not interfere with their job as an MP.'

'The trouble is that so many of today's MPs have little experience of real life. I think that an MP should have to be at least 40 years old.'

'If I had another job my employer would take a very dim view of it. How can they possibly do their job if they are off somewhere else doing another job? I'm a teacher. Imagine the reaction I would get if I said to my bosses 'sorry I can't take this class as I've got a taxi fare to the airport!'

'They should be like the Formula One drivers whilst in the House and they should wear baseball caps bearing their sponsors names.'

Activities

1 Make arguments for and against MPs having 'other jobs'.

2 Look at Figures 1.11–1.13 and answer the following questions.
   a) What evidence is there to suggest that the British public are totally cynical about political parties and politicians in general?
   b) Is there any evidence to suggest that MPs are still valued by the British public?
   c) What evidence is there that people are becoming more willing to demonstrate or protest?

3 'British politicians are totally selfish and just in it for themselves. There is no evidence to suggest that they care for anything other than their own popularity.'

   How far does the evidence in these figures support this view?

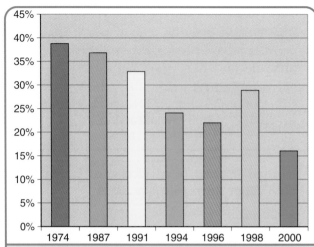

Figure 1.11 People who trust governments to put the needs of the country above the needs of the party. Percentage results by year.

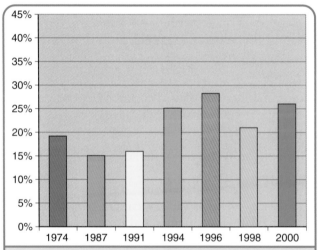

Figure 1.12 People who think parties are only interested in people's votes, not their opinions. Percentage results by year.

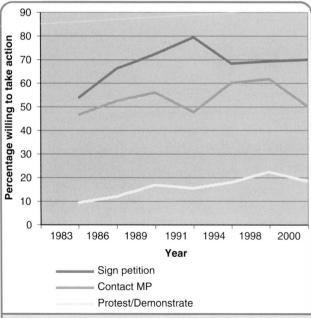

Figure 1.13 Percentage of people who are willing to take part in types of political action.

Political Parties

The political landscape of Britain has changed beyond recognition in the last twenty years. The traditional lines between socialist left and capitalist right have been redrawn.

In the 1970s the Labour party was left wing in outlook. This means it was committed to the welfare state, high taxation for the rich and the nationalisation of state assets such as coal, steel, railways, gas and electricity. Clause four of the Labour Party Constitution committed a Labour government to nationalisation.

The Thatcher election victories of 1979, 1983, 1987 and Major in 1992 changed all that. Britain swung to the right as Labour's traditional core support deserted it in millions. The Conservatives Party won support amongst 'middle England' voters because it championed low taxation, home ownership, strong law and order policies, privatisation and share ownership.

Many middle class and better off working class voters saw improvements in their earnings and standard of living through increased home ownership and the boom in house prices, access to credit and through buying shares in newly privatised companies, such as British Gas and British Telecom.

The Conservatives also encouraged people to provide for themselves and their families and not become reliant on the 'nanny state'. Welfare benefits were drastically reduced to 'encourage' people to seek work. Nevertheless, many people also lost their new found wealth through playing on the stock market. Unemployment increased and Margaret Thatcher's Poll Tax policy became deeply unpopular.

Labour seemed set to win in the 1992 election. At that time average earnings were £12,000 a year. Labour pledged only to increase taxes for those earning £20,000 and over. One of the main reasons Labour lost the election was that richer voters would naturally not want to pay more tax, but more importantly, that middle income voters in key constituencies, who aspired to earn more than £20,000 per year also did not want to have to pay more tax when they achieved higher earnings.

The 1992 election was a turning point for Labour. Neil Kinnock, the Labour Leader resigned and was replaced by John Smith, and after he died in 1994 by Tony Blair. Blair's 'New Labour' policies were directed at winning over 'middle England' voters.

Nationalisation policies within Clause four of the Labour Party Constitution were dropped along with the policy of high taxation. Labour promised big business that they could manage the economy better than the Conservatives.

Public disaffection with Tory sleaze and corruption (and the lack of a threatening alternative to Tony Blair's dynamic 'New Labour') won Labour 'middle England' votes and the elections in 1997, 2001 and 2005.

Labour's move to the right under Tony Blair has led to a re-alignment in British politics. Some Conservative policies such as restoring the link between pensions and earnings as well as abolishing top up fees are closer to the 'old' Labour left. The Liberal Democrats are now the high tax party. Some Conservatives regard Labour's law and order policies as too extreme. All three parties believe in choice both as a way of improving public services and satisfying the demands of the consumerist age.

Activity

Explain in your own words why Labour changed its policies in the 1990s.

The House of Lords

Figure 1.14 Inside the House of Lords

The House of Lords is sometimes regarded as the real opposition as they have regular opportunities to criticise and even defeat government bills.

The House of Lords has four main functions. To:

◆ **make laws (60 per cent of its work)**

◆ **scrutinise (look closely at) what the government is doing**

◆ **provide advise through committees or investigations**

◆ **perform judicial work – it is the highest court of appeal for all UK cases (excluding Scottish criminal law cases).**

Abridged Extract from House of Lords Order Paper 28th January 2004

Oral Questions
Lord Northbrook – what plans are there to legislate to change the way that the council tax or equivalent local government tax is levied?

Lord Tombs – how much new generating capacity (excluding wind power) is expected to be commissioned in England and Wales during each of the years 2004, 2005 and 2006?

Lord Sheldon – what action is being taken to produce a clear delineation of roles and lines of accountability between special advisers and permanent civil servants?

Debates
Bishop Lord Gardner of Parkes – the Post Office

Lord Blaker – Zimbabwe

Lord Rae – what is the assessment of the total costs to date in economic and human terms of the recent conflict in Iraq and the likely future costs of the occupation, reconstruction and rehabilitation of Iraq?

Legislation
Domestic Violence

Crime and Victims Bill [HL] – (Grand Committee 3rd day – Committee Rooms 3A and 4B).

Source www.parliament.uk

Reform of the Lords

The 1997 Labour manifesto included a reform of the House of Lords. Labour viewed the House of Lords as anachronistic (out of date) in a modern democracy. It was wrong that someone should have a powerful say in making laws because of the family they were born into.

The 1999 Lords Act reduced the number of hereditary peers to 92, until a more permanent plan for the Lords could be devised. The government also set up the Wakeham Commission to look at a permanent solution for the House of Lords. The report was superseded in late 2002 by the following options:

1 fully appointed – supported by traditionalists, could be more representative of society at large but appointees are as undemocratic as the hereditary and life peers they replace.

2 fully elected – simple and legitimate but could duplicate the Commons or even challenge it.

3 80 per cent appointed/20 per cent elected – a mixture of democracy and patronage but could be confusing.

4 80 per cent elected/20 per cent appointed – allows meaningful elections but keeps some appointed experts.

5 60 per cent elected/40 per cent appointed – seen as a good mix of democracy and stability but unclear.

6 60 per cent appointed/40 per cent elected – supported by those against fully elected house but again most will be unelected.

7 50 per cent elected/50 per cent appointed – very neat in terms of numbers and composition but could lead to deadlock.

Source *Guardian* 12 December 2002 (adapted)

Activities

Look at the text above (abridged extract from the House of Lords Order Paper for 28 January 2004) and answer the following questions.

1 What bill was the House of Lords involved in discussing?

2 What evidence is there of the House of Lords using its scrutiny powers?

3 What other activities took place that day?

4 From the list of functions given earlier, what was the House of Lords not involved in?

5 Why major criticisms did the Labour government have of the House of Lords?

6 What did the 1999 Lords Act do?

7 Look at the options for change suggested. For each one, state the points in favour and the points against.

8 Select one of these options and make a case in its support.

The Judiciary

Judges and the courts are formally separate from parliament and the government and are responsible for interpreting British and European law and protecting the rights of the individual and others.

The top court of appeal in the United Kingdom for all cases (except Scottish criminal cases) is the House of Lords. There are 12 Law Lords whose job it is to hear appeals from lower courts.

The judiciary can also come into conflict with the executive. For example, the former Home Secretary, David Blunkett, was judged to have acted illegally by deporting asylum seekers before they could put their case properly.

In theory, the judiciary are separate from the government (the executive). However, senior members of the judiciary are appointed by the PM, such as the Attorney General and the Solicitor General.

Who are the Judges?

Lawyer Laura Cox is one of the High Court's newest judges. Despite the fact that Cox is a prominent employment lawyer, her elevation is highly unusual. She became one of just seven women among a total of 107 judges serving in the court.

Although more women have been made judges over the last few years, the UK's judiciary remains elitist, white, male and aged. The average age is over 60. Only one per cent are from minority ethnic groups. The Commission for Judicial Appointments recently expressed the view that the current judiciary is 'overwhelmingly white, male and from a narrow social and educational background.'

Source: *Labour Research* December 2002 (abridged)

Court	All judges	Judges appointed since 1997
House of Lords	63%	66%
Court of Appeal	78%	86%
High Court	74%	70%
All Courts	67%	67%

Figure 1.15 Percentage of judges (England and Wales) who attended public school

Court	All Judges	Judges appointed since 1997
House of Lords	92%	100%
Court of Appeal	91%	95%
High Court	82%	81%
All Courts	60%	60%

Figure 1.16 Percentage of judges (England and Wales) who went to Oxford or Cambridge university

Adapted Source Labour Research December 2002

Activities

1   What is the role of the judiciary and what evidence is there to suggest that they are not totally independent of the executive?

2   In what way have the courts protected the rights of the individual against government action?

3   What evidence is there that judges are unrepresentative of:
    a)   women
    b)   minority ethnic groups
    c)   the people of Britain by age?

4   Look at Figures 1.15 and 1.16.
    a)   What is the school and university background of most senior judges?
    b)   What evidence is there that Labour has not changed this?

Activities

1   Using the table of current party policies say which party supports the greatest number of students going on to further education.

2   Which parties support fewer numbers?

3   On what policy areas is there greatest similarity between all three parties? Explain your answer.

4   Which of the three parties might pensioners favour most and why?

5   On which issue do all the political parties offer the consumer a choice?

6   Summarise the following policies in note taking form for all three parties:
    a)   taxation
    b)   law and order
    c)   welfare/pensions

7   Look back at the section on political change. Say which policies the Labour Government might find are opposed by 'old' Labour MPs.

GENERAL/CREDIT

Please note that the current policies of the political parties at Westminster for England (and Wales) may be different from the policies of the same parties in the Scottish Parliament or the Welsh Assembly.

Labour – New Labour

Education
Sure Start for pre-5s.
National testing.
Targets for schools.
More specialist schools.
50% of school leavers to go to further education.
Tuition fees of £3,000. Grants for poorer students.

Health
Foundation hospitals.
Work with private sector.
Cut waiting times.
More choice of hospitals.
Appointments online.

Pensions/Welfare
Pension credit.
Income guarantee.
Pensions linked to prices.

Crime
Anti-social behaviour laws.
Restrict right to trial by jury.
More community support officers.

Tax
Tuition fees, road tolls.
No increase in taxes.
Increase National Insurance.

Local Government
Localism: more freedom for best performing Councils.
Set up other local bodies. Council Tax Capping.

Conservatives

Education
Introduce US Head Start policy for pre-5s.
School Voucher scheme.
Support popular schools.
Funds for private schools.
Reduce 50% target of school leavers going to further education.
Scrap tuition fees.

Health
Support Private sector.
Patient chooses hospital.
Health screen immigrants.
Independent board to distribute NHS funds.

Pensions/Welfare
Pensions linked to wages.
Cut means-tested benefits.
Cut higher taxes.

Crime
Counselling for delinquent children.
Elected sheriffs to decide local police spending.
40,000 extra police.

Tax
Cut taxes.
Cut administration costs.
Reduce bureaucracy.

Local Government
More decentralisation.
Oppose regional assemblies.
Oppose local increases in local taxes.

Liberal Democrats

Education
One stop centres. Flexible curriculum. Vocational education.
Support poorer schools. Scrap targets and league tables.
Scrap tuition fees and top up fees.

Health
More money for NHS.
Regional NHS.
Flexible health.
Choice of hospital using a national database.

Pensions/Welfare
Increase pensions by up to £15 a week for 80s +.
Free long-term care.

Crime
Oppose aspects of anti-social behaviour orders.
Local crime reduction partnerships.
More community sentences.

Tax
Raise taxes on rich.
Local Health taxes.
Cut waste and bureaucracy.

Local Government
Regional Assemblies.
Local income tax.

Figure 1.17 The main political parties at Westminster and their current policies

The British Electoral System

The Westminster electoral system is known as First Past the Post or the simple majority system. There are 646 seats in the House of Commons. The candidates who are elected to represent these constituencies simply have to get more votes than any of the other candidates to win the seat. The political party with the most seats usually forms the government. If a party wins 324 seats or more it will form a majority government.

Safe Seats

Each of the 646 constituencies is contested in the General Election. Many of these seats have been won by very large majorities. The majority is so large that there is very little danger of the sitting MP losing the seat at the next election.

Marginal Seats

These are constituencies where the winning candidate has a very small majority and would be in danger of losing the seat at the next election.

Marginal constituencies are very important at a general election. Labour's success in 1997 was down to the fact that they targeted 60 key marginals. As it turned out they won these easily and many more. Their victory at the 1997 election was so resounding that many Conservative MPs even lost safe seats! In 2005, all the parties targeted the marginals. The overall swing to the Conservative and Liberal Democrat parties meant that Labour lost 47 seats. The Conservatives won 33 more seats and the Liberal Democrats gained 11.

Voter Apathy

There is evidence to suggest that the public are turning away from politics. People could not be bothered to vote. This is known as **voter apathy**.

Tony Lawrence, a 33 year old Liverpudlian, has never voted. 'Basically because there's no one I can decide on. I'm not going to vote for someone I don't believe in. It's just a lot of suits and faceless men and all your "Ra, Ra, Order, Order" on the telly'.

National turnout at the Westminster General Election fell from 71 per cent in 1997 to 59.4 per cent in 2001. In the European elections the turnout is even lower, in the low twenties.

A BBC study in 2002 found that two thirds of the population feel unrepresented by the political process. Even the Conservative leader Michael Howard said 'the British public view conventional party politics with contempt.'

The low turnout and alienation according to Liverpool MP Louise Ellman is: 'concentrated in the inner cities where there is a lot of poverty, a lot of mobility and a loss of a sense of community'.

Even in affluent areas there is evidence of voter apathy. In Runnymede and Weybridge in Surrey, one of the richest constituencies in the country, voter turnout has fallen from 80 per cent in 1992 to 71.5 per cent in 1997. In 2001 it fell to 56.1 per cent.

Guardian 25 November 2003 (adapted)

1 What is the name given to the Westminster electoral system?

2 Explain how a political party is elected to government.

3 Explain the difference between a safe seat and a marginal seat.

4 What evidence is there that marginal seats were crucial to the outcome of the 1997 election?

5 Look at source above and answer the following questions.
   a) What evidence is there of apathy at general elections?
   b) What did the BBC survey of 2002 conclude?
   c) To what extent are politicians aware of the problem?
   d) In what type of constituencies does apathy appear to be most acute and suggest reasons for this?
   e) What evidence is there that not just poor areas suffer apathy at election time?

How Fair is the British Electoral System?

If you look at Figures 1.28–30 you will note that the First Past the Post system appears to benefit the Conservative and Labour parties while at the same time penalising the smaller parties.

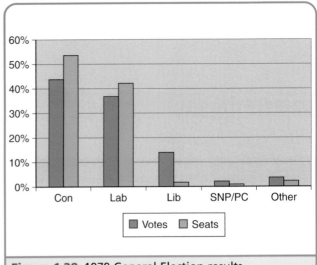

Figure 1.28 1979 General Election results

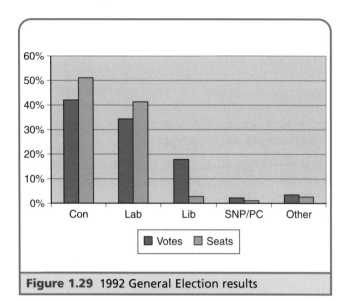

Figure 1.29 1992 General Election results

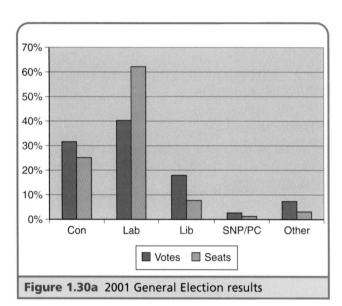

Figure 1.30a 2001 General Election results

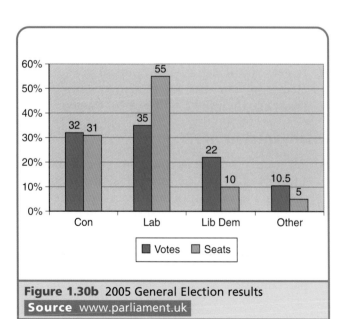

Figure 1.30b 2005 General Election results
Source www.parliament.uk

In the 17 Elections since 1945, Labour has won a greater percentage of seats than votes with the exception of 1951, 1955 and 1959. The Conservatives have won a greater percentage of seats than votes with the exception of 1945, 1966, 1997, 2001 and 2005. The Liberals/Liberal Democrats, SNP, Plaid Cymru and others have all won fewer seats (percentage-wise) than total votes cast.

The First Past the Post System

First Past the Post is a single member system. This means there are 646 separate constituencies across the UK and each one elects one single Member of Parliament.

In order to vote you simply place an 'X' beside the candidate of your choice. The candidate who gets the most votes wins. It is not necessary for the winning candidate to get over 50 per cent of the votes.

Under FPP there are millions of wasted votes. In the constituency results in Figure 1.31 the losing candidates' votes added together are more than the winning candidate. Under FPP there are no prizes for coming second.

Party	Votes	%
Labour	25,694	44.7
Conservative	23,369	43.5
Liberal Democrats	5469	10.2
UK Independence	880	1.6
Labour Majority	665	1.2
Turnout	53,752	67.4

Figure 1.31 Kettering constituency 2001

Advantages of FPP

◆ It is easy to use and simple to understand.
◆ The voter can express a view on the party he/she wishes to form the next government.
◆ It tends to lead to a two party system; this means that either the Conservatives or Labour form the government.
◆ It produces single party government with a mandate to implement its policies and it does not have to rely on other parties for support.

◆ It provides a close link between the constituent and the MP.

◆ The system represents the wishes of the people as the candidate with the most votes wins the seat.

◆ It has worked well for years so why change it.

Disadvantages of FPP

◆ FPP produces results where the winning party has a majority of seats in the House of Commons but only won a minority of support in the country, for example, in 2005 Labour got 35 per cent of the vote but won 55 per cent of the seats.

◆ Only one MP is elected to each constituency, so the voters who did not vote for the winning candidate have their votes wasted.

◆ There is a lack of choice for the voters. Candidates for the parties are selected by a small number of party members and voters can only choose between the parties. Electors may wish to vote for a party but might not like the candidate.

◆ Voters are represented unequally. In 2005 The Liberal Democrats won 22 per cent of the vote but got only 10 per cent of the seats.

◆ Constituencies are not all the same size. Prior to 2005 the smallest electorate was 21,807 in the Western Isles while the Isle of Wight has 106,305. This means it takes more votes in one constituency to elect an MP than it does in another.

◆ The system benefits the Conservative and Labour parties. They tend to have their support concentrated in certain geographical/regional areas. Those parties such as the Liberal Democrats tend to have their support thinly spread throughout the country and as a result their vote is smothered.

◆ It disadvantages women and ethnic minority candidates. Countries which use proportional systems have greater female representation.

Alternative Voting Systems

Alternative Vote (AV)

Like FPP, this system is a single member system. The same constituency boundaries are used and voters elect one person to represent them in parliament just as we do now.

However, rather than placing an 'X' against their preferred candidate, each voter ranks their candidates in order of preference, for example, 1 for first choice, 2 for second choice and so on. If a candidate receives a majority of first place votes, he/she will be elected as they would under the present system.

However, if no candidate manages to get more than 50 per cent of the vote, the second choice votes for the bottom candidate are redistributed. This process is repeated until one candidate gets an absolute majority.

The AV system is in effect a modified form of FPP and has its advantages.

Advantages of AV

◆ It keeps the same constituencies and so the link between the MP and their constituents is maintained.

◆ Extremist parties would be unlikely to gain support by this system and there would be little chance of coalition governments being formed, no more than at present.

◆ All MPs would have the support of the majority of their constituents.

◆ It prevents MPs being elected with a minority of the vote. In 1997 47 per cent of MPs were elected with less than 50 per cent of the votes in their constituencies.

◆ It gets rid of negative or tactical voting. The electorate can vote for their first choice knowing their vote will not be wasted.

Disadvantages of AV

◆ Although it ensures the winning candidate is supported by the majority of constituents, it does not give proportionality to parties with other opinions. Research has shown it could even give a more distorted result than FPP.

◆ It does not help those smaller parties who have traditionally been underrepresented in parliament.

Proportional Representation Systems

The Party List System

This system of voting is a multi-member system. Under this system, electors vote for a party in a multi-member constituency, or sometimes for a whole country. Each political party submits a party list with its candidates ranked in order of the party's preference. Voter then vote according to party of their choice on the ballot paper.

All the votes are counted and each party receives seats in the constituency in the same proportion as the votes it won in that constituency. Those who are placed high on the party list are most likely to become the party's MPs. Electors have no say in electing the candidates.

Arguments for Party List

◆ It guarantees a high degree of party proportionality. If a party gets 42 per cent of the vote it will get 42 per cent of the seats. If this system was used in the 2005 General Election Labour would have got 239 seats instead of the 356 seats it got under FPP.

◆ The system is simple for voters to use. They simply have to vote for a political party out of a small selection of parties.

Disadvantages of the Party List

◆ Voters have no choice over candidates and they only get a decision over which party forms the government.

◆ Party lists do not give fairer representation to traditionally under-represented groups in society. In fact party leaders when drawing up their lists are more likely to choose 'mainstream' candidates.

◆ The system puts power in the hands of the party not the voter.

◆ There is little accountability to voters and no link between the MPs and the voters.

The Single Transferable Vote (STV)

Again, like the party list system, this is a multi-member system. Under this system each constituency would elect between three and five MPs. Britain would therefore be divided into smaller multi-member constituencies. Voters rank the candidates in order of preference, putting a 1 for their first choice, a 2 for their second choice, a 3 for their third choice and so on. Each constituency is given a quota of votes a candidate much get before they can be elected. The quota is worked by using the following formula:

$$\frac{\text{Number of votes cast}}{\text{Number of seats} + 1} + 1$$

If there was a five-member constituency and 180,000 votes were cast, a candidate would need 30,001 votes to be elected. If a candidate gets over that quota they are automatically elected. Supposing Candidate A is elected on the first count then the 'surplus' votes of this candidate are redistributed among the candidates not yet elected.

The surplus votes are redistributed, based on 2nd, 3rd or 4th preferences. More candidates will meet this quota.

Finally, the lowest placed candidate is eliminated and then their 2nd, 3rd or 4th preferences are redistributed until candidates meet the quota.

Under this system most of the votes are used and far fewer votes are wasted.

Arguments for STV

◆ It puts power in the hands of the voter.

◆ Parliament reflects the wishes of the voters.

◆ It is simple for the voters to use.

◆ Only a party or coalition of parties with more than 50 per cent of the electorate could form a government.

◆ Voters can choose between candidates within parties demonstrating support for the different factions within political parties.

◆ There is no need for tactical voting. Voters can be confident that all their preferences will be used.

◆ It produces strong stable governments because they are founded on the majority support of the electorate.

Arguments against STV

- It does not produce the same proportionality as the list system or additional member system.
- It breaks the link between the MP and their constituents.
- MPs might have to spend far more time on constituency problems rather than focusing on the broader picture.
- It could lead to permanent coalition government and if parties fell out with each other the government would collapse.
- It is disliked by many politicians as it gives power to the voter. Many MPs who feel safe under the present FPP system might not be assured the same comfort under STV.

Activities

1 Discuss arguments for and against;
   a) First Past the Post
   b) Alternative Voting
   c) the Party List System
   d) Single Transferable Vote.

2 Why do you think Scottish voters would find less difficulty with the Party List System?

3 Overall, which system would you prefer for elections in the UK?
   Give reasons for your answer.

The Scottish Parliament

Figure 1.18 The Debating Chamber of the Scottish Parliament

On the 24th July 1997 the new elected Labour government published a White Paper on devolution. This White Paper was titled Scotland's Parliament. The government further outlined proposals to hold a referendum to let the Scottish people decide if they wanted it.

The referendum which was held on the 11th September 1997 asked the Scottish electorate two questions:

Do you want a Scottish Parliament?
Do you want the Parliament to have tax raising powers?

The result was 74.3 per cent voting for the Scottish Parliament. The Scotland Bill received the Royal Assent on the 19th November 1998. The first elections to the Scottish Parliament were held on the 6th May 1999 and on the 1st July 1999 the parliament was officially opened.

Both the Westminster and Scottish Parliaments have law making and financial powers over many issues which affect the lives of the people who live in Scotland. These law making and financial powers are divided up into reserved matters which are dealt with at Westminster and devolved matters which are dealt with in the Scottish Parliament.

Reserved Matters

There are certain matters the Scottish Parliament cannot deal with and these are reserved for the UK Parliament in Westminster. These areas are known as reserved matters.

The reserved matters are: foreign affairs, national security, laws on misuse of drugs, defence, trade and industry, social security, equal opportunities, broadcasting, electricity, gas, coal and nuclear energy

Devolved Matters

The main areas are: education, health, housing, justice, local government, social work, environment, fisheries, agriculture, police and fire service, food standards, tourism, culture and sport.

What Takes Place Inside the New Scottish Parliament?

In many ways the Scottish Parliament is similar to the Westminster Parliament. It votes, debates issues and legislation, it works in Committees, it scrutinises the work of the Scottish Executive and holds it to account. It also has the important task of choosing the First Minister.

Figure 1.19 Jack McConnell and Jim Wallace signed the Partnership Agreement in 2003

The Scottish Executive is the government of Scotland for devolved matters. The Scottish Executive is made up of the party or parties which have the majority of seats in the Scottish Parliament.

In the May 2003 elections the Labour Party did not have a majority necessary to form the Scottish Executive in its own right. Out of a total number of 129 MSPs, Labour only won 50 seats. Labour signed a Partnership Agreement with the Liberal Democrats who had won 17 seats. Both parties now form the Scottish Executive

The Scottish Executive is made up of the First Minister, Ministers, Junior Ministers and Law Officers.

Figure 1.20 Jack McConnell MSP, First Minister

The main difference between the Scottish Executive and the Labour Government is that the Executive is a coalition between the Labour and Liberal Democrat parties, whereas the Westminster Government is controlled by one party.

Although the Labour party is the biggest party in the Scottish Parliament, and a Labour MSP is the First Minister, Jack McConnell also had to agree to implement some Liberal Democrat policies if he was to be able to form a Scottish government.

He also had to agree to the appointment of Liberal Democrats to the Scottish Executive, including Jim Wallace as Deputy First Minister, replaced by Nicol Stephen in 2005.

Figure 1.21 Nicol Stephen, Deputy First Minister

The Scottish Executive has 18 Ministers and Deputies and two Law Officers. The Liberal Democrats have five of the 18 Ministerial positions; Nicol Stephen – Deputy First Minister, George Lyon – Deputy Finance and Public Services, Ross Finnie – Minister for Environment and Rural Affairs, Tavish Scott – Minister for Transport and Robert Brown – Deputy Minister for Education and Young People.

The Scottish Executive has three basic functions:

1 proposing legislation. It suggests the vast majority of legislation. A recent example might be the proposal to outlaw smoking in public places.

2 responsibility for government departments.

3 deciding the distribution of Scottish Expenditure.

What is the role of the Scottish Parliament?

The Parliament has four basic functions:

1 to scrutinise the work of the Scottish Executive through questions to ministers or in committees

2 to make laws, including approving the Scottish Executive's expenditure

3 to debate topics

4 to conduct inquiries and issue reports

It also has the power to raise or lower the basic rate of Income Tax in Scotland by 3p in the £1.

In Question Time the Scottish Executive and the minister responsible will be held accountable. On 11th December 2003, Rosie Kane MSP asked about the cost of the M74 extension. On 11th December 2003 the First Minister was asked by MSP John Farquhar Munro what the Scottish Executive was doing to cut drink driving offences.

Types of Bills

There are four types of bill:

◆ **Executive Bill – proposed by the Scottish Executive**

◆ **Committee Bill – proposed by the Chair of a Parliamentary Committee**

◆ **Member's Bill – proposed by an MSP**

◆ **Private Bill – proposed by a person or body.**

Passing a Bill

There are three key stages:

Stage 1 the bill is introduced and debated
Stage 2 a committee looks at the bill in detail
Stage 3 the bill is given final consideration, debated and voted on.

At each stage the bill is issued for consideration to interested bodies. For instance, outline proposals for an Executive bill to protect workers in emergency services such as the fire and ambulance services was sent to all the trade unions with members in these services.

These trade unions can submit detailed comments and also present their views at the Committee Stage. Full details of Scottish Executive and parliament consultation documents can also be accessed on each website.

Activities

1 What evidence is there that the vast majority of Scottish people supported devolution?

2 What are the reserve matters the Scottish Parliament cannot deal with?

3 Why do you think this is the case?

4 Why is the Scottish Executive made up of two parties?

5 Give examples of how the First Minister and the Scottish Executive are held to account.

6 **Internet Task**: type in www.scottish. parliament.uk/education and try and give current examples of the four main types of bill.

Elections to the Scottish Parliament

Figure 1.22 Scottish MSPs elected in May 2003

Elections to the Scottish Parliament are different from Westminster elections. When proposals to set up a Scottish Parliament were being discussed, there was a strong view that the number of seats each party wins should more closely reflect the wishes of voters.

Systems which do this are called Proportional Representation. The Scottish system of proportional representation is called the Additional Member System (AMS). It uses 'First Past the Post' to elect MSPs for constituencies and a topping up procedure to elect MSPs by region. This ensures that the total number of MSPs elected more closely represents the proportion of the votes each party has won.

Constituency MSPs

When the Scottish Parliament was being set up there was also the view that the link between the new MSPs and his/her constituency should be maintained. 73 of these MSPs are elected by the 'First Past the Post' system on a constituency basis, the same way an MP is elected to Westminster.

Voters simply put an 'X' beside the name of an individual candidate, for example, Mike Watson (Labour). The candidate in the constituency with the most votes is then elected as a Constituency MSP. Constituency MSPs look after the interests of their constituents as well as their work in the Scottish Parliament.

Regional List MSPs

Figure 1.23 Tommy Sheridan, MSP

Scottish voters have a 'second regional vote'. The remaining 56 MSPs are elected under a form of 'proportional representation' called the Additional Member System. Voters choose the party they wish to support rather than the individual candidate.

The second vote constituencies are very large and there are eight of them covering the whole of Scotland. There are seven additional seats in each region. These are divided up between the parties on the basis of the proportion of votes they get.

To even up the number of seats in order that parties get seats roughly proportionate to their votes, parties which have already won several seats under the First Past the Post system in a region are effectively put to the end of the queue.

Parties who have won no or a small number of first past the post seats are more likely to get Regional List additional member seats. Voters also have a greater chance of having an MSP whose party they support or voted for. List MSPs look after the interests of all their regional constituents as well as their work in Parliament.

Activities

1 Explain why the Scottish Parliament's Additional Member System can be described as fairer than the Westminster system.

2 How has the link between the Constituency and the MSP been maintained?

3 'Constituency MSPs regard List MSPs as second class, because they were not directly elected by the voters.' Give arguments for and against this statement.

Independent MSPs

In May 1999, Dennis Canavan was elected a constituency Independent MSP for Falkirk West after the Labour Party tried to stop him standing. He was re-elected in 2003.

Dr Jean Turner stood as an MSP for the first time in 2003. She campaigned as a constituency MSP in the Bearsden and Strathkelvin seat to save Stobhill Hospital from closing. She narrowly defeated the sitting Labour MSP.

John Swinburn also stood for the first time as an MSP. He was top of the list for the Scottish Senior Citizens Party in central Scotland. His party was formed because he regarded that the voice of pensioners was not being heard in parliament.

Margot McDonald was placed low on the SNP list for the Lothians and she believed that she would not be re-elected as an MSP. Instead, she stood as an Independent, won 27,143 votes and was elected as a Regional MSP.

Activity

1 Look at Figures 1.24–1.26 and answer the following questions.
   a) Which party would have won if 'First Past the Post' had been used for the Scottish Parliamentary elections?
   b) Which parties would have been represented in the Parliament and which would not have been if 'First Past the Post' had been used?
   c) 'It is only the smaller parties that benefit from the additional member system'. Give evidence for and against this statement.
   d) In what way can AMS not be described as truly proportional?
   e) Which parties would have gained and which would have lost seats if a truly proportional system had been used instead of AMS?
   f) What possible form would the Scottish Executive have become if a truly proportional system had been used?

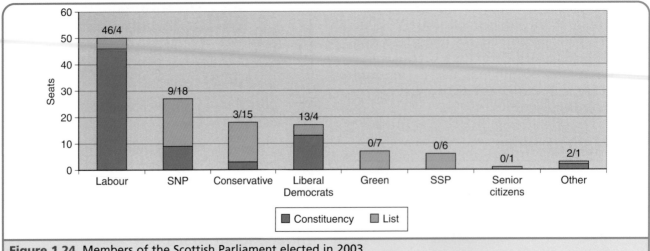

Figure 1.24 Members of the Scottish Parliament elected in 2003

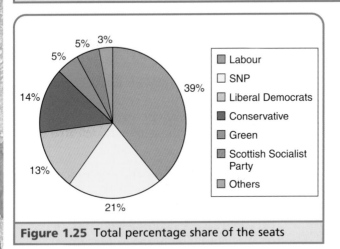

Figure 1.25 Total percentage share of the seats

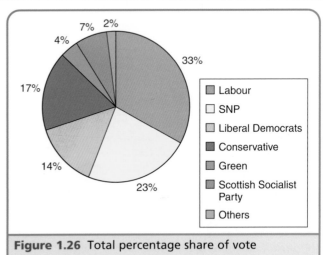

Figure 1.26 Total percentage share of vote

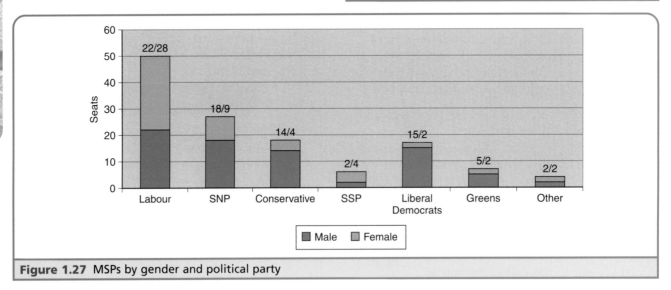

Figure 1.27 MSPs by gender and political party

Improved Representation

Currently, women make up 51.2 per cent of the Scottish population. 39.5 per cent of MSPs are women. The Scottish Parliament has the fourth highest percentages of women members of parliament in the world. Only the Welsh Assembly

G E N E R A L / C R E D I T

(50 per cent), Rwanda and Sweden have higher percentages.

In 1999, 48 women were elected MSPs. This rose to 51 in 2003.

Political Parties are allowed to take positive action under the terms of the Sex Discrimination (Electoral Candidates) Act 2002 to improve the number of women representatives. At the 2003 election, only the Labour Party and the SSP chose to make use of the Act.

The Scottish Parliament also enjoys 'family friendly' hours and is in recess during Scottish school holidays. Many MSPs can also return home from Edinburgh at night after meetings in the Parliament. However, there are no minority ethnic MSPs in the Scottish Parliament.

Activities

1 What evidence is there that the Scottish Parliament enjoys a high representation of women?

2 What evidence is there that women's representation is greater when parties take positive action?

3 Explain why 'family friendly' hours and the location of the Parliament might make it easier for women to participate as MSPs?

4 What evidence is there that minority ethnic groups might feel unrepresented?

The Role of the MSP

MSPs have a representative as well as a legislative function. They can ask questions of the First Minister and other members of the Scottish Executive. They can also suggest new laws to go before the Parliament. They can also pressurise the Executive into action.

In 2002, many MSPs expressed concern about the lack of scrutiny over people who were allowed to work with young people. As a result, the Minister for Education and Young People announced a change to the Protection of Children (Scotland) Bill.

MSPs can also work in committees. There are two types of committee:

Subject Committees – these deal with issues such as communities, education, enterprise and culture, environment and rural development, health, justice and local government and transport

Mandatory Committees – these deal with issues such as audit, equal opportunities, European affairs, finance, procedures, public petitions, standards, subordinate legislation

As part of their representative function MSPs must deal with correspondence from their constituents. Much of their time is taken with constituency work. They hold surgeries where they meet with constituents in an attempt to redress any grievances or complaints they might have.

MSPs now deal with many of the queries formerly dealt with by the MP. This is because MSPs deal with devolved matters many of which were the 'bread and butter' issues such as education, health and care of the elderly previously dealt with by MPs.

This is one of the reasons that the number of Scottish MPs in the House of Commons was reduced from 72 to 59.

Making a Difference in Scotland?

From its first session in 1999, the Scottish Parliament had passed 64 Bills (by December 2003). Most Bills which became laws were Executive Bills. These range from the Abolition of Feudal Tenure, Land Reform, National Parks, to Standards in Scotland's Schools, Graduate Endowment and Student Support, Community Care and Health to Dog Fouling.

In 2001, a Private Members' Bill, (Tommy Sheridan's Abolition of Poindings and Warrant Sales Bill) became Law. This stopped poorer people (or people in debt) from having their furniture and other possessions sold off to pay debts.

The number of Acts of Parliament have increased each year from 12 in 2000 to 19 in 2003.

Most Scottish Executive Bills arise from policies included in the Labour and Liberal Democrat election manifestos. The Partnership Agreement between Labour and the Liberal Democrats includes agreement on policy options which both parties regarded as vital.

Some Bills are also similar to Bills being proposed by the Labour Government at Westminster. These Bills cover devolved areas which the Westminster parliament did not have the power to act upon. For instance, the Education (Disability Strategies and Pupils' Educational Records) Scotland Act 2002 applied a Westminster Act of Parliament to Scotland.

Devolution Differences

Some Westminster Acts on devolved matters are passed by the Scottish Parliament. Others are amended at Committee stage. Some Scottish Parliament Acts have been radically different.

The major reasons for the differences are:

◆ **Scotland has a different education and legal system**

◆ **the Scottish Executive is a coalition of Labour and the Liberal Democrats who are bound by a Partnership Agreement which includes major policies from each party's manifestos**

◆ **Scotland is a smaller country and there is greater opportunity within the Scottish Parliament for interest groups such as trade unions to make their voices heard.**

Some practical differences:

◆ **Scottish pensioners enjoy free person personal care while English pensioners have to pay for it**

◆ **Scottish students studying in Scotland do not have to pay top-up fees unlike students in England**

◆ **The Scottish Executive also does not support Tony Blair's flagship policy of foundation hospitals**

◆ **The Scottish Executive is also now proposing a local governance Bill introducing proportional representation for the election of Scottish councillors and for payment of councillors**

In February 2004, there were nine Executive bills going through Parliament, three Members' bills, and three Private bills brought by individuals or groups of people.

Current Executive Bills

Scottish Expenditure – Budget (Scottish Executive)

Education – Additional Support for Learning

Health – National Health Service reforms, Primary Medical Services

Local Government – Local Governance

Environment – Nature Conservation

Law – Antisocial behaviour, Criminal Procedures, Vulnerable Witnesses

Members Bills

Breastfeeding

Fire Sprinklers in Residential Premises

Prostitution Tolerance Zones

Private Bills

Stirling – Alloa-Kincardine Railway

Waverley Railway (Edinburgh to the Borders)

Edinburgh Tramline

Activities

1 What evidence is there that the Scottish Parliament has increased the number of bills passed since 1999?

2 Why might the Scottish Executive seek to have some Westminster bills passed by the Scottish Parliament?

3 What are the main reasons why laws passed by the Scottish Parliament are different from Westminster laws?

4 Give examples of differences between the Scottish and Westminster parliaments affecting ordinary people.

5 Look at the titles of bills. Suggest what the main differences might be between the types of bill proposed by the Executive, MSPs and private individuals or bodies.

6 'The Scottish Parliament is too busy discussing dog dirt to make a real difference to people's lives.' Give reasons why the person making this statement might be accused of being selective in use of the facts.

The Public and the Scottish Parliament

The Scottish Parliament can also hear petitions from members of the public. The Parliament will respond to the petitioners and take action if required. The following are examples of petitions lodged in early 2004.

◆ **petition by Alex and Margaret Dekker calling for action to be taken in relation to the Crown Office's decisions and considerations in prosecuting road traffic deaths.**

GENERAL/CREDIT

- petition by Grandparents Apart (self-help group) calling for the Scottish Parliament to consider amending the Childrens' (Scotland) Act 1995 to name grandparents in the Act as having an important part to play in the lives of their grandchildren.

- petition by Technology Teachers Association calling for the Scottish Parliament to advance technical/technology Education within Scottish Secondary Schools as a national priority.

- petition by Councillor Sam Campbell calling for the Scottish Parliament to take the necessary steps to re-regulate the bus service in Scotland to enable rural communities that depend on it to have an adequate bus services.

Source www.scottishparliament.uk

Activities

1. Suggest reasons why the Dekkers put forward their petition.

2. What do the Grandparents Apart (self-help group) want the Parliament to do?

3. What do the Technical Teachers want the Parliament to do?

4. What is Councillor Campbell's main area of concern?

5. List the four petitions in order of importance. State the ones you would expect the Parliament to act upon. Give reasons for your answers.

Local Government

An important part of representative democracy is local government. In 1996 Scottish local government was reorganised. In Scotland we now have 29 councils on the mainland and three island authorities.

Local government is the democratically elected tier of government at the local level consisting of 1, 222 councillors in Scotland within 32 unitary authorities. Scottish local government is a major influence upon the economy of Scotland. In 2002–2003 local government in Scotland spent over £8bn. Scottish local government employs over 290,000 staff – 185,000 full-time and 108,000 part-time.

Source: www.scottishparliament.uk – Local Government briefing paper

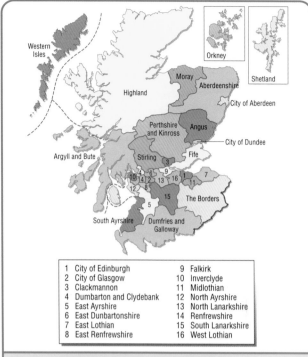

1. City of Edinburgh
2. City of Glasgow
3. Clackmannon
4. Dumbarton and Clydebank
5. East Ayrshire
6. East Dunbartonshire
7. East Lothian
8. East Renfrewshire
9. Falkirk
10. Inverclyde
11. Midlothian
12. North Ayrshire
13. North Lanarkshire
14. Renfrewshire
15. South Lanarkshire
16. West Lothian

Figure 1.32 Scotland's local authorities
Source www.scottishparliament.uk

Local government is under political control and most councillors represent a political party. The majority party on each council is known as the 'ruling group' or 'administration group'. Local councils are responsible for providing services in their areas such as education, social work, roads, leisure activities, housing, libraries refuse collection.

Most of the funding for these services comes from the Scottish Executive in the form of grants. Only about 15–25 per cent of the costs of services are funded from the Council Tax which is based on the value of the property. Other sources of funding are charges which councils make for certain services such as swimming pools, five a side football pitches, leisure centres etc.

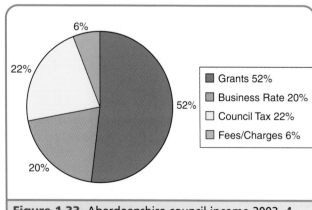

- Grants 52%
- Business Rate 20%
- Council Tax 22%
- Fees/Charges 6%

Figure 1.33 Aberdeenshire council income 2003–4
Source www.aberdeenshire.gov.uk

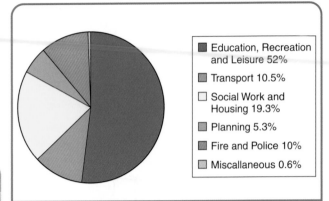

Figure 1.34 Aberdeenshire council expenditure (2003–4)
Source www.aberdeenshire.gov.uk

- Education, Recreation and Leisure 52%
- Transport 10.5%
- Social Work and Housing 19.3%
- Planning 5.3%
- Fire and Police 10%
- Miscellaneous 0.6%

Activities

1 How is local government in Scotland organised?

2 What services do local authorities in Scotland provide?

3 What are the four sources of funding for local authorities in Scotland?

4 Rank the main areas of expenditure by size.

The Work of the Local Councillor

Local councillors represent the people in their electoral ward in the same way an MP or MSP represents the people of their local constituency. The local councillor listens to the problems of the people in their ward and tries to get these problems solved.

The councillor's surgery is the usual way people go to their councillor with problems. Many people believe that the local councillor is more likely to get a problem solved than the individual themselves. People identify with their local councillor as they normally live in the area and know the problems of that area.

Councillors also attend council meetings which make decisions affecting the people in their area, such as whether or not to close schools or even build a new one.

Local Councillors are mostly part-time and usually have a job. They are given time off work to attend to their council duties. They are not paid but receive attendance allowances for attending meetings.

Councillor Profiles

The average local councillor in Scotland is white, male, mid-fifties in age, educated to degree level and owns his own house and car.

Just over 25 per cent of councillors would call themselves 'full time'. Of those councillors who have jobs, approximately 70 per cent are in professional or managerial jobs.

For those who work, the majority tend to be in the private sector followed closely by those in the public sector. As far as gender is concerned, female representation was 21.8 per cent in 2003. This is a fall from 22.6 per cent in 1999.

In terms of ethnic minority representation, the number of councillors from ethnic minorities has doubled. There are 14 ethnic minority councillors in Scotland, which is one per cent of the total. However the ethnic minority population of Scotland is 2 per cent.

Source www.cosla.gov.uk

Should Councillors Work Full Time?

This question has been asked many times. There are some arguments for having full time councillors who get paid a salary like the MP or MSP.

- Councillors would have more time to deal with the problems raised by local people. They cannot perform their role properly if they cannot attend council meetings because of work commitments. Full time councillors could also come from a more representative cross section of the population.

- People complain about MPs having other jobs such as consultancies so why should we be satisfied with part time representatives in local democracy?

- However full time paid councillors would be a huge cost to the Scottish taxpayer given the fact there are 1,222 of them. Full time paid councillors might also duplicate the work of council officers who already receive a salary.

- There is also the argument that full time paid professional councillors might not necessarily make them better councillors.

- Councillors are local people living and working in the community this already gives them the advantage of knowing what the needs of the community are.

Activities

1 In what ways are councillors different from the MP or MSP?

2 Look at Figures 1.35–8 and answer the following questions. The results contained within the tables refer to a Scottish Executive/CoSLA survey of councillors carried out in 2003.
   a) What evidence is there that full time councillors spend more time serving the needs of the people at local level? Use Figures 1.35–6 only.
   b) What evidence is there that councillors are better educated in comparison to the rest of the adult population?
   c) 'Councillors are self centred, career-seeking people with no regard for the people they serve'. How far does the evidence in Figure 1.38 this statement?

3 'Women and ethnic minorities continue to do well in representation at local authority level.' How far does the evidence support this point of view?

4 Write a report stating whether or not you think councillors should become full time paid representatives. You must use the information and sources above.

Hours per week	Full-time councillors working those hours (%)	Part-time councillors working those hours (%)
Under 21	6.5	35.6
21–30	15.9	37.9
31–40	28.8	17.0
Over 40	48.8	9.5
Average hours per week	**42.9**	**27.2**

Figure 1.36 Estimated weekly council workload by employment status
Source www.cosla.gov.uk

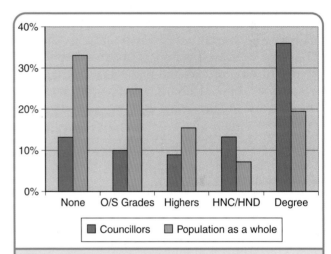

Figure 1.37 Percentage highest education qualification of councillors compared with the Scottish population.
Source www.cosla.gov.uk and www.gro-scotland.gov.uk

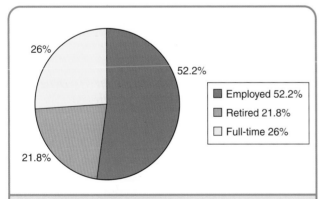

Figure 1.35 Employment status of councillors
Source www.cosla.gov.uk

Reason given	%
Interest in community	45
Duty/public service	10
Improve services	10
Career/personal development	9
Promote party objectives	8
Other	18

Figure 1.38 Top five reasons for standing for election as a councillor

A Lifetime of Service

Abridged Extract from CoSLA Connections No 7 December 2003 by Councillor Pat Watters, President, CoSLA

Jimmy Jennings had been a Councillor for 45 years: from 1958 until 2003.

Times were hard and at that time he had four children to feed and clothe, and to go into elected office meant giving up any chance of promotion at the steelworks.

This is something that still remains a problem in 2003 and perhaps a reason I reacted so angrily to the recent 'part-timers' tag labelled against Scotland's 1,222 elected members.

Despite this, Jimmy gave elected office his all. His house was used as his surgery and despite people turning up day and night – no one was ever turned away. If Jimmy was ever out, one of the kids had to take details and then pass the problem on.

There is not a town or village in the Garnock Valley that he has not been involved in during his 45 years as a councillor.

Kilbirnie Police station is known locally as (Jinning's Jile).

Local government and local politicians can at times get poor press coverage. Even our partners in central government often under value the work of local councillors.

I also think that even certain sections of the communities we serve, our electorate, can also treat us with contempt.

Obviously we are not in local politics for the money. However, when Jimmy retired in May he left with a certificate and a presentation. He has no pension to show for 45 years public service.

Jimmy will not be the first councillor in Scotland to be in this position. But in the 21st century he should be the last.

I am sure that every party, indeed every council, will have their own Jimmy Jennings. Sadly, I think that the days of the Jimmy Jennings of the political world are gone forever, never to be replaced.

Activities

Using the abridged CoSLA source answer the following questions:

1 'We are not in local politics for the money.' What evidence is there that this was the case with regards to Councillor Jennings?

2 In what ways does Councillor Watters feel that the work of councillors is not recognised the way it should be?

Central and Local Government

The Scottish Parliament is elected by the Scottish people. MSPs are elected on the basis of their manifesto promises to the Scottish electorate. The Scottish Executive is the government of Scotland and is charge of devolved matters, such as education, social work, police fire, housing.

At the same time, local councils are elected by the people at local authority level and will make political decisions regarding local public services. Councils have local and political priorities which may be different from those of the Scottish Executive. Councils make decisions at local level on how much money should actually be spent on their priorities and how local public services are delivered.

Since the election of the Labour Government in 1997 and the Scottish Parliament in 1999, the Scottish Executive has taken a stronger role in influencing the work of councils.

Best Value – Introducing Continuous Improvement in Public Services

The previous Conservative government introduced Compulsory Competitive Tendering (CCT) for a range of council services. Councils' own direct labour organisations (DLOs) such as roads and repairs departments had to compete openly with private sector companies for council contracts.

The Conservative's aims were not only to open up council contracts to private firms but also to drive down the price for doing these jobs. Lower prices could also mean lower council taxes.

Unfortunately, much of the time council departments would have spent doing the jobs was actually taken up drawing up very time consuming tender documents.

Some council workers also lost their jobs when the contracts were won by the private sector, or were re-employed by the private firms to do the same job, but with worse employment conditions.

Labour replaced CCT with Best Value. Councils are now obliged to carry out 'best value reviews' of council services. The Scottish Executive's Audit Unit is in charge of ensuring that councils implement Best Value in their areas.

Under Best Value, councils look at their services by applying the 'Four Cs':

◆ **Challenge – looking closely at how the service is operating**

◆ **Compare – look at how other councils or private firms are operating similar services**

◆ **Consult – ask local people what they want from services and how they think they should improve**

◆ **Compete/cooperate – introduce improvements by doing it better than others or working in partnership with other service providers to deliver better public services.**

Best Value in Practice

In East Dunbartonshire Council, a Best Value Review was set up to look at Community Transport. One of the aims was to look at improving school transport.

The review group was made up of senior council officers, a primary, secondary and special school headteacher, members of the local community and the three main trade union representatives in the council, including the EIS (the main teachers' trade union). During the review the group:

◆ **identified the challenge – working with councillors, they decided the main issues to be addressed**

◆ **found sources for comparison – information was gathered from other councils in Scotland**

◆ **undertook consultation – a market research company was employed to draft questionnaires and conduct 'focus group' meetings with groups who had an interest in the issue.**

Schools throughout the council were asked to participate. The EIS trade union representative was also a Modern Studies teacher and he worked with the market researcher and three S3 Standard Grade Modern Studies classes to find out what pupils

wanted. This became part of the pupils' work on Enquiry Skills. The Standard Grade Modern Studies pupils drafted school questionnaires for each year group to find out the views of other pupils and to report their findings to the council.

The council decided to introduce improvements suggested by pupils and parents, including:

◆ **a code of conduct on school buses to be drafted by the pupils themselves**

◆ **seat belts on all school buses**

◆ **better training for adults on buses**

◆ **investigating cycle routes to schools and more lockers for pupils in schools**

◆ **improved safety on 'walking routes' to schools**

◆ **improved transport arrangements for pupils going to special schools based on the needs of the child**

◆ **not to increase the qualifying limit for free school transport from two miles to three as the council's lower limit was regarded as one of the best in Scotland.**

Activities

1 Explain why there might be conflict between central and local government.

2 Why did the Conservative government introduce CCT?

3 What were the main drawbacks of CCT?

4 Explain in your own words how a council carries out a Best Value Review.

5 Describe how pupils in East Dunbartonshire participated in the Community Transport Best Value Review and how the council acted to improve or maintain services for its 'customers.'

6 What further suggestions would you like to see your council introduce to improve your school transport.

Modernising Local Government

In addition to Best Value, the Executive set up two groups to look at the relationship between the Scottish Parliament and local government and to improve the way local councils operate.

The MacIntosh Commission (1999) looked at local government and the Scottish Parliament. The Kerley Working Group (2000) looked at renewing local democracy. After MacIntosh and Kerley reported, the Scottish Parliament passed the Local Government Scotland Act (2003).

On introducing the Bill, the Executive stated that the aim of the bill was 'to provide a framework to enable the delivery of better, more responsive public services.'

The Act:

1 places a duty to secure Best Value.

2 created a statutory basis for 'Community Planning'. Community planning is a process by which a local council works in partnership with other public bodies such as health boards, chief constables and joint police boards, fire boards, Scottish Enterprise, Highlands and Islands Enterprise and Strathclyde Passenger Transport Authority and the local community to plan and provide improved services in a local authority area.

3 provides a 'power to advance well-being' which gives local authorities the power to undertake activities which will promote or improve the well-being of an area.

4 introduces a 'prudential' system of council borrowing for big building projects (such as schools) if they can show they can afford to pay back the loans either from their own resources or even by raising the Council Tax.

Many councils had already begun to change the way they operate through Best Value Reviews, working closely with health boards on jointly funded projects such as community health initiatives, working with other neighbouring local authorities and improving transport before the 2003 Local Government Act was passed.

Councils were also critical of the Scottish Executive.

Scottish local government has long-standing concerns that require immediate attention if it is to fulfil its potential as local government rather than merely local administration carrying out the wishes of national government.

Under-funding, unnecessary interference and control from the centre, the inexorable growth of nationally imposed initiatives and partnerships are just some of the issues that need to be tackled if local government is to be allowed to flourish.

CoSLA will make a strong case for:

◆ **reductions in ring-fenced funding (in other words, the Scottish Executive saying where councils should spend the money)**

◆ **the Scottish Executive supporting the real cost for local services**

◆ **full funding for new initiatives**

◆ **additional funds for poorer and rural councils.**

Adapted Extract from CoSLA Manifesto 2003

Activities

1 What is the aim of the Local Government Scotland Act 2003?

2 Who are the main partners in community planning?

3 What limitations are there on 'prudential borrowing'?

4 Outline CoSLA's main criticisms and what it wants the Executive to do.

How Representative are Councils?

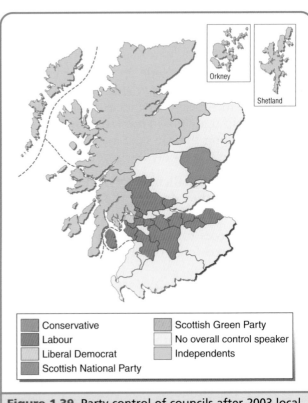

	Conservative		Scottish Green Party
	Labour		No overall control speaker
	Liberal Democrat		Independents
	Scottish National Party		

Figure 1.39 Party control of councils after 2003 local government elections
Source www.alba.org.uk

2003 Council Election results

Party	% Vote	% Wards	Seats
Labour	47.6	89.9	71
SNP	20.5	3.8	3
SSP	15.6	1.3	1
Conservative	7.6	1.3	1
Liberal Democrats	7.6	3.8	3
Total			79

Figure 1.40 Glasgow (turnout 40 per cent)

Party	% Vote	% Wards	Seats
Independent	44.3	61.5	16
SNP	25.3	11.5	3
Labour	12.7	19.2	5
Liberal Democrats	7.9	.9	1
Other	5	0	0
Conservative	4.3	3.9	1
SSP	0.6	0	0
Total			26

Figure 1.41 Moray (turnout 44.5 per cent)

Party	% Vote	% Wards	Seats
Labour	48	76	51
SNP	29	13.4	9
Conservative	12.9	3	2
Liberal Democrats	5	3	2
Independent	3.1	4.5	3
SSP	2.3	0	0
Total			67

Figure 1.42 South Lanarkshire (turnout 49.5 per cent)

Party	% Vote	% Wards	Seats
Labour	44.2	55.6	10
SNP	41.4	33.3	6
Independent	6.6	5.6	1
Conservative	5.8	5.6	1
Liberal Democrats	2	0	0
Total			18

Figure 1.43 Clackmannanshire (turnout 55.3 per cent)

Sources www.alba.org.uk (abridged)

Renewing Local Democracy

One of the recommendations of the MacIntosh Report was that local councils should be more representative of the voters wishes.

'We believe that, as far as is practicable, every vote should count, and that Councils, in their composition, should reflect the range and balance of views within the communities which they serve. It is critical that the democratic credentials of councils should be no less strong than those of the Parliament. Since the Parliament has been elected under a form of proportional representation we see this as a compelling reason for adopting PR for Scottish local government too.'

Source: MacIntosh Report (p. 22)

Activities

1. From Figure 1.39, which geographical areas were won by:
   a) Independents
   b) Labour
   c) SNP
   d) Liberal Democrats
   e) no overall control?

2. 'Councils should reflect the range and balance of views within the communities they serve.' In what ways can the results in:
   a) Glasgow
   b) Moray
   c) South Lanarkshire
   d) Clackmannanshire

   be described as unrepresentative of the range and balance of the electors in their areas?

MSPs are elected by a form of proportional representation while councillors are still elected by 'First Past the Post.'

The Scottish Executive's Partnership Agreement between the Labour and Liberal Democrat parties contained many proposals which would affect local government.

All sections of the Agreement include:

◆ **proposals and commitments to legislate that will have an impact on local government. It includes over 400 commitments, around 350 of which will be delivered through local government.**

◆ **key priorities such as the war against anti-social behaviour and youth disorder, the** environmental agenda, the drive to push up educational standards and the reform of public services will all rely on local government to deliver at a local level, policies that will be determined at the national level.

Source: CoSLA Connections No. 1 June 2003 (abridged)

The Partnership Agreement also included proposals that a form of proportional representation – Single Transferable Voting (STV) should be introduced for local government elections.

'for the next local government elections the proportional Single Transferable Vote system of election. The multi-member wards would have either three or four members, depending on local circumstances.'

Source: Partnership Agreement 2003

The Local Governance (Scotland) 2003 Bill will also introduce a new remuneration package for councillors (pay and pensions and severance payments for councillors) and reduce the age at which people can stand for election to a local authority to 18.

Many of the councils which make up the Convention of Scottish Local Authorities (CoSLA) are opposed to electoral change as they see it as breaking the important link between the councillor and his/her ward.

The First Past the Post system provides for strong political leadership of a council, with a clear mandate to carry through the programme of measures put to the electorate. It also provides a clear member-ward link and gives a fair opportunity for independent councillors to be elected.

... CoSLA feels that undue account has been taken of issues of proportionality in the decision to adopt the STV system of proportional representation.

The council agreed previously to support the retention of the First Past the Post system and to oppose the introduction of PR into local government elections, on the basis that PR will increase the number of hung councils, thereby causing political instability within local government and reducing the openness and accountability of Scottish local government by threatening the direct link between voters and their representatives. This is an inherent strength of local politics and is valued by all constituents no matter what their political persuasion.'

Source: CoSLA submission to consultation on local governance Bill

Activities

1 What evidence is there that local government plays a major role in implementing decisions of the Executive?

2 What benefits will the local governance bill give councillors?

3 Using Figures 1.40–1.43, state reasons for and against the introduction of STV for local government elections.

Pressure Groups

A pressure group can be described as an organised group that is set up to influence governmental policy and decisions without seeking to win political power. Pressure groups offer the public an alternative means of putting forward their points of view in addition to voting in elections.

The term pressure group is a wide definition that does not distinguish between the different groups that come under that term. Some pressure groups are huge organisations such as the CBI (Confederation of British Industry) which represents over 100,000 British businesses.

Others are very small almost unknown groups formed on the basis of specific functions and interests such as the Ladies Sidesaddle Association.

There are two types of pressure group: sectional and promotional.

Sectional Pressure Groups

These groups seek to represent the common interests of a particular section of society. These groups are sometimes called interest groups. Members of these groups are restricted to those with a shared background, or performing a common socio-economic function.

Trade unions, employers associations and professional bodies are all sectional groups. These groups exist to protect members' self interest and as a result their membership is restricted.

Examples of sectional groups are the British Medical Association (BMA), National Union of Farmers (NUF) and the Law Society.

Since their aim is to look after the interests of all people in that section of society, sectional groups tend to aim to recruit as many eligible members as possible to join that group i.e. to get all doctors to join the BMA.

Promotional Groups

These are groups which seek to promote a particular cause and for that reason they are sometimes called 'cause' groups. Their objectives are not directly beneficial to a particular profession or socio-economic group.

Examples of promotional or cause groups are Shelter, Campaign for Nuclear Disarmament (CND), Greenpeace, Action on Smoking and Health Scotland (ASH Scotland), Royal Society for the Protection of Children (RSPCC).

Figure 1.44 Shelter's logo
Source www.shelter.org.uk

Figure 1.45 An Ash Scotland campaign
Source www.ashscotland.org.uk

Cause groups aim to promote a cause which might be supported by anybody regardless of their profession or socio-economic status. Membership is therefore not restricted.

Some cause groups do not have a large membership but have a great deal of influence. Liberty has a membership of approx 5,000 and exerts influence on the Labour Party when in opposition and now in government.

Cause groups can be divided into the aims they pursue. Sectional cause groups aim to protect the interests of a section of society. Attitude cause groups aim to change people's attitude about an issue or policy.

Activities

1 How do we define pressure groups?

2 What are sectional groups and why can their membership be said to be restricted?

3 What are cause groups and why is their membership open?

4 Put the following pressure groups into either cause or interest groups:
Child Poverty Action
Friends Of the Earth
British Road Federation
Institute of Directors
Age Concern
Liberty
Prison Reform Trust
National Association on Health
Chief Superintendents Association
Royal College of Surgeons.

What Tactics do Pressure Groups Use?

Many pressure groups are also referred to insider and outsider pressure groups. Insider groups have strong links with the decision-makers – the government. They have direct access to the corridors of power. They are experts and the government consults them and listens to their advice.

The Law Society, representing the legal profession, would have a large input into any proposed changes to the law with regard to the rights of suspects. Likewise any change to legislation with regards to human embryo research would have a large input from the medical profession in the form of the BMA.

The status of insider groups sometimes depends on which government is in power. During the

Conservative governments of the 1980s and 90s, the TUC was marginalised while employer groups such as the Institute of Directors (IOD) had ready access to government.

Outsider groups, on the other hand, have none of the advantages of insider groups. They cannot be expected to be consulted on changes to Government policy or gain access to government ministers and civil servants.

In the 1980s the CND was excluded from the consultation process because the then Conservative Government was very much in favour of Britain increasing its nuclear capability.

Figure 1.46 CND protesters

Many pressure groups lobby MPs and MSPs and even employ consultants or paid 'parliamentary officers' to make their views heard.

Many outsider groups work closely with the opposition in the hope that when the opposition wins the election they might achieve insider status. A good example of this was the Low Pay Unit which was responsible for influencing Labour in its policy of implementing the national minimum wage.

Activity

Explain in detail the difference between insider and outsider pressure groups.

Protest and Demonstration

Common tactics of some pressure groups are staging protests and demonstrations in the hope of achieving publicity for their cause.

In 2000, petrol tanker drivers went on strike over what they considered were the exorbitant fuel prices in the UK. The country was brought to a standstill and after two weeks it called off the strike when the government began to listen to its case.

In February 2003, the largest demonstration ever held in Britain took place in London against the possibility of war against Iraq. An estimated two million people took part. Similar demonstrations took place throughout the world.

Glasgow also had its biggest demonstration ever. Protests and demonstrations continued throughout 2003 and 2004.

Figure 1.47 Anti-war demonstration September 2003

Some pressure groups use violent protests to voice their opposition. A good example of these are the various anti-globalisation groups who attack what they perceive to be symbols of international capitalism and domination such as McDonalds, the City of London.

Figure 1.48 A demonstration against McDonalds

Various animal rights groups have resorted to trespassing and vandalism against animal farms. GM crop farms have in recent years become the target of such tactics.

Other organisations try to achieve the same ends by peaceful means. Recently pressure groups have developed extensive websites which give information about their activities and seek to recruit new members. Many pressure groups' Internet websites have links to other similar organisations in the UK and internationally.

Figure 1.49 Friends of the Earth campaign badge
Source www.foe-scotland.org.uk

Activities

1 What tactics did the lorry drivers use and were they successful?

2 What evidence is there that the government doesn't always pay attention to large demonstrations?

3 List some other tactics used by pressure groups.

Pressure Groups and Democracy

Pressure groups have grown in size and influence, particularly in the last twenty years. Single issue pressure groups such as the Stop the War Coalition have also been successful in attracting people of all ages and social classes, but particularly the young.

Pressure groups are also becoming more sophisticated in their approach, particularly through the use of the Internet and Internet links with like-minded groups or individuals.

The Internet and websites are alternatives to the traditional news media, many of whom support mainstream political parties and views. Mobile phones also mean that people can be contacted

quickly to turn up in large numbers and demonstrations and events.

This is also at a time when voter turnout at elections and individual membership of most political parties is declining.

On the other hand, Proportional Representation in the Scottish Parliament has also led to the election of MSPs representing groups who might not previously have got representation.

There are now seven Regional List Green MSPs. Dr Jean Turner was elected a Constituency MSP who stood on a platform to Stop the Closure of Stobhill Hospital. John Swinburn was also elected as a Regional List MSP for the Scottish Senior Citizens' Unity Party.

Proportional Representation makes it more likely that single issue or pressure group type MSPs and Councillors at local government level will be elected in the future.

Pressure groups also have the opportunity of bringing petitions to the Scottish Parliament or seeking to have a Private Bill introduced. The 'First Past the Post' system for Westminster elections, on the other hand, makes it also likely that the traditional parties will continue to win all the seats and dominate on a UK basis.

Some argue that pressure groups add to democracy:

◆ **they improve government by challenging its decisions**

◆ **they are a product of freedom of association**

◆ **they offer an outlet for people not interested in mainstream politics**

◆ **they allow new issues and concerns to reach the political agenda**

◆ **they help social progress, for example, women's groups and environmentalist groups**

◆ **they act as a check on government, for example, Liberty.**

However, many take the view that pressure groups are self interested and represent a threat to democracy. Here are some negative views about pressure groups:

◆ **they are not representative of their members**

◆ **their leaders are not elected**

◆ **large scale demonstrations can lead to violence**

- powerful pressure groups can slow down or block change
- **pressure groups benefit the well organised but disadvantage the weakly organised** – in this sense they work against rather than in favour of the public interest.

Activities

1 Describe how pressure groups have successfully made use of new technology.

2 How has proportional representation helped the election of pressure group-style MSPs?

3 'The benefits of pressure groups to democracy far outweigh the disadvantages.'

   How far do you agree with this statement? Answer in detail.

GENERAL/CREDIT

Participation at Work: Trade Unions

Trade unions are groups of workers who get together to try to improve workers' rights, pay and conditions. Early unions were made up of skilled workers, called **craft unions**, and later as unskilled workers became organised, they also set up trade unions which are known as **general unions**.

Following these early unions, office, shop and professional workers have arranged themselves into what are called **white-collar unions**.

In recent years there has been a move towards having fewer, but bigger, unions – **super unions** – like Amicus and UNISON.

Unions demand 4% for local government workers

Trade unions have lodged a pay claim of 4% plus £200, on behalf of one million local government workers across England, Wales and Northern Ireland.

The claim, which could benefit 800,000 UNISON members, includes a demand for a £6 an hour minimum wage, increased annual leave, better maternity provision and improved parental leave.

The pay bid could set up a tough confrontation between the unions and local government employers, who had already warned unions against asking for an 'unrealistic' sum.

But UNISON head of local government Heather Wakefield insisted this was a 'modest claim' on basic pay.

'UNISON believes that now is the time to deliver for local government workers,' she said.

Figure 2.1 UNISON action for its members
Source 30 January 2004

The major political parties recognise the importance of trade unions to British industry but they have different ideas about what part the unions should play in the making of industrial policy.

At times the unions have been at odds with the government's policy and this has led to **industrial conflict**. The Conservative governments from 1979–1997 passed many laws in an attempt to control the power of trade unions.

The Labour party was originally set up by the trade unions to represent workers' interests in parliament. New Labour was elected in 1997. Despite pressure from the trade unions, the Labour Government (under Tony Blair) did not change the anti-trade union laws introduced by the previous Conservative government.

However, it has been responsible for a number of social policies which have improved workers' welfare. For example,

◆ paid holidays for part-time and full-time workers

◆ introduction of the national minimum wage

◆ statutory sick pay and paternity leave

◆ flexible working arrangements for working parents.

In recent years there has been an increase in industrial conflict. Train drivers, fire fighters, postal workers and nursery nurses have all taken industrial action.

Industrial action takes place normally only if **negotiations** (talks) between employers and trade unions break down. The most common reasons for industrial action are over issues such as pay and conditions, job losses and in recent times threats to workers' pensions, as can be seen in Figure 2.2.

Strike threat to Christmas mail

Postal unions are threatening to strike during the Christmas rush in a row over pensions.

The union is angry at Royal Mail Group's plan to sell the Cash Handling & Distribution (CHD) part of the business, which supplies post offices with cash and stamps.

RMG say the sale is vital to cut losses of £1.2 million a day.

The union is demanding that if the deal goes ahead, the 3000 staff affected must be allowed to remain in the Royal Mail pension scheme.

Mail chiefs say staff will be moved to a private scheme with 'broadly comparable terms'. A strike ballot of CHD members is expected to begin a week tomorrow.

If, as expected, there is an overwhelming 'yes' vote, the union is thought to be considering balloting the wider Royal Mail membership.

This could lead to a strike in the run up to Christmas, which could cost the organisation £100 million a day.

Figure 2.2 Newspaper article from 14th October 2004

Source *Daily Record*

Reasons for Joining a Trade Union

People join trade unions for many different reasons. These include:

- **pay** – unions can negotiate pay rates, paid holidays, bonuses and hourly rates

- **working conditions** – healthy and safe working conditions can be improved through union negotiation

- **job security** – protecting members' jobs is a part of the union's responsibility

- **victimisation** – a union's strength is unity, and a case of one person being picked on brings support from all members

- **benefits** – ill workers can receive money from the union to see them through their illness, some unions have holiday homes for retired members

- **legal matters** – lawyers are provided to represent members who are in need of legal advice

- **political** – pressure can be applied to politicians through **lobbying** and some unions sponsor MPs to present their view in parliament.

The number of employees (workers) belonging to trade unions has fallen to the lowest level since the Second World War.

For the last 15 years there has been a decline in trade union membership but 1995 saw the third biggest decline in over 25 years. There are now only 8.3 million trade union members compared with 13.3 million in 1979 – only 1/3 of the workforce.

The biggest decline is in the number of men. In 1994 male membership fell by 8.7 per cent, while female membership rose by 1 per cent in the same period.

(Source: *Financial Times*, 9th February 1996 – abridged)

Trade union membership has declined since the 1970s. Most workers in Britain today are not members of trade unions as the article above shows:

This trend has continued with the estimated figures of union membership now at about 6.7 million, a drop from over 12 million in 1979. Anti trade union legislation, the decline of traditional industries (a male dominated traditional union strong hold) and the increase of flexible working practices such as part-time working, seasonal working etc. has contributed to this situation. In Scotland there are now only just over 600,000 trade union members.

Reasons for Not Joining a Trade Union

About 70 per cent of the working population are not members of a trade union and there are a number of reasons why this is the case:

- some well-paid workers don't see the need to join a union

- some jobs are difficult to organise a union for, like North Sea oil workers, shop workers and home workers

- workers in small family firms can negotiate for themselves

- some workers are self-employed
- some companies do not recognise trade unions
- part-time and temporary workers tend not to be in trade unions due to the cost of membership and trade unions have not actively recruited members in this area in the past.

Activities

1 What are trade unions?   *(2 marks)*

2 What type of trade union organises the following:
   a) white-collar workers?   *(1 mark)*
   b) skilled workers?   *(1 mark)*
   c) unskilled workers?   *(1 mark)*

3 Why was trade union legislation introduced in the 1980s?   *(2 marks)*

4 List the ways in which the social policies of the Labour Government have improved workers' conditions.   *(4 marks)*

5 Give a recent example of industrial conflict. *(2 marks)*

6 From Figure 2.1, what demands is UNISON making for their members?   *(2 marks)*

7 Give four reasons to join a union.   *(2 marks)*

8 What type of union has seen an increase in membership?   *(2 marks)*

9 What are the reasons for the decline in union membership?   *(3 marks)*

10 How many trade union members are there in Scotland?   *(2 marks)*

11 Give four reasons why people do not join trade unions.   *(2 marks)*

Types of Union

In the past, unions could easily be categorised into four main types and they all offered their members similar benefits. The types of union were based on the type of worker and the place of work, not the service given by the unions.

Changes in British industry, but in particular the decline of manufacturing and increase in public and service sector jobs, has led to the decline in 'traditional' unions and an increase in unions covering a wide variety of workers. Many smaller trade unions have joined together – 'amalgamated' – in order to serve their members better.

Type of union	Membership type
Craft	Skilled workers in one trade such as electricians, plumbers, engineers.
Industrial	Workers in a particular industry.
General	Workers in different types of industries and different skills.
White-collar	Office workers, professionals, civil servants.

Figure 2.3 Unions and members

Examples of Change in Trade Unions

Craft to General
The Electricians' Trade Union (ETU) joined with the Plumbers' Trade Union to form the EEPTU. The EEPTU joined with the engineer's trade union to form the AEEU. The AEEU joined with the scientific trade union MSF to form the general union, Amicus.

Industrial
The National Union of Mineworkers used to be one of the strongest trade unions in Britain and represented all mineworkers. Following the mass closure of pits in the 1980s and 1990s, membership in Scotland has declined from around 200,000 to only 1,500.

White Collar to General
Nalgo, which represented white collar local government workers, joined with NUPE which represented lower paid manual council and health service workers, and COHSE which represented other health service workers to form Unison.

Professional
Your teacher's trade union may be the EIS, Educational Institute of Scotland or the SSTA, Scottish Secondary Teachers' Association. The EIS represents all Scottish teachers, college lecturers, educational psychologists, advisors and school librarians. The SSTA represents some secondary teachers.

Trade Union Negotiations and Industrial Action

Trade unions represent their members in negotiations with management on the pay and working conditions of employees. Both sides sit down together to discuss the issues and try to reach an **agreement**. This is known as **collective bargaining**.

If both sides can't reach agreement they are in **dispute**. If the union members feel strongly about it they can decide to vote on whether they should take **industrial action** to try to put more pressure on management. In some cases, industrial action may lead to agreement being

Types of industrial action	What it involves	Effect
1. Work to rule	Workers only do what they are paid to do. For example, no 'tidying up' after a job is finished.	Problem for employers.
2. A 'go-slow'	Workers don't work at their normal pace.	Productivity falls.
3. Overtime ban	Workers refuse to work overtime.	Problem for employers as production falls. Workers lose some pay.
4. Token strike	Usually one day.	Warning that union members are not happy. Employers lose a day's production. Workers lose a day's pay.
5. Unofficial or 'wildcat' strike	Does not have union backing and breaks the law.	Creates a bad 'public image' of the union. Workers lose pay.
6. Official strike	By law, a secret ballot must be taken to get an idea of the support for strike action.	Costs the union money because workers receive strike pay from the union. The production of the company is on hold during the strike. The employers will lose customers when they cannot complete orders. It is bad for worker and manager relations. Strikers lose out on their regular pay.

Figure 2.4 Types of industrial action

reached quite quickly or it may lead to a more serious rift between managers and unions.

Although unofficial strike action or 'wildcat strikes' are quite uncommon, a recent example was the postmens' action in Edinburgh.

Activities

1 Why have some small unions merged with each other? *(2 marks)*

2 What is 'collective bargaining'? *(2 marks)*

3 What happens if managers and unions fail to agree? *(2 marks)*

4 Name three types of industrial action. *(3 marks)*

5 What is a 'wildcat' strike? *(2 marks)*

How are Individual Trade Unions Organised?

The ordinary trade union members are called the '**rank and file**'. They are the people who are members of a trade union. Another term for them is the **grassroots** members. The rank and file members vote for a **shop steward** who represents their interests in the work place.

Trade union members participate in their union in the following ways:

◆ paying membership fees (union dues).

◆ attending meetings in the workplace

◆ by voting in ballots

◆ by supporting industrial action which needs to be approved by a secret ballot

◆ by picketing their place of work (up to a maximum of six people if a strike is legal).

Trade unions have many rights and responsibilities.

Rights

◆ Protecting members' interests

◆ Representing members in negotiations

◆ Taking industrial action

Responsibilities

◆ To act within the law at all times

◆ Not to use violence

◆ To hold secret ballots

◆ To control the number of pickets to the lawful limit.

Unions are organised in the following way:

Shop Steward in the Workplace
The shop steward represents members in the union at the place of work dealing with pay, health and safety, overtime, victimisation and many other issues. The shop steward does not get paid for carrying out union duties. Other shop stewards' duties include recruitment and the communication of important information

The Branch
Lowest level of union activity. The shop steward and a local committee are elected by members of the branch.

District Committee
Shop stewards of different branches get together.

National Conference (yearly)
Delegates of the union meet to work out the union's plans for the next year. The conference elects the National Executive in some unions.

National Executive
Elected union officials run the union between National Conferences. They are supported by full-time officials who are employed to do the daily business of the union and also to support and give expert advice to branches and shop stewards.The General Secretary leads the union.

The Trade Union Congress

The TUC is a collection of 71 member unions, representing approximately 6.7 million workers in 2003. It meets once a year to work out the

common policy of all trade unions for the forthcoming year. The TUC:

- lobbies the government for worker friendly policies
- campaigns on economic and social issues
- represents workers on public bodies
- carries out research on employment related issues
- helps unions to develop services for members
- help unions to avoid clashes with employers or other bodies.

In Scotland, the Scottish Trade Union Congress (STUC) does a similar job to the TUC. Scottish trade unions belong to both the STUC and the TUC

Activities

1   What is another name for ordinary union members? *(1 mark)*

2   How do members participate in their unions? *(3 marks)*

3   What are the rights and responsibilities of unions? *(4 marks)*

4   What are the duties of a shop steward? *(4 marks)*

5   What is the TUC? *(2 marks)*

6   How many unions are members of the TUC? *(1 mark)*

7   How does the TUC represent the interests of the union members? *(2 marks)*

Changes in Union Membership

Year	Number of members	Number of unions
1979	12.12 million	109
2001	7 million approximately	76
2003	6.7 million	71

Figure 2.5 Changes in union membership

Figure 2.5 indicates that there is a decline in the popularity of unions (reflected by falling membership) as well as a reduced number of unions. What are the reasons for this decline?

- Attitudes towards trade unions have changed. The late 1970s brought chaos to many British industries and some people felt that the trade unions were responsible for this.
- More part-time and temporary working have led to a reduction in trade union membership as these workers are less likely to be union members.
- Laws have been introduced to reduce the union influence in industry and its ability to take industrial action.
- The Labour Party has reduced the influence of trade unions on its actions and policies.
- The type of employment which has been increasing has been in the service sector which is predominantly part-time, temporary and mainly female (such as call centers) with low union membership.

The biggest fall in union membership has been in the traditional industries, such as coal-mining, shipbuilding and engineering due to a decline in these industries.

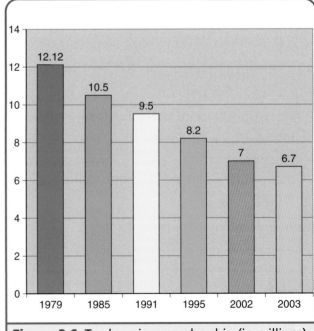

Figure 2.6 Trade union membership (in millions)

Changes in Employment

In the 1980s the British economy was hit by a large number of closures of factories. This created the large levels of unemployment which were experienced at that time. Many factory closures were in the traditional industries which had high levels of trade union members.

Some areas were worse hit by factory closures and unemployment than others. The areas which traditional industries like steel-making, coal-mining, engineering and shipbuilding were badly hit. These areas included:

◆ Northern Ireland

◆ Scotland

◆ North East England

◆ North West England

◆ South Wales.

Trade union membership is still high in the above areas but low in the south of England where **service industries** like banking and insurance are large employers.

There is growth of **white collar unions**, for groups such as office staff, civil service, managers and professionals. In the past, white collar workers had security from unemployment as most job losses were in the **manufacturing sector**. In the 1980s many job-losses began to affect these workers and the need to join trade unions became important.

> 'In the 1980s the middle classes are getting the same treatment as the working classes as they face unemployment'
> Source: John Monks,
> General Secretary of TUC

On the other hand, self employment and part-time employment in call centres and the leisure industries are now responsible for a large section of the working population most of whom are not union members.

Activities

1 What are the main reasons for the decline in union membership? *(4 marks)*

2 In which industries has union membership fallen the most? *(2 marks)*

3 In what parts of the country is union membership still high? *(4 marks)*

4 In what parts of the country is membership low? *(2 marks)*

5 What types of trade unions are growing in membership? *(2 marks)*

6 Why is this the case? *(2 marks)*

7 In what kinds of job is union membership still low? *(4 marks)*

Women, Ethnic Minorities and Trade Unions

Women and ethnic minorities are under-represented in unions. Females in particular, who make up over 50 per cent of the population, have lower overall membership of trade unions than men.

In the past women have been under represented in trade unions because:

◆ trade unions were male dominated

◆ women were mostly in part-time employment

◆ union fees were off-putting

◆ meeting times were unsuitable

◆ women were perceived as weaker than men when it comes to negotiation with management.

Under representation of women appears to be changing. For example, UNISON has over 60 per cent female membership.

Trade unions are seeking to recruit members in areas of employment where trade union membership is low, and in particular are seeking to recruit women into unions. Trade unions have been successful in promoting 'family-friendly' policies, which allow women workers to change their employment patterns to suit their home circumstances. This particularly benefits women workers.

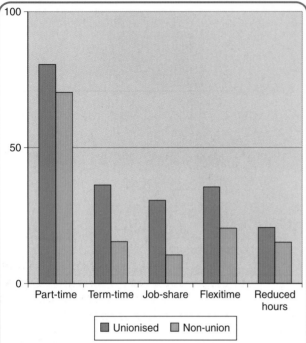

Figure 2.7 Types of companies with work–life balance policies (where workers can change their employment patterns to suit their home circumstances)

Source DTI 2003 (abridged)

Activities

1 Which two groups are under-represented in trade unions? *(2 marks)*

2 Why are there fewer women in unions? *(4 marks)*

3 Look at Figure 2.7. What benefits does being in a union give women? *(4 marks)*

Conservatives and Trade Unions

Conservatives believed that trade unions were bad for the British economy for the following reasons:

◆ they gave a 'bad image' to British industry and they frightened-off foreign companies

◆ they stopped the creation of jobs

because they did not accept wage cuts when companies were in trouble

◆ they affected customers if they went on strike

◆ sometimes they acted unlawfully.

When Mrs Thatcher was Prime Minister she described the unions as the '**enemy within**', and she brought them under government control. Her government introduced a number of laws to control the unions.

The trade unions say that industrial action has fallen over the last 20 years because it may lead to the loss of jobs. The level of unemployment has 'frightened' union members from taking industrial action.

Activities

1 Why did the Conservatives believe that unions were bad for the British economy? *(4 marks)*

2 Explain why the level of industrial action has fallen over the last twenty years? *(2 marks)*

The Labour Party and Trade Unions

The Labour Party has always had strong ties with the trade unions, as it was set up to represent the workers in parliament. A lot of the money to support the Labour Party comes from trade union members in the form of a **political levy**. Another way that the trade unions provide finance to the Labour Party is through the '**sponsoring**' of MP's. One of the most famous sponsored MPs is the current Prime Minister Tony Blair who is sponsored by the TGWU.

In the past the trade unions were given quite a big say on the policies of the Labour Party in return for their support. However, since 1997, under the premiership of Tony Blair the influence of trade unions on party policies has been dramatically reduced.

FOUNDATION/GENERAL

The influence of the trade unions on the Labour Party was seen by many as a reason why the Labour Party was not elected in the 1987 and 1992 general elections. The Miners' Strike of 1984–85 brought back the memory of the '**winter of discontent**' of the late 1970s.

The Labour Party leadership felt that the influence of the unions would have to be reduced if they were to have a chance of winning a general election.

Reform of the Labour Party began in the 1980s with Neil Kinnock, and continues to the present day as Figure 2.8 shows.

Year	Leader	Changes
1983	Neil Kinnock	Begins to reduce power of unions.
1992	John Smith	'One Man One Vote' (OMOV) passed. Union power over Labour Party policy reduced.
1994 –	Tony Blair	Seeks to increase Labour Party membership to reduce the need for trade union financial support. Reduction of union sponsorship of MPs.

Figure 2.8 Labour Party reform and trade unions

The traditional relationship between the Labour Party and the trade union movement appears to be broken. After 1997, the Labour government has continued to distance itself from the trade unions and failed to repeal Conservative anti-union legislation.

Some trade unions are now considering reducing financial support for New Labour and transferring their support to political parties which are closer to their aims. In addition, many trade unions have elected leaders who are strongly opposed to New Labour policies.

Rail Union's Final Labour Split
One of Britain's biggest unions severed its ties with the Labour Party in Scotland.

The Rail, Maritime and Transport Union is allowing its branches in Scotland to affiliate (join) to other political parties, including the Scottish Socialists (SSP).

Other unions will now come under pressure to disaffiliate from the Labour Party highlighting dissatisfaction with Tony Blair's policies.

Tommy Sheridan, leader of the SSP said, 'New Labour represents the millionaires in society and is the enemy of socialist policies. More and more trade unionists are willing to accept this reality'.

Source: *Daily Mail* – 8th February 2004 (abridged)

Activities

1 Explain the traditional link between the Labour Party and the unions in the past. *(2 marks)*

2 What has happened to the Labour Party and its union links since 1977? *(2 marks)*

3 What changes have occurred since 1994 in the Labour Party's relationship with unions (see Figure 2.8)? *(3 marks)*

4 According to Tommy Sheridan, why did the RMT decide to let its Scottish branches join the SSP? *(2 marks)*

Trade Union Reforms

Low pay is another area of change. The **national minimum wage** legislation was introduced in the late 1990s. In 2004, low pay is still a big issue as can be seen in Figure 2.9.

Alarm as gender pay gap widens

The pay gap between men and women grew last year for the first time in two decades.

Full-time women workers made £383 a week on average compared to £514 for men.

A 10 per cent hike in the national minimum wage late in 2001 had been expected to narrow the pay gap.

But this was more than off-set by bigger wage increases for men in highly-paid jobs.

Women are more likely to work as shop assistants, cleaners and in clerical jobs, while more men work in management, a new report said.

The gap in pay is widest in high-powered finance jobs – male company financial managers and treasurers earn 40 per cent more than their female colleagues.

The overall pay gap hit almost 19 per cent last year.

Women's average hourly wages were £10.22, compared to £12.59 for men.

The gap had been closing at a rate of around 0.5 per cent a year since the 1980s but grew by 0.3 per cent from 2001.

The new figures dismayed equal pay campaigners.

Figure 2.9 Newspaper article about the gender pay gap
Source *Paisley Daily Express*

Trade Unions and Europe

In some European countries (like Germany), trade unions have a bigger influence on their government's policy than they have in Britain. British workers now co-operate closely with European trade unions. The European Union also appears to have taken European workers seriously and introduced the Social Chapter of the Maastricht Treaty which was not introduced into Britain.

However, some European legislation has found its way into Britain. For example, the **working time directive** provided rights for part-time workers, allowing them the right to paid annual holiday leave. It also covers the working times of lorry and coach drivers. Workers should not work more than 48 hours per week.

The latest important piece of European legislation is the new **information and consultation directive** which will force companies to consult workers on all significant decisions affecting them. This will be introduced in European countries in 2005.

Equality at Work

Another European Union initiative is the goal of equality of opportunity for all. The fact that there is still an 18 per cent pay gap between male and female earnings in Britain is receiving attention in Strasbourg.

The following article shows the pay-gap in 2004 between male and female workers has not been reduced.

Scottish Low Pay Unit hits out at Job Centre adverts

A new report from the Scottish Low Page Unit reveals that Job Centres in Glasgow are advertising positions in the Catering, Leisure and Tourism sector which offer 'astonishingly' low rates of pay.

In Glasgow, 91.1 per cent of the vacancies surveyed pay rates at lower levels than the Scottish Low Pay Unit's Minimum Wage Target (£5.55 at the time of the survey).

Amongst the vacancies surveyed in 'Scottish

Jobcentre Survey 2002: Analysis of Vacancies within the Catering, Leisure and Tourism Sector', positions in the area were recorded with pay rates as low as £2.43 per hour.

SLPU director John Wilson said: 'Due to the fact that it would be illegal to pay such low rates to most employees over the age of 18, companies offering this type of position are ensuring that only the youngest jobseekers can apply.

Figure 2.10 Newspaper article from 22nd January 2004
Source *Daily Record*

Activities

1   What is the Scottish Low Pay Unit's minimum wage target for an adult per hour? *(2 marks)*

2   What rate per hour is being offered in some industries? *(2 marks)*

3   Which age group is being targeted in these industries? *(2 marks)*

4   How many hours a week does the European Union's 'working time directive' state as a maximum that a person should work? *(2 marks)*

5   Why is this pay gap causing concern at the European Parliament? *(2 marks)*

6   What is the size of the pay gap between men and women? *(1 mark)*

FOUNDATION/GENERAL

Representation in the Workplace

What are Trade Unions?

Trade unions are organisations that represent the interests of people who work. Not all workers belong to trade unions. Some workers choose not to do so, for various reasons, which will be looked at later.

Trade unions have grown in the last one hundred and fifty years with the industrialisation of the British economy. Today they are modern, sophisticated organisations representing the interests of millions of workers.

Their main purpose is to improve the pay and working conditions of their members. In addition they offer other benefits to their members, such as discounted insurance and health benefits such as private health schemes.

Trade unions also campaign for laws and policies which will benefit workers and society as a whole. They act as pressure groups in society. They not only function to look after the interests of their members, but also have been responsible for bringing benefits to the wider society.

In the past, trade unions co-operated closely with government, especially Labour governments. This is because, historically, the trade union movement helped form the Labour Party.

Some examples of social legislation which has been passed for the benefit of workers and society in general have been:

- **paid holidays**
- **the national minimum wage**
- **statutory sick pay and maternity leave**
- **flexible working arrangements for working parents.**

Trade unions cover all sorts of industries and jobs. Some people who work in a specific job or industry might be represented by one particular trade union, for example, the Fire Brigades Union (FBU) represents fire fighters in the United Kingdom.

On the other hand, the car manufacturing industry tends to have different trade unions representing the workers in that industry, reflecting the diversity of the jobs they do, such as Amicus and TGWU. Other examples would be journalism and the media – the National Union of Journalists (NUJ) represents journalists.

The largest unions tend to include a mixture of workers in different types of employment. The biggest are Amicus, GMB, TGWU and UNISON. These large unions represent people working in a range of different occupations in the public and private sectors. This is mainly because unions have **amalgamated** (joined together) to increase their membership and influence.

Activities

1   What is the main purpose of trade unions?

2   In what ways do trade unions act as pressure groups? Give specific examples of successes.

3   In what ways can trade unions be said to represent a wide range of workers?

Types of Union

There are basically four main types of trade union in Britain today. They cover all types of workers and employees. Some are larger than others and some are more powerful than others depending on the job they do.

Craft Unions

These are the oldest and smallest unions. They date back to the time when individual skills were very important. Many are skilled workers, for example, musicians, cobblers and coopers. Unfortunately, many of the skills are no longer in demand as these jobs can be done by machinery. Membership of these unions is falling as a result.

Industrial Unions

These used to have a very strong influence in the past and were mainly to be found in the manufacturing side of the economy, for example, heavy engineering, shipbuilding and car manufacturing. These unions were dominant at the height of trade union power. They have declined rapidly since 1980 as the British economy has moved from being a manufacturing economy to being a service sector economy.

General Unions

These unions take in workers from a variety of jobs, for example, the Transport and General Workers Union (T&G) and UNISON. These unions are growing in membership but mostly through amalgamations.

White Collar Unions

These unions represent office workers, professional people, government officials and clerical workers. They are the fastest growing type of union as many people are joining to protect themselves against impending redundancy and privatisation, for example, civil servants.

Activities

1   Why have both craft unions and industrial unions declined?

2   What types of trade unions have been growing in membership? Give reasons for these changes.

Why People Join a Trade Union

People belong to trade unions for many different reasons, but these are considered to be the most important:

◆   **to be able to negotiate the best possible working conditions such as paid holidays, health and safety, and higher rates of pay**

◆   **to have job security, to consult over possible redundancies**

◆   **to prevent victimisation of workers through the idea 'unity is strength'**

◆   **to ensure benefits for workers who are not working due to illness, stress or old age**

◆   **to provide legal backing and advice for members**

◆   **to exert political power through sponsorship of MPs and the political levy.**

Reasons for Not Joining a Union

There are reasons why people may not wish to join a trade union:

◆   **many workers are well paid and don't see the need to join a union**

◆   **some workers are in jobs where union activity is difficult to organise, for example, shopworkers, homeworkers and part-time workers**

◆   **many workers are employed in small family firms and can negotiate for themselves**

◆   **many workers are self employed**

◆   **some employers refuse to recognise or deal with unions (now outlawed as employers must recognise a union where a majority of the workforce vote for it)**

◆   **people can get the benefits of union membership without actually joining.**

Activity

Look at the reasons for and against joining a union. Overall, do you think the benefits of membership outweigh the disadvantages? You must answer in detail.

Trade Union Negotiations and Industrial Action

Negotiation

This is the process which takes place at various levels. This is where union representatives discuss with management issues which affect people working in an organisation. The union takes on board the wishes of its members and communicates these wishes to the management of the company.

There may be a difference of opinion between management and unions over issues and 'negotiation' is about finding a solution to these differences. This process is known as 'collective bargaining' (the union bargains on behalf of all employees with management). The issues which are normally negotiated under the process of collective bargaining are pay, working hours, holidays and changes to working practices.

Agreements reached between the employer and trade unions through collective bargaining will apply to all workers in that company or workplace.

Case Study: British Airways Dispute

In summer 2003 there was a dispute at British Airways, centering on management plans to introduce an electronic clocking in and out system for British Airways staff who worked at the check in counters at Heathrow Airport.

This Automated Time Recording system would allow British Airways to manage and record attendance as well as plan shifts and rosters. BA hoped this 'smart' chip would allow them to store information about how long someone has worked, when and where.

Here are the management and unions' views on the proposed change:

BA – the system will allow us to monitor working patterns and organise shifts more accurately as well as upholding the new working time regulations due to come into effect (restricting the number of hours a worker could work in any one week). We are already losing a substantial number of staff from the business and this system will help us record, monitor and manage our staff. 2000 baggage handlers already use the system.

The unions – this system will be used to stagger and change shift patterns and holidays. BA might decide to cut the numbers on certain shifts, leading to redundancies or wage cuts for staff paid at an hourly rate. Many of those affected by these proposals are women who rely on current shifts to fit in with child care. Changes could lead to inconvenient working patterns, with staff sent home during quiet periods and as a result hourly paid workers would lose money.

The proposed changes caused walk outs by union members in July 2003, causing thousands of passengers to suffer delays to their holidays. This unofficial action is known as a wildcat strike.

In most cases management and trade unions seek to achieve a resolution through negotiation which both parties can accept. In this case it was not possible and ACAS acted as a 'referee' between the two sides.

The dispute was settled when union members were allowed to voluntarily use the new clock in/out system if they so wished. ➤

So many hours, so little time

'Employers want increasing flexibility, involving more hours and less pay for workers. But workers need flexibility to work for them.

In the case of the BA check-in staff, they were very anxious to get recognition of the balance in their lives. This summer's dispute involving British Airways check-in staff was notable not least for being about time, rather than pay.

Threatened with changes to working hours, the largely female check-in staff walked out. It was the prospect of losing control over their work-life balance that proved the last straw for them, as BA found out to its cost.'

Source: TGWU Record October 2003

Activities

1   What arguments could BA have put forward in negotiations?

2   What arguments would the trade union put forward?

3   How did the ordinary workers respond to the proposals and how did this affect BA's customers?

4   What evidence is there that direct negotiations between the trade unions and management did not succeed?

5   Who won? Give reasons for your answer.

Industrial Action

The main task of trade unions is to negotiate pay and conditions for their members.

Negotiations are most successful when both sides think they have won something for their side, sometimes called 'win, win'.

When negotiations between management and unions break down, there are many actions a trade union can take to put pressure on the employers.

Action by the union is often described as 'escalating', that is, the action gets more serious as the length of any dispute goes on. Strike action is only taken as a last resort. There are many tactics a union can employ to get what they want short of strike action. These are know as restrictive practices.

Restrictive Practices

Overtime ban: workers refuse to work overtime and production is slowed down. Although union members lose money as a result, this is seen as vital as employers have orders to meet and they do not want to lose business. Employers also use overtime as it is much cheaper than employing more full time workers.

Go-slow: this is where workers slow down the production process which ultimately costs the employer money as much less is produced in the normal working day.

Work-to-rule: this is where workers adhere strictly to working at what they get paid for. Workers refuse to do any 'extras 'such as tidying up etc.

Strike Action

Token strike: this usually takes place as a warning to employers that the union is not happy with pay or conditions of employment. It usually lasts for a day.

Unofficial strike: this is a strike which takes place without union backing. These were very common in the past but are now very rare. Government legislation means that employers can sue for compensation if a union has failed to take adequate legal steps before calling for a strike.

Lightning strike: these occur on a spur of the moment basis. The recent dispute at Heathrow (summer 2003) is a good example of this. Union members walked out after a new clocking in system was introduced.

Official strike: this is the most serious form of industrial action. A strike can only be called after a compulsory ballot of members has been held. The firemen's dispute 2002–2003 is a good example of an official strike. When a strike has been declared official then those on strike are entitled to strike pay from their union but this is usually much less than the worker would have earned if he/she had remained at work.

Figure 2.1 Scotland's nursery nurses on an official strike in 2004

More than 4000 of Scotland's nursery nurses still in dispute with local councils will ballot on an all-out indefinite strike next month unless there is a resolution to their two-year old claim, UNISON said today.

UNISON's UK Industrial Action committee agreed unanimously yesterday to authorise the escalation in an attempt to bring the nine-month ➤

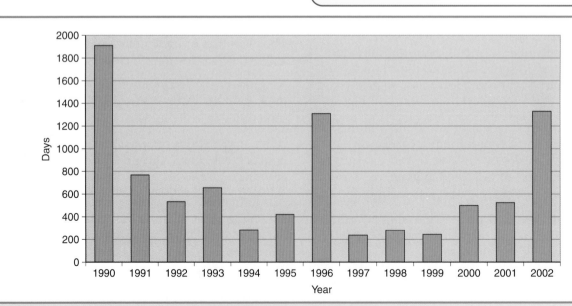

Figure 2.2 Number of working days (thousands) lost due to strike action.

Abridged Source *Guardian* 3 September 2003

Case Study: Scottish nursery nurses continued

campaign of industrial action to a head. The union will also call three days of action prior to the indefinite strike.

Joe Di Paola, UNISON said 'Despite days of action, and selective strikes, petitions and concentrated lobbying by nursery nurses and parents, CoSLA has continually failed to recognise the value of the nursery nurses' job, and the need for their grading to be tackled.

We have been consulting with nursery nurse members across Scotland and they have told us that they feel they no longer have any alternative but to move towards all-out strike action. We have only moved to this stage with the utmost reluctance. Even now we are proposing to ballot our members, to give an opportunity for CoSLA to come back to the table, or for any other initiatives to avoid this action.'

Source: www.unison-scotland.org.uk

Activities

1 What are the main types of trade union action?

2 What are restrictive practices?

3 Explain why an overtime ban is damaging to both unions and employers.

4 Look at the Unison source.
   a) How long have the nursery nurses been seeking improved salaries?
   b) How long has the campaign of industrial action been going on?
   c) How is the union further escalating the industrial action?
   d) What other forms of action has the union undertaken in order to try to win their case?
   e) What are the union's main complaints against CoSLA?
   f) How do Unison members wish to bring the dispute to a head?
   g) What does Joe Di Paola suggest CoSLA do?
   h) What will the effect of all out strike action be on:
      ◆ nursery children and parents
      ◆ members' incomes,
      ◆ the union's strike fund.

5 Look at Figure 2.2. 'The 1990s were periods of industrial stability. Now we are returning to the days of industrial militancy.' In what ways can the speaker be accused of being selective with the facts?

How are Individual Trade Unions Organised?

Union Members
↓
Shop Steward/Representative
↓
Union Branch
↓
District and Regional Offices
↓
National Office

Figure 2.3 Typical structure of a trade union

Trade unions are democratic organisations, that are accountable to their members for their policies and actions. Figure 2.3 provides a typical trade union structure.

Who's Who in the Trade Union Structure?

Members: these are referred to as the 'rank and file', the ordinary workers who pay their union subscriptions to belong to the union. They are the backbone of the union. The larger the union the more industrial muscle it can exert and the more money it has to support members.

Shop Stewards: these are the elected by the members in the workplace and are given time off by the management to do their trade union duties. The shop steward is the first 'port of call' when a member has a question or a problem. They are also the people who are most likely to recruit new members.

They are unpaid union officials. In large factories or sites there are sometimes shop steward committees composed of shop stewards from the same union. In cases where there are different unions representing workers, a joint shop steward committee may be formed.

The role of the shop steward is a crucial one. They basically have four main functions; recruiting, informing, giving advice and representing. They will usually keep the membership informed through regular union meetings and distributing union literature.

The role of the shop steward has become more

complex in recent years with the increase in legislation which both employers and employees have to adhere to, for example, the introduction of flexible working time for parents in 2003. Trade unions inform shop stewards of changes in the law and organise training. It is also not unusual for the shop steward to know more than the employer about changes in employment law.

The Branch: this can be the grouping of members in a workplace or a group of workplace branches together. Members meet in the branch to discuss and decide on local issues. There is usually a branch secretary who is elected by the local members. The branch can also send motions to the union's annual conference to be debated.

District/Regional Office: these are the local headquarters of the union. They are staffed by full-time paid officials (FTOs) who offer advice and support to branches, shop stewards and their members.

The National Office: this is the union headquarters which manages the affairs of the union. National paid officials give support to districts, branches and individual members.

The General Secretary: these are usually directly elected by all the union members and becomes a paid official of the union. He/she has a very high profile and represents the image of the union to the media. In the 2002–2003 firemen's dispute Andy Gilchrist, leader of the FBU (Fire Brigades Union), adopted a very high profile in the negotiations and final settlement.

The National Executive: this is made up from full-time paid officials and elected union officials (lay officials) from throughout the country. The head of the National Executive is the General Secretary or the Union President, who is usually elected for one year and is the top lay official. The job of the National Executive is to ensure union policy is implemented between annual union conferences.

Annual National Conference/Annual General Meeting: members elected from local branches are delegates to the National Conference/AGM. Delegates debate and vote on a wide number of issues which, if passed, become union policy.

STUC/TUC Conferences: The Scottish Trades Union Congress (STUC) brings together all the trades unions and trades union councils (local groups of trade unionists) with members in Scotland. The Trades Union Congress (TUC) operates similarly on a UK basis. Trade union delegates at STUC or TUC conferences vote on issues affecting all trade unionists at Scottish/UK level. The STUC Conference is sometimes referred to as the 'Scottish Parliament of Labour.'

Activities

1   Why is the shop steward so important?

2   What main functions does the shop steward have?

3   How do unions keep shop stewards up to date and what unusual effects can this have?

4   What is the role of:
   a)   the branch
   b)   the district/regional office
   c)   the national office
   d)   the General Secretary
   e)   the National Executive
   f)   the National Conference?

How Unions Represent their Members

There are four main functions which trade unions perform for their members: giving information, giving advice, representation and negotiation.

Information

Much of the work of trades unions deals with day to day issues in the workplace. Trade union shop stewards have a wealth of information which is very useful for their members in their workplace. Information is also available on union notice boards, through leaflets, trade union journals/newspapers or on the union's website.

Advice

Shop stewards/union representatives give advice on a whole range of 'salaries, terms and conditions issues' such as the correct salary for the job, holiday entitlement, maternity leave and maternity pay. Trade unions are also currently recruiting and training 'Learning Representatives' who can help members with training needs and advises them on training courses which they can attend.

Representation

Trade unions also represent individual members when they have a problem at work. If an employee feels that they have been unfairly treated, he or she can ask for a union representative (usually the shop steward) to help them discuss the issues with management to sort out their problem.

If the problem cannot be solved by the shop steward at the place of work, the matter can then be referred to a full-time trade union official (FTO) who is employed full-time by the union. The FTO usually has much more experience than the shop steward and can often put more pressure on management to listen to the worker's problems.

Discussions between management and the individual member's trade union representative about the member's problems can be informal.

In other cases, a formal procedure is started called 'grievance'. The member's representative puts the case at a Grievance Hearing which is conducted by one of the company's senior managers. A Grievance Hearing is a bit like a court, except that the 'judge' may not entirely be independent.

If the matter cannot be resolved through grievance, the trade union can decide to refer the matter to an employment tribunal.

ACAS (the Arbitration Conciliation and Advisory Service) usually gets involved at this stage. The role of ACAS is to try to get an agreement between the union and the employer before it goes to tribunal.

If this fails, the employment tribunal will hear the case. The tribunal is made up of an independent chair (usually a lawyer), a member who has been nominated by the trade unions (such as the STUC) and one who has been nominated by the employers (for example, the CBI).

The trade union bringing the case will represent the worker, either through an FTO or through a lawyer who specialises in employment law. Most workers would not be able to afford to pay for an employment lawyer themselves. The lawyer's fees are usually quite high and are paid for by the union. The employer is also usually represented by an employment law specialist.

The job of employment tribunals is to make sure that current employment legislation is being properly adhered to by both employers and employees. Most disputes that reach employment tribunal level are about pay, unfair dismissal, redundancy or discrimination at work.

Employment tribunals decisions become 'case law' and have strong powers to enforce their judgements, including forcing employers to pay compensation. They can decide that an employer should re-instate a worker who has been sacked unfairly. However, employment tribunals cannot enforce this. If the employer refuses to re-instate the worker, the tribunal can decide to enforce higher levels of compensation.

The employer can appeal to an employment appeals tribunal and to the House of Lords. If the employer does not appeal within 40 days, the employment tribunal's decision becomes law.

Look at Figure 2.4 and answer the questions which follow.

Member believes employer is acting unfairly

↓

Shop steward listens to member, advises whether the member has a case or not

↓

Shop steward seeks informal resolution with employer. If not resolved shop steward refers matter to FTO.

↓

FTO seeks to resolve informally with employer. If not resolved . . .

↓

FTO represents member at Grievance Hearing. If not resolved . . .

↓

Union lodges Employment Tribunal Application. ACAS involved in talks with FTO and employer. If not resolved . . .

↓

Employment Tribunal Hearing. FTO or union's employment specialist lawyer represents member.

Figure 2.4 Grievance procedure involving trade unions

Activities

1   What further measures can a trade union take if a member's problems cannot be resolved informally in the workplace?

2   What is ACAS's role?

3   How does the make up of employment tribunals ensure balance between union and employer interests?

4   What advantages would a union member have over a non-union member in bringing a case to an employment tribunal?

5   What are the main issues which come before employment tribunals?

6 What kinds of powers do employment tribunals have?

7 What can employment tribunals do if employers refuse to re-instate a worker who has been sacked unfairly?

8 When does an employment tribunal's decision become law?

Decline in Trade Union Membership

In 1979 there were over 12 million union members in the UK. Trade union membership has declined in the 80s and 90s although there has been some increase since 1997.

In autumn 2001 there were only 7.6 million people in employment who belonged to trade unions. The number of people in trade unions is now approximately 29.1 per cent of those in paid employment. However, the number of employees in workplaces in the UK where trade unions were present was 11.9 million. There are many workers who do not belong or may not want to belong to trade unions.

In the past decade there has also been an overall decline in union membership and this has been steeper for men than for women.

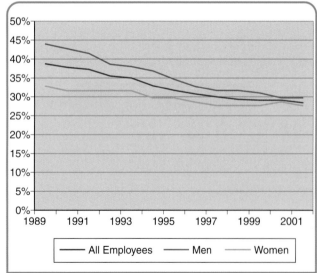

Figure 2.5 Union density Great Britain (employees who are union members as a percentage of total number of employees)

Source Labour Force Survey 2002 www.gov.uk

There are various reasons for this decline:

◆ a change in the British economy – we have moved from a manufacturing-based economy with a traditionally high union density (most workers in trade unions) towards a service-based economy where union membership is low

◆ high unemployment in the 1980s and 1990s cost unions dearly in terms of membership

◆ a fall in traditional full-time employment and an increase in part time and temporary employment where workers are less likely to join unions

◆ an increase in the number of small companies employing a small workforce who find it difficult to organise themselves into unions and achieve union recognition

◆ government legislation in the 1980s which made it more difficult for unions to operate.

The Trade Union Congress

Each year the TUC Conference takes place. It is a very important event in the TUC calendar. At this conference various issues are discussed and debated and motions passed. Some of the issues at the 2003 TUC annual congress were university tuition fees, foundation hospitals, privatisation and private finance initiatives, manufacturing and employment rights, pensions and Iraq.

The leader of the TUC is Brendan Barber. He represents the new style of trade unionist who preaches social partnership between government, employers and workers.

What is the Role of the TUC?

The Trades Unions Congress (TUC) is an umbrella organisation which represents the vast majority of trade unionists in Britain. It brings together Britain's unions and tries to draw up common policies. It is also influential in lobbying government to introduce legislation which will benefit workers.

It acts as one of the most important pressure groups in Britain. It also campaigns on major social and economic issues such as pensions, social security benefits etc.

The TUC has also been instrumental on carrying out research on employment related issues such as gender

GENERAL/CREDIT

and race. It also runs extensive training programmes for shop stewards and trade union representatives.

Activities

1 What is the role of the TUC?

2 Outline the main functions of the TUC.

3 What type of issues were discussed at the 2003 TUC Conference?

4 What type of trade union leader is Brendan Barber?

Trade union general secretaries were asked what they would change in the union movement.

Derek Simpson, Amicus, general secretary: 'Reduce the number of unions. There is no need for more than three unions in Britain: a public services union, private sector skilled and a professional union, closer relations with unions abroad to deal with globalisation.'

Dave Prentis, Unison, general secretary: 'Loads more young people joining and more women becoming active, make being a member fashionable, speak up about the big issues and not concentrate solely on narrow workplace concerns, learn from the past, not be stuck in it.'

Mary Bousted, ATL, general secretary: 'Trade unionists are articulate, intelligent and committed, and want to engage in a social partnership with the government. There are still a lot of blokes from the north, but women like me are helping to change this.'

Mick Rix, Aslef, general secretary: 'The movement is now united on policies for peace, employment rights and social justice. We need to see action by millions of trade unionists to impose those policies on government and bad employers. More members, more struggle, and more socialism.'

Source: *Guardian* September 2003 (abridged)

Activities

1 Which of the four union leaders appears to want the most union reform? Explain your answer.

2 What evidence is there that the trade union movement wishes to lose its old fashioned image?

3 Which of the four union leaders appears most left wing in their opinion as to the role of trade unions? Explain your answer.

Changes in Union Membership

Since Labour took office in 1997, trade unions have been keen to take the opportunity to increase their membership. In many cases it means trade unions have to compete with each other in the recruitment of new workers.

They offer many inducements and benefits to prospective members. Trade unions can offer discounts on credit cards, cheap home and car insurance, discounts on holidays, cheaper health care for their members and their families.

The cost of recruiting new members is very high and some unions are running deficits to do that. The GMB union ran a deficit of £5.1 million in 2002. Among the remaining 'big four', only the Transport and General Workers Union (T&G) and engineering and professional combine Amicus (AEEU and MSF) are in surplus.

Unison, a major public service union, says its numbers are on the rise again (2003). More than half of its costs are administrative, with 1,100 full time officials to support. Due to members changing jobs or retiring, Unison has on average 120,000 people a year to replace, roughly 10 per cent of its membership.

The CWU (Communication Workers Union) faces particular problems. Most of its members are in the Royal Mail and BT. The Royal Mail has lost 20,000 jobs to date in 2003 and BT has lost 10,000 jobs in 2003.

Unions such as the CWU recognise that if they are to survive they will have to diversify (branch out and recruit from other areas of employment).

Activities

1 What is the major problem facing trade unions today?

2 How have trade unions responded to the challenge?

3 What particular problems does the CWU face in 2003?

Union Characteristics

An LFS (Labour Force Survey) in autumn 2001 showed that employees in the UK aged 40+ have the highest union density (35 per cent–38 per cent) and the lowest union density was those under the age of 20 at 5 per cent.

Representation in the Workplace

Union density was 29 per cent for white employees and 26 per cent for all other ethnic groups. Black employees had the highest density at 30 per cent.

In terms of educational and academic qualifications, union membership was highest among those with higher education qualifications below degree level (at 44 per cent) compared to 37 per cent for those with a degree or equivalent.

In terms of gender, men and women were almost equally likely to join a trade union, although in terms of ethnicity there are some differences as women from ethnic minorities were more likely to join a union than their male counterparts from ethnic minorities.

Union membership is also higher for full-time workers than for part time workers. Again when we compare public to private sector, union membership is significantly larger in the public sector, almost three times higher.

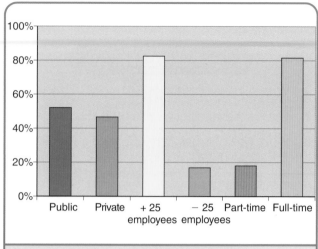

Figure 2.8 Union membership by type of employment, size of workplace and sector

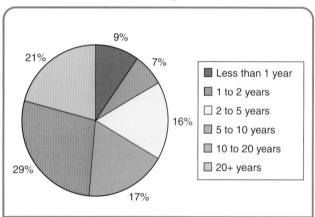

Figure 2.6 Union membership by length of service

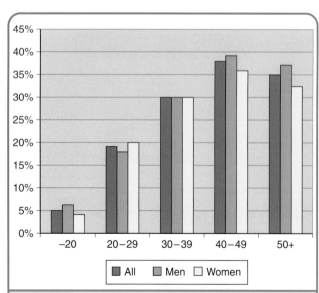

Figure 2.7 Percentage of each age group who are members of trade unions

Activities

1   What evidence is there that workers who have worked longer for a company are more likely than younger workers to be union members?

2   Why do you think that workplace size is a crucial factor in determining union membership or not?

3   Public sector workers are more likely to be union members than private sector workers. To what extent is this statement true?

4   Using Figures 2.7–9 how would you describe the 'average trade unionist'?

Investigation

5   Look at the trade union websites at the end of this book. What evidence is there that trade unions are trying to change this image?

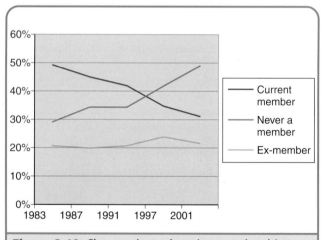

Figure 2.10 Changes in trade union membership 1983 – 2001

Abridged Source *Guardian* 20 September 2003

GENERAL/CREDIT

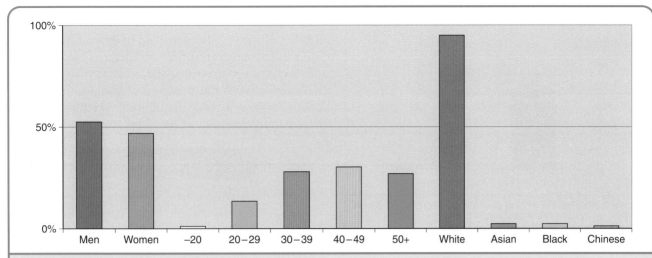

Figure 2.9 Trade union members by gender, age and ethnic origin

Source Labour Market Trends July 2002 ww.gov.uk

Recruitment and Retention

One of the major problems facing trade unions today is recruiting and retaining membership. Membership of unions fell from just under half the workforce to a third. The blame for this decline is usually put on the collapse of heavy manufacturing industry, the rise in white collar work and the new 'casualised' service sector.

A British Social Attitudes Survey 2002 reveals a bleaker picture. The decline is spread across every type of workplace. It has been greatest in traditional male manual work. The lowest paid in most need of unions are least likely to be members. Much of the decline has been among the new workers not choosing to join even where there is a union.

David Coats, TUC Head of Economic and Social Policy, said that unions had been unable to establish its presence in workplaces set up since 1980, most notably in the private sector.

Research has shown that the so called 'never members' were highest among young workers, those in non-union workplaces, the low paid, places employing less than 25 workers, the south of England and the private sector.

The TUC is even more worried by the fall in membership in unionised workplaces. In response to this crisis, the TUC has set up an organising academy, training some 40 recruiters a year, from all ages and backgrounds. It is targeting such employers as Pizza Express where a few members are already established.

Activities

1   What has been the traditional cause for the fall in union membership?

2   What evidence is there that the picture is bleaker than was first thought?

3   What are the typical characteristics of a non union member?

4   How has the trade union movement responded to this crisis?

Job Security and Pay

Trade unions seek to protect members from unfair dismissal. Trade unions also have a legal right to be consulted when employers decide to reduce the number of employees through redundancy. Trade unions try to avoid compulsory redundancies or to reduce the number of workers who may be made redundant.

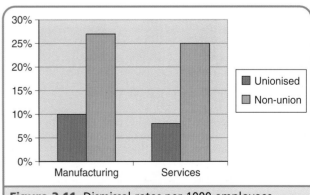

Figure 2.11 Dismissal rates per 1000 employees

Source TUC website www.bized.ac.uk

Trade unions also seek to negotiate higher wages for members.

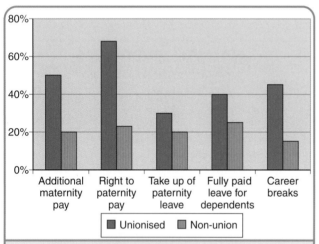

Figure 2.12 Types of companies with low paid workers
Source TUC website www.bizid.ac.uk

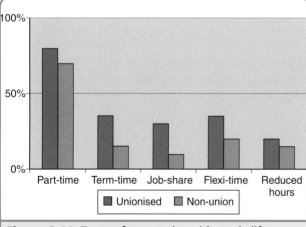

Figure 2.13 Companies with agreed parental rights
Source DTI 2003 (abridged)

Figure 2.14 Types of companies with work–life balance policies (where workers can change their employment patterns to suit their home circumstances)
Source DTI 2003 (abridged)

Securing a Work–Life Balance

Trade unions are also involved in ensuring that laws are actually applied in the workplace. One key area of recent government legislation is to provide a balance between the world of work and life outside of it. This can involve negotiating anything from better maternity pay to the right to go part time.

Activities

1 What evidence is there that trade unions are successful in:
  a) protecting members from dismissal or redundancy
  b) achieving better pay for members
  c) achieving better rights for members with families
  d) negotiating rights so that members can change their patterns of employment?

Conservatives and Trade Unions

During the 1980s and 1990s the membership of trades unions fell quite dramatically due to unemployment and changes in the economy. The Conservative governments under Margaret Thatcher and John Major also introduced laws which made recruitment and organisation of workers in trade unions more difficult.

Union practises and types of industrial action were also severely curtailed. This made trade unions less effective and forced them to change how they operated in order to represent their members.

The following changes were made law by the Conservative governments in the 1980s and 90s:

◆ **closed shop made illegal** – previously you had to join a union to get a job in a particular place of work

◆ **compulsory election of union leaders every four years**

◆ **union members had to vote on the political fund levy** (whether or not to fund political campaigns or donate part of their union fees to the Labour Party)

◆ **introduction of compulsory secret ballots before a strike can take place**

◆ **outlawing of secondary industrial action** – unions were prohibited from trying to influence disputes by putting pressure on companies which were not the direct employers of the workers (for example, suppliers or customers of the company in dispute).

Activities

1 How might banning the 'closed shop' affect union membership?

2 What intention do you think the Conservative government had in imposing ballots on members on whether their trade union could campaign politically or give money to the Labour Party?

3 What do you think the purpose of 'secondary industrial action' was and why do you think the Conservatives banned it?

The Labour Party and Trade Unions

The Labour government elected in 1997 did not repeal the Conservative's trade union laws. Instead it passed legislation saying that employers must legally recognise unions where a majority of the workforce vote for it. This came into effect in summer 2000 as the Employment Relations Act 1999.

Only three out of 44 firms with over 25,000 employers are union-free zones. Two retailers – Marks and Spencer and John Lewis – continue to be two of only three large companies which are union free. The other is the McDonalds burger chain.

Last year, Usdaw recruited 8,500 new members in Safeway. In Sainsbury's 3,000 new union members were recruited over a six month period and the union now has 100 new stewards.

However, the retail sector remains a hard nut to crack with a high staff turnover, particularly of young workers.

Source: *Labour Research* September 2002 (abridged)

Activities

1 What evidence is there that unions have made successful use of the new legislation?

2 What particular problems do unions face recruiting members in the retail sector?

Some companies do not want to have their workers belonging to a trade union. In these companies trade unions are not 'recognised'.

Culina Logistics – owned by the Müller yoghurt company – used blatant threats to put the kibosh on a recognition campaign by TSSA.

The union had recruited more than 1/3 of the workforce. More than 70 per cent had signed a petition for union recognition.

Culina launched a major anti-recognition campaign beginning with the sacking of Culina's leading activist. It held mass meetings and one to one surgeries. According to the union, staff were also 'threatened with derisory pay deals, reductions in breaks, loss of bonus schemes, petty disciplinaries and ultimately job losses if TSSA won recognition'. TSSA lost the recognition ballot.

Following a BECTU recognition campaign, BSkyB threatened to close the call centre completely and relocate 9,000 jobs overseas.

Source: *Labour Research* (abridged) January 2004

Activities

1 What tactics did Culina use to persuade workers not to join TSSA?

2 What was BSkyB's ultimate threat to its workforce if the voted for union recognition?

Issues for Trade Unions in the 21st Century

Source A
Tony Blair's plea to the unions to step back from confrontation over PFI* was rebuffed yesterday despite desperate attempts to avoid defeat on the issue at next weeks' Labour Party conference.

Links between the Labour Party and the unions have become weaker since 'privatisation' became an issue after the 2001 general election.

The PM's plea to unions not to become 'prisoners' of an outdated welfare state in their resistance to PFI was not just rejected by union leaders but also by a pro-Labour think tank.

➤

John Edmonds of the GMB, the most vociferous of PFI's critics, called for a proper inquiry into PFI to see if that it will bring value for taxpayers' money. The unions are fearful that extra funds for doctors and nurses will be siphoned off for private profit. Bill Morris of the TGWU said 'we don't want to see another Railtrack fiasco. Some things are too important to be left to privatised commercial companies.'

According to the think tank, PFI is only sometimes good value as in road building and prison building schemes. In terms of hospitals and schools it is only marginally good value.

But the think tank also criticises some union leaders for their 'ideological' dislike of the private sector in general and their calls for a return to the mythical past when the private sector had no involvement in the public service.

Source: Michael White, Political Editor
Guardian 28 September 2002 (adapted)

***PFI (Private Finance Initiative)** – private companies will build, refurbish and run schools and the government will pay for the lease of them.

Source B

. . . no one can be insulated against change whether you work in the private, voluntary or public sector. Trade union's ideological opposition to PFI is totally misguided. Some union leaders are like latter day Canutes holding back the tide of change. The pressure for change from the public is so great and their members are tax paying consumers of public services as well.

PFI underpins public service reforms. Without it, government plans for 100 new hospitals in the NHS won't happen. Some PFI hospitals have been completed ahead of time. Would you want your family treated in a poorly equipped Victorian hospital or a new state of the art PFI hospital? I know what I'd prefer.

In terms of education PFI has meant new schools being built or refurbished and containing state of the art ICT equipment. This is clearly

progress but sadly the unions want to deny the country this advance.

Digby Jones, CBI Director

Guardian 30 September 2003 (adapted)

Activities

1 Write a short report summarising the differences of opinion over PFI.

2 Contrast Mr Blair's criticisms of the unions' position on PFI with that of Digby Jones.

3 What moral argument does Bill Morris use against PFI?

4 How does Digby Jones argue for PFI in the health service?

5 Overall, do you think the advantages of PFI outweigh the disadvantages? Explain your answer.

Outsourcing

This is the term used to describe a recent trend in UK employment practises as part of globalisation of labour markets and service delivery. British companies export jobs abroad where wages and costs are much cheaper. Trade unions are almost powerless to do anything about this.

British Telecom

In March 2003, BT confirmed that it was going ahead with its plan to set up call centres in India.

They are the latest in a long list of high profile companies including BA and HSBC setting up in India where they can reduce labour costs by 30 per cent. In October 2003, the National Rail Enquiries Centre intimated that it might be moving to India.

Unions are so worried that they are going to send a delegation to India to investigate conditions at call centres.

BT is going to open call centres in India creating 2,200 jobs. The Communication Workers Union (CWU) is considering strike action. BT has pledged that no jobs will be lost in Britain. Powergen have also stated that moving 300 jobs to Delhi by the end of 2003 will not cause job losses in the UK, just natural wastage and loss of agency staff.

Average British call centre worker
Lives in: London, Glasgow or South Wales
Works: seven hours a day with one hour lunch break
Wage: £10,000–£13,000
One third of workforce are graduates
Number of jobs: 510,000

Average Indian call centre worker
Lives in: Delhi
Works: eight hours a day, three shifts, start at 5am
Wages: £2,500
Almost all graduates
Number of jobs: up to 100,000 call centre jobs in India by 2008.

Activity

Using only the BT source above, what economic reasons can be used to support the idea of outsourcing?

Case Study Dyson

In August 2003, Dyson the vacuum cleaner and washing machine manufacturer announced that it was moving production of its hi-tech washing machines from Britain to Malaysia.

Last year, the same company closed its vacuum cleaner production plant with the loss of 800 jobs.

Dyson have argued that its shift was part of the globalisation process and this would enable his company to expand its Research and Development centre in the UK, helping safeguard Britain's technology base. They argue that the products would still be designed and engineered in Britain.

Derek Simpson, co-leader of the engineering union Amicus, said 'the latest export of jobs by Dyson is confirmation that his motive is making even greater profit at the expense of UK manufacturing and his loyal workforce. Dyson is no longer a UK product'.

James Gray, Tory MP, whose constituency is affected by the Dyson move, said 'It just goes to prove that we cannot maintain profitable manufacturing in the UK.

He (Dyson) is not doing this for fun, it's because he cannot make a profit here.'

Activity

'The trade union movement cannot justify its opposition to globalisation.' How far does the evidence in the sources support this point of view? You should mention reasons for and against.

Trade Unions and Europe

The European Union has passed a number of laws (known as 'directives') which are intended to make the lives and working conditions of people in the EU better. Some of these laws do not apply to the UK because the previous Conservative government blocked the legislation on the grounds that too much red tape would be bad for the British economy.

Since Labour was elected in 1997 they have implemented various EU Directives, but sometimes not in the ways trade unions would have liked.

The following now apply:

European Works Council Directive: employers are required to set up information and consultation structures involving the workforce. Companies with less than 50 employees do not need to do this.

Directives on Family Leave: this gives workers the right to take three months parental leave for each child he/she is responsible for (effective from 1999).

In December 2003 the Labour government hinted at giving parents statutory rights to take time off work to tend to their children. This may be extended to six months and employers will be required to keep the job open for the father, but unlike some other countries neither the state nor the employer would be required to pay the father.

Directives for Workers on Fixed Term Contracts: this came into effect in 2000/01 and gives workers on fixed term contracts the same statutory rights as full time workers.

Part Time Work Directive: this gives part time workers the same rights in principle as full time workers (took effect April 2000)

There are other directives which apply such as four weeks paid holidays each year and a maximum compulsory 48-hour working week.

Trade unions support EU legislation which will benefit their members. However, the employers' federation (CBI) take a different view …

Representation in the Workplace

1 Using information on EU directives and the *Independent* newspaper article write a report detailing whether or not you think the benefits of adopting EU directives outweigh the disadvantages.

A proposed EU directive for full and immediate rights to temporary workers would cause 'irreparable damage' to Britain's job market … half the businesses would cut their use of agency workers if the proposals went through.

The CBI has some support from an unlikely quarter. The British government wants to delay for a year any proposal to give equal status to temporary workers.

The CBI quoted a recent survey by Pertemps which said that 47 per cent of employers would cut the use of agency temps … 'a large number of people choose only to do flexible work as it suits their lifestyles. Forcing these people out of the economy would be to the detriment of the economy'.

The EU measures are supported by British trade unions who believe it is unfair to give temporary workers less rights to pay, holidays and maternity leave in comparison with full time workers.

A TUC representative said that the survey was just another attempt by employers to deny British workers their rights … 'these were the same people who said the national minimum wage would cost thousands of jobs'.

Source: *Independent* 29 May 2003 (abridged)

Investigating Trade Unions

Part of your external exam will be the investigating question. It can be examined in any of the four syllabus areas. If it appears in Changing Society as Representation in the Workplace, here are some worked through examples which may be of help.

Question: you are investigating the role of the shop steward in modern industrial relations. Suggest a relevant hypothesis. (Remember a hypothesis is a statement you can either prove or disprove.)

1 The shop steward is still the most important union functionary in the workplace.

2 The role of the shop steward has become increasingly complex in modern day industrial relations.

3 The shop steward will always support the members on the shop floor.

Write down two aims to help you with your investigation.

1 What is the role of the shop steward in the workplace?

2 Is the ability of the shop steward important in determining the outcome of a dispute?

3 Is the role of the shop steward more than just about representing the membership?

4 Is the shop steward adequately trained for modern day industrial relations?

5 Is the shop steward there to represent the members or the union?

6 Can the role of the shop steward ever be compromised over redundancy issues?

Choose suitable methods of enquiry to help you with your aims:

♦ **contact a local trade union office**

♦ **use the various union websites**

♦ **invite a shop steward to school for an interview**

♦ **write a letter to a local trade union that might put you in contact with local shop stewards.**

It is unlikely that using books, newspapers or the local library will be of use to you in this case because of the nature of the subject you are investigating. Credit pupils are expected to be discerning in their use of hypotheses and aims.

Methods of enquiry are very much dependent upon the subject matter to be investigated. Credit pupils are expected to:

1 formulate sophisticated hypotheses

2 devise appropriate aims to help them with their hypotheses

3 use appropriate methods of enquiry linked to a particular aim or aims.

Remember that methods of enquiry that may be appropriate in a particular case, such as the personal interview may not be appropriate in others, for example, investigating an issue concerning the USA.

Candidates are expected to know the advantages and disadvantages of using particular types of enquiry, such as the questionnaire:

◆ **types of questions-open or closed?**

◆ **where to carry out the sample?**

◆ **sample size?**

◆ **collation of data?**

◆ **how reliable is a questionnaire?**

Using the Internet:

◆ **immediate advantages?**

◆ **up to date information – is this always the case?**

◆ **accessibility – easy to use in school or at home?**

◆ **cost – free if used in school**

◆ **does the internet always have the obvious advantage over the more traditional methods of enquiry such as books and newspapers?**

These are the type of questions that Standard Grade Modern Studies candidates should be asking themselves in preparation for the exam.

Employment/Unemployment

The labour force of the United Kingdom is made up of all the people who are able and eligible to work and who are in or seeking work. The Census of 2001 showed the following:

UK population in 2001	Millions
Males	28.5
Females	30.2
Total population	58.7
Labour force	29.1

Figure 3.1 UK population and workforce, 2001
Source Department of Employment (abridged)

Figure 3.1 shows that about 50 per cent of the UK population are not available to work. The list below identifies some of the groups of people who, for a number of reasons, do not work:

◆ housewives
◆ pensioners
◆ carers of sick relatives
◆ persons under the legal age for work
◆ students
◆ people suffering from an illness

These groups are not included in the labour force.

Not all of the available working population are in employment. Many are unemployed, while others are participating in some form of government training scheme.

The Labour Force

Figure 3.2 shows the age structure of the British labour force. When you look at it you can see how the age structure of the labour force has changed in the last 20 years.

A major change has been in the number of young persons under the age of 24 in the labour force, which was about 5.8 million in 1981 and is now only 4.2 million, a fall of around 1.6 million. This has occurred at a time when the working population rose to 29.1 from 26.2 million. This is mainly due to the increased numbers of young people who continue in some form of education after they leave school, as well as a general decrease in the birth rate in the country.

Age group				
Year	16–24	25–44	45+	Total
1981	5.8	11.3	9.05	26.2
1991	5.5	13.8	8.7	28.1
2001	4.2	14.6	9.9	28.8

Figure 3.2 UK labour force breakdown by age (millions)
Source Department of Employment (abridged)

Who are the Unemployed?

In simple terms, the unemployed are those members of the population who would be part of the work force if they had a job. To be counted as an unemployed person you must be:

◆ out of work and available for employment

- on the unemployment register
- receiving some form of unemployment related state benefit.

Unemployment became a serious problem in the UK during the 1980s and 1990s. It is a major cause of poverty and long-term unemployment, for example, among workers aged 25–49 years is increasing.

Calculating the real level of unemployment has become increasingly more difficult. The previous Conservative government made some 30 changes to the way unemployment statistics are calculated.

One of the current methods used by the Labour Government is called the **claimant count**. That is a count of those signing on, claiming and receiving unemployment benefit as a percentage of the work force.

Year	UK
1996	7.0
1998	4.6
2000	3.6
2002	3.1
2004 (January)	2.9

Figure 3.3 Percentage of UK workforce counted as unemployed (claimant count)
Source Office for National Statistics

Unemployed People Who Do Not Count

Critics of the government argue that the claimant count method hides the real level of unemployment in the country. The following groups listed are not included in the figures:

- **women** – women in particular are often not counted in the unemployment figures. This is because many unemployed women are unable to claim benefit, as they have not paid enough national insurance contributions. Many other women are part-time workers whose earnings are too low to pay national insurance.

- **young unemployed** – unemployed people who are under 18 years. This group does not qualify for income support and are not claimants.

- **people on schemes** – other people who are on government training schemes. They are not unemployed, but neither are they in full time paid employment.

- **intentionally unemployed** – people who have left a job through their own choice. They are banned from 'signing on' for 26 weeks. They are not claimants, so do not count.

There are other ways of counting the unemployed. The International Labour Organisation (ILO) way of measuring unemployment uses the Labour Force Survey count (LFS). Under the LFS system, the unemployed are classified as people who have not done any work for pay in the week that the count was taken. People must also want to work, be available to start work in two weeks and have looked for work in the last four weeks.

Many think that this is a better way to measure unemployment. The LFS count of unemployment in December 2003 was 4.9 per cent compared with a Claimant Count of only three per cent.

Types of Unemployment

There are three different types of unemployment which affect the UK. These are:

- **structural unemployment** – this is the worst type because the lost jobs are never likely to return. This occurs when an industry is in decline, for example, mining.

- **Cyclical unemployment** – this occurs when the economy is in a slump.

- **Seasonal unemployment** – some jobs like Santa Claus helpers in shops at Christmas only last for a short time. Some workers will lose their jobs at the end of a season.

Activities

1 List the reasons why some people are not available for work? *(2 marks)*

2 In what way has the age structure of the British labour force changed in the last 20 years? *(2 marks)*

3 Who are the unemployed? *(3 marks)*

4 What is the name of the current method of calculating the number of unemployed? *(2 marks)*

5 Why is this method criticised? *(2 marks)*

6 Which groups are not included in this method of calculating the unemployed? *(3 marks)*

7 What other method of calculating the unemployment is seen as being better? *(1 mark)*

8 List the three types of unemployment. *(3 marks)*

9 Which type of unemployment is the worst and why? *(3 marks)*

Changing Patterns of Employment

Since the 1980s the United Kingdom has seen two major changes in the job sector. These are a decline in the number of industrial and manufacturing jobs and a rise in available employment in the service sector.

The greatest job losses have been in what is called the traditional industries, such as:

◆ shipbuilding

◆ mining

◆ steel

◆ car production

◆ textiles.

However many thousands of new jobs have been created in the service sector. This includes banking, insurance and finance as well as hotels, catering, transport and communications.

Figure 3.4 shows the changes in these industries in the period 1971 to 1994.

	Year		
Industry	1971	1994	% change
Agriculture	2 %	2 %	0
Energy and water supply	5 %	2 %	−3
Manufacturing	41 %	28 %	−13
Construction	8 %	6 %	−2
Distribution – hotels and catering	13 %	20 %	+7
Transport and communications	10 %	9 %	−1
Financial and business services	5 %	13 %	+8
Other services	15 %	21 %	+6
Total number of all employees (thousands)	13,425	10,539	

Figure 3.4 Percentages of UK male employment by industry
Source Office for National Statistics

FOUNDATION/GENERAL

Since 1995, there has actually been a rise in the numbers in employment. Employment in Scotland actually grew by around 2 per cent over the 1990s and by 1.5 per cent in Great Britain as a whole.

Figure 3.4 shows how employment levels in the different industries have changed since 1971. There has been a move away from manufacturing towards the service sector. The number of people employed in the financial and business sector has also increased.

Overall, women accounted for 38 per cent of employees in 1971 compared with almost 50 per cent in 1994 and by 2003, they made-up 53.6 per cent of the workforce in the service sector industries.

Since 1994 the communications sector has been growing with many new jobs being created because of advances in cable, satellite and mobile phone networks. Another major growth area for jobs has been in the call centre service industry. These are jobs where women are in demand.

Figure 3.5 A typical UK call centre

One problem of traditional sector jobs being replaced by jobs in the service sector is that many of these jobs are part-time, lower paid and less secure.

Activities

1 What are the two major changes that have occurred since the 1980s in the jobs market? *(2 marks)*

2 List the main traditional industries that have lost jobs over the last 20 years or so. *(5 marks)*

3 In which types of employment has there been a big increase in the number of jobs? *(3 marks)*

4 In which industry was there the biggest increase in the number of jobs in terms of percentages? See Figure 3.4. *(2 marks)*

5 Which industry saw the largest fall? *(2 marks)*

6 What was the percentage of women in total employees in service sector industries in 2003? *(2 marks)*

7 List three types of job where women are in demand. *(3 marks)*

8 What is the most recent area for employment growth? *(2 marks)*

9 Why are service sector jobs sometimes seen as being a problem? *(2 marks)*

The North–South Divide

Some people say that it is easier to find a job in certain areas of the UK than it is in other parts. Unemployment has traditionally been higher in areas such as Scotland, the north of England and Northern Ireland than it was in the Midlands and the south of England.

In 2004, Scotland had an unemployment rate of 5.8 per cent while in the east it was 3.5 per cent and in the south east it was 3.8 per cent. In some Scottish cities unemployment can be as high as 30 per cent.

These figures led many people to believe that in terms of jobs a North–South divide existed in the UK. Others disagreed with this view pointing to the fact that recent large increases in unemployment in the Midlands and the south of England have shown that the North–South divide no longer exists.

Region	Percentage unemployed
London	7.0%
Northern Ireland	6.3%
Scotland	5.8%
South West	3.1%
South East	3.8%
East	3.5%
West Midlands	5.8%
East Midlands	4.4%
Yorkshire	5.1%
North west	4.8%
North East	6.4%
UK average	4.9%

Figure 3.6 Unemployment by region in December 2004
Source Office for National Statistics

Figure 3.6 shows that the unemployment rate (the percentage of the labour force who are out of work) was 5.8 per cent in Scotland. In the East Midlands it was only 4.4 per cent.

The figures do not tell the whole story because if we look at a smaller area than Scotland, for example, Glasgow, the unemployment rate is much higher in the east end of Glasgow where the unemployment rate is over 30 per cent. It is a similar story in many other inner-city areas in the UK.

Does the North–South Divide Exist?

Different rates of unemployment between regions of the UK are used by some people as evidence that the North–South divide does exist. Others say that things are just as bad 'down South' and give the example of West Midlands where there is 5.8 per cent unemployment or the very high levels of unemployment in the inner-city areas of London.

The information that Figure 3.6 does not show is that over the last 30 years or so the North has consistently had high levels of unemployment. Over the same period in the South the opposite has been the case.

The types of jobs that are available in Scotland have changed over the last 10 or 15 years. There has been a shift away from jobs that males tended to do and a move towards female-oriented employment. A problem has arisen as a result of the shift towards female employment is that many of these jobs are part-time, temporary and poorly-paid.

Official statistics for the unemployment rates in Scotland in January 2004 indicate that the rate was the lowest it has been for over 30 years at 4.9 per cent.

Scotland's Labour Force in the 21st Century

The shift towards **service sector** industries and the growth of female employment are the two major changes that have affected Scotland's labour force. There are other things happening that will affect it in the near future:

◆ the Scottish population will fall and this will effect the size of the labour-force

◆ fewer young people will enter the job market

◆ an increasing percentage of the population will retire or will be near retirement

◆ fewer teachers or nursery teachers may be required and more hospitals and care facilities will be needed.

The Scottish Executive has recognised these problems and is planning ways to get round them. Some suggestions include attracting foreign workers to Scotland, using some of the asylum-seekers or encouraging young Scots to stay in Scotland.

Another possible solution could be the raising the retirement age, which would also allow the skills, and experience that older workers have to be made use of for the benefit of the country.

Activities

1 In which areas of the UK are the levels of unemployment the highest in December 2004? *(3 marks)*

2 What was the unemployment rate in Scotland in December 2004? *(1 mark)*

3 Why do some people not believe that there is a North–South divide? *(2 marks)*

4 What is the UK average unemployment rate? *(2 marks)*

5 What can we say about the levels of unemployment in inner-city areas? *(2 marks)*

6 Give one reaon for and one against the idea that a North-South divide exists. *(4 marks)*

7 What was the unemployment rate in Scotland in January 2004? *(2 marks)*

8 What are the major changes in employment that have taken place in Scotland in recent times? *(2 marks)*

9 The increase in female jobs has created a new problem. What is it? *(2 marks)*

10 List the other factors that will affect the Scottish in the near future? *(4 marks)*

11 How might the Scottish Executive get round these problems? *(4 marks)*

New Technology

New technology is probably not recognised by young people as being **new** at all, but to older generations most of the household appliances that are used today have been introduced in the last 20 years or so and are therefore very much new.

Many of the new technology appliances in the home have led to time being saved in the household duties like cooking or cleaning-up.

Figure 3.7 A range of appliances used in the home

More leisure time is therefore available and this may be spent playing the latest computer game on a PlayStation 2 or other type of games console.

For most householders, the extra time could be used to find a job because the new 'must have' technology is expensive to buy and extra income is therefore necessary.

There is a range of new technology that a person could buy for the home, including some of the following:

◆ home computers with broadband Internet access

◆ Dyson washing machines with washer-dryer facilities

◆ phones with small TV screens so that you can see the person you are speaking to

◆ DVD players with re-recordable ability

◆ mobile phones.

In shops, the introduction of bar codes and scanners helps reduces the queues at the checkout and also alerts the shop managers when items have to be reordered.

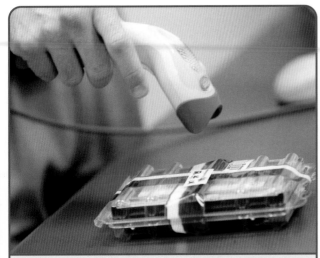

Figure 3.8 Technology has changed the every-day shopping trip

Many shops offer Internet Shopping (Asda, Tesco, Iceland and Somerfield to name a few) so that even a trip to the shops may be a thing of the past for some people.

In factories, the use of robotics and computer-assisted machines are now commonplace.

Banks are very highly computerised. Cash dispensers allow customers to have a range of services other than withdrawing cash and the use of 'Switch' cards could eventually lead the way to cashless shopping. Banks can make a lot of money out of 'intelligent banking'. Recently, the Royal Bank of Scotland reported record profits of over £7.1 billion.

Hospitals and doctors surgeries use medical technology that can help doctors diagnose and treat illness. Doctors in cities can even use technology to treat people in rural or island communities via video-conferencing links.

The use of laser technology has led to a reduction in the need for spectacles for a large number of people.

The use of computers and word processors in offices have made businesses more efficient and easier to run.

Case Study – The Office

Figure 3.9 Modern offices are full of technology

New technology has changed even the smallest offices. They have many of the office machines that cut down time-consuming and boring jobs and they have become more efficient. Some of the more common uses of new technology are shown below.

Computers – files and information are now kept on computers or disk, saving space and time. No need for filing cabinets or for staff to take up as much time doing this filing.

Typewriters have been replaced by computer word processing software which can alter mistakes very easily. A great deal of time and effort is saved.

Fax – allows copies of documents to sent to other areas of the country/world instantly.

Call Connect Systems – modern phone network system which can 'queue' calls, divert calls and tell you when someone else is trying to get through to you.

Video Conferencing – businessmen wanting to have face to face meetings no longer have to travel. This allows them to see and speak to each other while seeing what their reactions and facial expressions are.

Internet/Teletext – instant access to large amounts of current information using the TV

Case Study – The Office continued

and phone network can be used for passing information, advertising or specialised data.

One result of the introduction of new technology is that many workers' jobs have been lost. The development of the technology itself has meant that other types of new jobs have been created to replace some of those lost. However, many of the people losing jobs might not have the skills to fill the newly created jobs.

The Case For New Technology

◆ Cheaper and better quality goods. More will be sold. This will increase the firms' profits and the entire country will benefit.

◆ More workers will be needed to produce the new technology – including, household electrical appliances, home and office computers, robots, personal mobile phones and the miniaturised computer chips that they use.

◆ Jobs which are repetitive, boring or dangerous to human life can sometimes be done by computers.

◆ Employee costs could be reduced. Fewer workers will be needed. This means that firms will make savings on their wages bill.

◆ Jobs which cannot be done due to a shortage of skilled labour will be carried out by machines or robots. This could lead to a shorter working week or even an earlier retirement age.

◆ An increasing number of people are able to work from home as a result of advances in computer and telephone technology.

The Case Against New Technology

◆ Unemployment will increase as machines and robots take over the jobs of working people.

◆ New technology leads to the de-skilling of jobs (de-skilling means that many of the old skilled jobs will disappear). Skilled workers may become machine minders.

◆ New technology will change jobs so much that retraining will be needed. This may not be a problem for younger workers but this may cause stress among older workers.

◆ It could be harder for trade unions to recruit members and protect their interests. This could lead to a worsening of pay and conditions of employment.

◆ New technology can cause job losses. British employers prefer to cut workers rather than cut the working week.

◆ Home workers are amongst the lowest paid workers in Britain and very difficult to organise into trade unions.

Ever-changing technology can lead to job-losses in the new technology industries themselves, as Figure 3.10 shows.

Motorola Shocks Workers

Motorola, the world's second biggest maker of mobile phones, has today announced plans to cut 7,000 jobs. Management blame the job losses on a reduced demand for their larger chip phones, as consumers want the new, more fashionable mini phones. The Scottish factory's technology cannot produce such phones. Shocked workers left the factory devastated after today's announcement knowing they would soon be jobless.

Figure 3.10 News report on job losses at Motorola

Source BBC News Online, June 2002

Activities

1 Explain some of the ways in which new technology affects everyday life. *(3 marks)*

2 Look at the case study about the office and answer the following questions:
   a) give two reasons why video conferencing would be of benefit to the businessperson. *(2 marks)*
   b) explain the benefits of two other types of technology used in the office. *(2 marks)*

3 Look at the arguments for new technology. Choose one point you consider to make the strongest case for increased new technology. Copy it out and explain why you have chosen this one? *(3 marks)*

4 Which points against new technology do you consider to be the strongest? Give a reason for your answer. *(3 marks)*

5 Why is it difficult to organise home workers? *(2 marks)*

6 What effect has new technology had on jobs? *(4 marks)*

7 Look at Figure 3.10 from BBC News Online and answer the following questions:
   a) what happened at Motorola? *(2 marks)*
   b) how did the workforce respond? *(2 marks)*

New Technology Job Creation in Scotland

'Silicon Valley' is in Northern California, USA. It is the largest centre for new technology in the world. Central Scotland has also been successful in attracting leading electronics firms to come and open factories. The result of this success is that this area of Scotland is now known as 'Silicon Glen'

Figure 3.11 Silicon Valley, California

The companies have set up in towns like:

Greenock	IBM
Ayr	DEC
Erskine	Compaq
East Kilbride	Motorola
Livingston	Unisys
Glenrothes	Hughes
Cumbernauld	Tenma and OKI

These companies have created over 50,000 new jobs by deciding to set up factories in Scotland. Most of the companies – over 80 per cent – are foreign owned. They come mainly from the USA and Japan, with an increasing number from Korea.

In 1994, Motorola announced a multi-million pound investment in new facilities in East Kilbride. This project created 200 new jobs. In the same year, British Sky Broadcasting announced a new £10million project in Dunfermline, creating up to 1,000 full time jobs by the year 2000.

During 1995, Locate in Scotland, a part of Scottish Enterprise brought 97 projects to Scotland, with a planned investment of £1110 million. These were mainly Japanese and American companies and they were expected to create and safeguard 12,300 jobs. Among the largest of them was the massive £260 million Chunghwa Picture tube factory lured to Lanarkshire in 1995.

FOUNDATION/GENERAL

However, Chunghwa is now closed and other foreign new technology companies such as Motorola have also closed or radically reduced their workforces.

Scottish Secretary Michael Forsyth will today give details of one of the largest investments yet by a Korean company in Scotland, bringing with it up to 200 jobs.

Officials from the government's inward investment agency, Locate in Scotland, have highlighted the ready supply of educated and available labour.

The Secretary of State will have been emphasising to the Koreans, during his present sales mission to the Far East, that employment in Scotland is very flexible through Britain not signing up to the EU's Social Charter.

His sales mission took him to Japan last week where he was able to give details of two new Japanese investments in Scotland: a £5 million expansion by Tenma in Cumbernauld and a £6.5 million location by the Kohdensha Company in Dunfermline.

Source: *The Herald* 29 May 1996

Scottish Secretary Michael Forsyth crowned his two day visit to South Korea yesterday with the announcement that Shin Ho Tech plans to build a new £8.6m factory to assemble computer monitors in Glenrothes. It should bring another 280 jobs to Fife.

Source: *The Herald* 30 May 1996

Activities

1 Where is the largest centre for new technology in the world? *(1 mark)*

2 What are the main advantages of Scotland having a 'Silicon Glen'? *(2 marks)*

3 From which countries have the new technology companies come from? *(2 marks)*

4 List four Scottish towns where new technology companies have been set up. *(2 marks)*

5 Name six new technology companies that have been set up in Scotland. *(3 marks)*

6 How many jobs did Motorola create in East Kilbride? *(2 marks)*

7 What is Locate In Scotland? *(2 marks)*

8 What reasons does the first newspaper article give for Scotland being able to attract foreign investment? *(3 marks)*

9 From which country is the company that Mr Forsyth attracted to Glenrothes? *(2 marks)*

10 How has new technology created jobs? *(2 marks)*

11 What evidence is there that new technology jobs are not safe? *(3 marks)*

Unemployment in Europe

Unemployment is not only a problem for Britain, it is also a European problem. In December 2003, 8 per cent of all Europeans were out of work. Figures 3.12 and 3.13 show the percentage of unemployed workers in Europe for different age groups.

Employment/Unemployment

Country	Percentage of unemployment
Italy	26.5 %
Greece	26.1 % (2002)
France	20.7%
Belgium	22.1 %
UK	11.8 %
Denmark	11.1%
Ireland	8.2%
Austria	7.4%

Figure 3.12 Unemployment in Europe, ages 15–24, 2003
Source Eurostat

Country	Percentage of unemployment
Italy	8.4 %
Greece	9.6% (2002)
France	9.5%
Belgium	8.1%
UK	4.9%
Denmark	6.0%
Ireland	4.6%
Austria	4.5%
EU average	8.0%

Figure 3.13 Unemployment in Europe, all ages, 2003
Source Eurostat

European Action on Unemployment

The European Union (EU) has specific policies for those in and out of work. It is estimated that Scotland has received some £1.3 billion in grants from the EU in the last ten years. This comes mostly in the form of European Structural Funds.

The most important of these funds are:

◆ European Social Fund – this supports a wide range of projects designed to teach unemployed people new skills and improve their chances of finding a job.

◆ European Regional Development Fund – supports specific projects such as building roads to improve Scotland's links with other parts of the EU as well as projects aimed at improving the environment.

◆ Rechar and Reneval Funds, which specifically help areas, which have lost jobs in the coalmining and shipbuilding industries.

Not all of the funds to help unemployment are taken up. This is because the rules say that these funds must be in addition to what the government would spend anyway, and must be matched by money from UK central and local government. This does not often happen, and the UK loses out on financial help because the government will not match EU spending.

Activities

1 How does the unemployment rate in the UK compare with the EU average in Figures 3.12 and 3.13? *(2 marks)*

2 List the most important European Structural Funds. *(3 marks)*

3 For what reasons might the UK lose out on EU financial help? *(2 marks)*

Women and Work

In Scotland, women make up over 50 per cent of the population and in 2002 approximately 47 per cent of the workforce were female.

The jobs that most women in the UK had were:

◆ local government
◆ civil service
◆ health service
◆ retail
◆ hotels and catering.

However, despite the fact that more and more women are going out to work, they still face problems in the job market. Since 1970 the government has found it necessary to introduce laws to make discrimination against women illegal in respect to jobs and pay.

The two major laws that were originally introduced are:

The Sex Discrimination Act 1975 – this act makes it illegal to discriminate against women in jobs

The Equal Pay Act 1970 – means that women can expect to be treated equally with men when it comes to pay.

Employment by Industry

Despite these laws and the fact that women account for 47 per cent of the entire work force, women are much more likely to be employed in part-time jobs, where pay is low and the working conditions are not as good as those for full time employees.

There are several reasons why so many women are in part-time employment:

◆ male unemployment – many women have gone out to work to make up for the loss of their husband's earnings

◆ many women need to work in order to make ends meet as the cost of living has gone up over the years

◆ many new jobs created tend to be part-time, un-skilled and low paid and these are normally taken by women, while full time skilled jobs, employing well paid men are lost.

Figure 3.15 A UK job centre

Type of industry	1983	2003
Agriculture	140	88
Energy and water	78	57
Manufacturing	1665	1020
Construction	172	210
Hotels and catering	2788	3573
Transport and communications	215	482
Finance and business	3421	4897
Public administration, education and health	1400	2660
Other services	620	915
Total number of employees	8443	12,528

Figure 3.5 Female Employees by Industry (000s)
Source National Office of Statistics

FOUNDATION/GENERAL

Reason given for not seeking work	Men	Women
Waiting result of job application	1%	1%
Student	16%	7%
Looking after Family/ home	6%	53%
Temporary sick/disabled	5%	8%
Long-term sick/disabled	23%	3%
Believes no job available	22%	9%
Not yet started looking	7%	7%
Other reasons	20%	13%

Figure 3.16 Reasons for not seeking work
Source Department of Employment

In 2002 the Scottish unemployment rates for men and women were 7.8 per cent for men and 5.6 per cent for women. The fact that the unemployment rate for women is lower does not mean that women find it easier to gain employment. Also, many women and men do not seek work and are not included in the unemployment figures.

Figure 3.16 shows that the main reason given by women for not seeking work was family responsibilities.

When women do get jobs, they tend not only to be part-time, but also to have lower status and pay than men. One other area of concern is the types of jobs that women occupy and their promotion prospects in their jobs. While 52 per cent of the population is female they still hold less than 10 per cent of the most influential jobs in politics, the law, education and business.

Activities

1 What percentages of the population and the workforce are female?   *(2 marks)*

2 Describe the types of work that many women do?   *(2 marks)*

3 How did the government respond to the problems faced by women in jobs and pay? *(4 marks)*

4 What is the percentage of women that were unemployed in Scotland in 2002?   *(1 mark)*

5 Give four reasons why women might not work or look for part-time work. *(4 marks)*

Inequality in the Workplace

Differences between women's and men's earnings are partly explained by the different jobs they work in. Women and men have equal rights to enter almost any occupation, but women often end up in low-paid jobs.

Figure 3.17 lists six high paid occupations and six low paid jobs, with the percentage of women working in each.

Income level	Employment	Women as a percentage of all in employment
High	Marketing, advertising, HR, ICT, public relations and other specialist management	27%
High	Managers in banks, post offices and other offices	56%
High	Managers in distribution, storage and retail	30%
High	Doctors, psychologists, pharmacists, opticians, dentists and veterinarians	54%
High	Teachers, lecturers and other teaching professionals	64%
High	Accountants, economists, brokers, financial advisors and other business professionals and associates	36%
Low	Nursing assistants, ambulance staff, dental nurses, care assistants etc.	84%
Low	Call centre agents and operators and other customer care jobs	65%
Low	Cleaners and domestic workers	81%
Low	Sales and retail assistants	77%
Low	General office assistants and clerks	80%
Low	Hospital and hotel porters, catering assistants, waiting and bar staff and other elementary personal service jobs	70%

Figure 3.17 Percentage of high and low income employment sectors which women work in
Source EOC

Women. Men. Different. Equal.
Equal Opportunities Commission Scotland

Figure 3.18 The Equal Opportunities Commission logo
Source Equal Opportunities Commission

Findings by the EOC (Scotland) point to the fact that the position of women at work has not seen a big improvement, even with the laws introduced since the 1970s.

Engender, a Scottish women's organisation, found the following:

♦ more women are in work
♦ women are paid less than men
♦ more women than men are in low-paid jobs
♦ fewer women are in well-paid jobs

In Education

♦ Girls do better than boys in examination results.
♦ 32 per cent of girls go on to full time education compared to 27 per cent of boys.
♦ Fewer girls go to university.

In Teaching

♦ Fewer women reach the top jobs than would be expected.

125

Employment/Unemployment

◆ Women make up 99 per cent of nursery teachers, 91 per cent of primary teachers but only 66 per cent of primary head teachers.

◆ Women account for 46 per cent of secondary teachers, but only 3 per cent of secondary head teachers.

In Politics

◆ 15 per cent of MPs are women.

◆ 24 per cent of Scottish councillors are female.

◆ 38 per cent of MSPs are women.

In Business

◆ Only two of the top 150 company directors are women.

◆ There are only three women on the boards of the top twenty Scottish companies.

In Law

◆ Scotland has only one woman judge.

◆ 54.2 per cent of all solicitors qualifying in 1994 were women.

◆ When women seek to move up the legal profession they will find that the ratio of women to men changes rapidly.

Activities

1 What types of job do women usually end up in? *(2 marks)*

2 From Figure 3.17 use the information to make a list of the three highest paid jobs and the three worst paid jobs. *(6 marks)*

3 What four factors did Engender find with regard to the work that women do? *(2 marks)*

4 List the five areas of employment where women are treated unequally in Scotland. *(5 marks)*

Race and Employment

In Scotland, ethnic minorities made up only 1.6 per cent of the population in 1999. This works out at about 86,000 persons. (Figure 3.20 shows the breakdown of the Scottish population).

Most of the ethnic minorities stay in the major Scottish cities like Glasgow, Edinburgh and Dundee. But in the last 10 years or so a number of the ethnic minorities have moved into the smaller towns and villages to set up small businesses. A large number of these are employed in the catering business or small shops, but some others are becoming involved in other types of jobs like local government, the civil service and the police force.

Force targets ethnic recruits

Strathclyde Police has launched a drive to recruit more officers from ethnic minorities.

A special team has been set up to ensure the force fully represents the different communities it serves.

The Diversity Recruiting Team will target minority communities to encourage anyone interested in working for Strathclyde Police to apply.

Chief Constable Willie Rae said: 'As an employer, the force values, respects and embraces ethnic diversity.

'Our Diversity Recruiting Team plays a vital role in supporting a recruitment policy which is open to people from all walks of life.'

The force is currently looking for police officers, special constables and police cadets.

Figure 3.19 News article on the recruitment of ethnic minorities 22 January 2004

Source *Evening Times – 22.01.2004*

Ethnic group	Percentage
White	98.4
Non-white	1.6
Black	0.2
Indian	0.2
Pakistani/Bangladeshi	0.6
Chinese	0.3
Other ethnic minority groups	0.3

Figure 3.20 Population by ethnic group in Scotland 1999

Source Office for National Statistics

Since the 1970s there has been a number of laws introduced to try to stop any form of discrimination against any person from an ethnic minority background.

A series of race relations acts make it illegal to discriminate on the grounds of colour, race or religion. Nevertheless, members of ethnic minorities still continue to encounter different treatment in employment.

Ethnic Minorities and Unemployment

Unemployment rates vary a great deal between ethnic groups in Great Britain.

'Black and Betrayed', a recent report from the TUC reveals that the unemployment rates for black workers is double that of white workers. The situation in Scotland is more complex.

	All	Male	Female
Scotland	7	8	5
White	7	8	5
Indian	8	7	9
Pakistani/Bangladeshi	12	12	14
Chinese	9	8	9
Other	13	14	11

Figure 3.21 Unemployment in Scotland
Source GROS

The figures from Figure 3.21 show that in 2001 the unemployment rate for white workers was 7 per cent, the highest unemployment rate was 12 per cent and this was for Pakistani and Bangladeshi workers.

FACTFILE

In 1999, 1.6 per cent of the Scottish population were from an ethnic minority. Over one third of Scottish people from ethnic minorities were from a Pakistani or Bangladeshi background.

The age profile of the ethnic minority population is younger than the white population. 57 per cent of the ethnic minority population were under 30 years old compared with 38 per cent of the white population.

46 per cent of non-whites living in Scotland were born in the United Kingdom.

In Scotland 25 per cent of non-whites work more than the legal number of hours per week (over 48 hours), compared with 16 per cent of whites.

Just under 0.5 per cent of police officers in Scotland are non-white. However over the last five years the number of non-white officers has increased by 71 per cent.

50 per cent of employed ethnic minority young people work in hotels, catering and repairs.

One in six of the Indian community are in social class 1, compared with one in 20 in the white community.

12 per cent of ethnic minority employed males and 34 per cent of females work in a family business as compared to 3 per cent and 1 per cent white males and females.

23 per cent of whites compared with 14 per cent of non-whites own their own home.

FOUNDATION/GENERAL

Activities

1 Where are the ethnic minorities most likely to stay in Scotland? *(2 marks)*

2 In recent times what changes has there been in the locations where ethnic minority groups have chosen to stay? *(2 marks)*

3 What are the main types of jobs that ethnic minorities are employed in? *(2 marks)*

4 In which new types of jobs are the ethnic minorities now to be found? *(2 marks)*

5 What percentage of the Scottish population are ethnic minorities? *(1 mark)*

Age and Employment

Many unemployed middle-aged and older people have great problems in finding a job regardless of the experience, skills or qualifications they have.

Long-term unemployment is more heavily concentrated among older people. Employers also appear to provide less job-related training to those over 50.

Employers often point out that younger people can be hired for lower wages and that older workers do not have the skills needed for today's modern workplace and that training is expensive.

There are around 19 million people aged 50 and over in the UK, 40 per cent of the adult population. The percentage of older people in the population is growing. The report 'Winning the Generation Game' published in April 2000 states that by 2020 the 50 plus age group will have increased by a further three million.

Employment Rate

The category of 'older workers' includes women aged 50 to 59 and men aged 50 to 64.

At present there are over six million people between 50 and the state pension age who are in work. This means that older workers have an employment rate of 69–71 per cent for men and 66 per cent for women.

FACTFILE

Since 1997 the employment rate of older people has risen faster than that of the working population as a whole.

The average length of time in current employment is much higher for older workers, 13 years compared with seven years for those aged 25–49.

Many have no formal qualifications.

Older people want to work and are prepared to work beyond normal retirement age.

A recent survey by 50 Connect found that 59 per cent of those questioned were in favour of working beyond state pension age. They say that younger workers can bring enthusiasm and willingness to the workplace, while older workers bring experience and reliability. Employers need both.

David Appledore, Executive Director at 50 Connect said:

'People who enjoy their work should have the option of continuing in employment until they feel ready to retire, rather than the current trend of being forced out of work before they're ready. People should be allowed to be flexible to do what they want or need to do with their later years.'

Source: Age Positive, July 2003

Age Legislation

The European Union has put forward a proposal, the Employment Directive on Equal Treatment, which requires that all member countries introduce laws to ban discrimination at work on the grounds of age, sex religious belief and disability.

The UK government has adopted the Employment Directive on Equal Treatment and will introduce age legislation by 2006. The time taken will allow the government to consult with individuals, employers and expert groups in order to try and pass the most appropriate legislation for this area.

But it may be quite a while before everyone can expect their age to be no barrier to getting a job, being promoted or staying in their job. Governments may pass laws, but it is very difficult to change people's attitudes

Emma Parry, of the Cranfield School of Management Human Resource Research Centre, points out that currently 43 per cent of all UK organisations have no plans for an anti-ageism policy and 65 per cent have no plans for flexible retirement options. She thinks that 'policies are just the first step, changing attitudes is the bigger challenge.'

She also says that population change, not laws, will force a change in attitudes. With the number of young people falling and the overall population ageing, it does not make business sense to discard those over 50, along with all their experience and skill.

Source: *Sunday Times* 2 November 2003 (abridged)

Andrew Smith, former Secretary of State for Work and Pensions said:

'We need to make sure we put in place options for people to work longer if they choose. Working a few years longer can make a huge difference to retirement income. For business it promises a more experienced skilled workforce. We believe people should have greater choice over how long they work, and when they retire. But people won't be able to exercise this choice unless we tackle the discrimination that all to often affects employment opportunities for older people.

We need to challenge stereotypes and discrimination and show the benefits of an age diverse workforce. New legislation will highlight the need for all of us to change

culture and attitudes to older workers. Discrimination is unfair and it is bad for business.'

Case Study: B&Q

B&Q is a company which has taken positive steps to recognise the skills and experience older employees bring with them. Today B&Q's older employees enjoy working with younger people as part of a team, while younger employees appreciate the extra skills and life experience, which mature workers bring to the job.

'As a business which attracts DIYers and gardeners of all ages, it's common sense to make sure that we have people of all ages to serve them. We find that our customers associate older people with having DIY knowledge and they feel comfortable asking them for advice.'

Bill Whitting, Chief Executive
Source: B&Q Newsletter

Activities

1 Why do many older people face problems in finding a job? *(2 marks)*

2 What reasons do employers give for not employing older people? *(2 marks)*

3 What do older workers bring to a job that young workers don't have? *(2 marks)*

4 'Very few people are interested in working beyond retirement age. It is a myth that many do.' Explain why this statement may not be true. *(3 marks)*

5 What is the EU doing to stop age discrimination? *(2 marks)*

6 What effect will population change have on the job market for older workers? *(2 marks)*

7 Why does Emma Parry think it will be a bad idea to discard older workers? *(2 marks)*

8 What is the view of the government with regard to older workers? *(3 marks)*

9 What benefits do older workers bring to B&Q? *(2 marks)*

Disability and Employment

Another group of people who often face problems at work are those with disabilities. Workers with disabilities often face prejudice from employers and fellow workers.

To try and combat this the government introduced the 1995 Disability Discrimination Act. This law aims to protect disabled people against discrimination, in employment, when using a service or facility, buying or renting property and in the use of public transport.

The government has introduced this law in three separate stages.

◆ In 1996 it was made illegal to treat disabled people less favourably.

◆ In 1999 businesses had to make reasonable adjustments for disabled staff, like providing additional support or equipment. They had to start making changes to the way they provided their services to customers, for example, providing gas or electricity bills in large print.

◆ In 2004 businesses have to make physical alterations to their premises to overcome access barriers. The example most people think of is installing ramps or special toilets for wheelchair users.

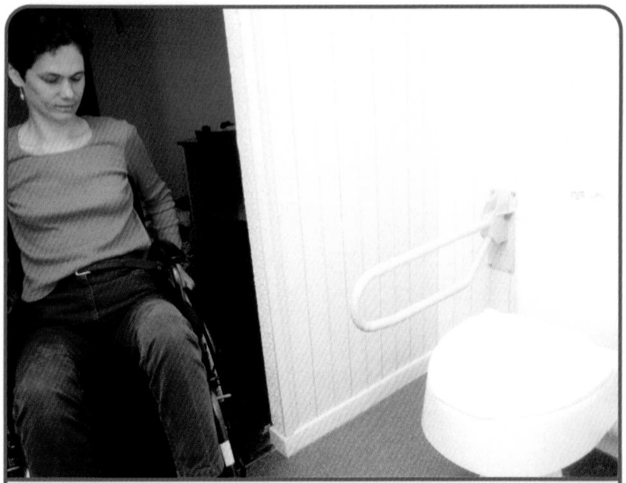

Figure 3.22 Facilities which meet the Disability Discrimination Act's demands

The law will apply to all businesses, no matter how many or how few employees they have.

This law may cause problems for employers due to the costs involved but many can see the advantages of employing more disabled workers. These advantages may include:

◆ employing staff from all sections of society – this will get a balance between staff and customers that creates a better atmosphere

◆ disabled people contributing an estimated £40 billion spending each year – this is too large a market to ignore

◆ with disabled people making up 18 per cent of the British working population, it makes sense to use the skills, expertise and resources that the disabled can offer

◆ with the shortage in skilled workers, disabled workers can help fill this gap.

FACTFILE

There are almost nine million disabled people in the UK.

6.8 million disabled people are of working age. This represents 18 per cent of the workforce.

Only 42 per cent of working age disabled people have paid employment. The average for non-disabled people is approximately 80 per cent.

Disabled people are six times more likely to be unemployed.

Almost half the 2.4 million disabled people on benefits and out of work would like to work.

Almost 70 per cent of disabled people in Scotland live in households where their annual income is less than £10,000.

Source: www.scotland.gov.uk

True Statements About Disabled Employment

◆ Disabled employees prefer to work in the same range of jobs as non-disabled people.

◆ Disabled employees have the same range of skills as non-disabled people.

◆ Disabled employees have skills developed through living everyday life situations.

◆ Disabled employees are more loyal than non-disabled employees.

◆ Disabled employees have fewer days off sick and less non-illness related absence than non-disabled employees.

◆ Disabled employees have a better than average health and safety record. Less than 5 per cent of the disabled use a wheelchair. This is contrary to popular beliefs held by many employers.

False Statements About Disabled Employment

◆ Disabled people can only work in factories or as cleaners.

◆ Disabled people are not as clever or as useful as non-disabled people.

◆ Disabled people would not be able to cope with the stress of work and would not be able to deal with everyday problems that arise.

◆ Disabled people do not stay in jobs for long.

◆ Disabled people will always be off sick.

◆ Disabled people are a danger to their fellow workers and the workplace. Their wheelchairs will block fire exits thus creating a health and safety hazard.

Source: Employers Forum on Disability website

Activities

1 Why did the government introduce the Disability Discrimination Act? *(2 marks)*

2 What benefits does this law bring for disabled people? *(3 marks)*

3 'Employers can gain benefits from employing disabled people.' What are the benefits that employers could gain? *(3 marks)*

4 Describe the three stages of the government's laws against discrimination towards the disabled. *(3 marks)*

5 What are the advantages to employers of hiring disabled workers? *(4 marks)*

6 Link up two 'myths' with two related 'realities' of disabled workers. *(2 marks)*

Low Pay

Changes in the Scottish and UK job market has led to an increase in the number of low paid workers. These changes have included:

◆ the loss of manufacturing jobs

◆ an increase in the 'casual' work available

◆ an increase in the amount of part time jobs, mainly for women.

Being in work is, however, no escape from poverty and for many people being in work can mean the loss of state benefits making them worse-off than before. In 1999 the government brought in the national minimum wage to help the people who were in work and had low pay. Figure 3.23 shows the levels of the national minimum wage since it was introduced.

Recent research has shown that despite the introduction of the minimum wage, almost 33 per cent of full time workers in Scotland are paid below the national average. Also, it was found that there are twice as many women on low pay than men.

FOUNDATION/GENERAL

	18–21 year olds	22+ year olds
April 1999	£3.00/hour	£3.60/hour
June 2000	£3.20/hour	£3.60/hour
October 2000	£3.20/hour	£3.70/hour
October 2001	£3.50/hour	£4.10/hour
October 2002	£3.60/hour	£4.20/hour
October 2003	£3.80/hour	£4.50/hour
October 2004	£4.10/hour	£4.85/hour
October 2005 (proposed rate)	£4.25/hour	£5.05/hour
October 2006 (proposed rate)	£4.45/hour	£5.35/hour

Figure 3.23   National minimum wage rates 1999–2006

Source LPC

In April 2003, there were 260,000 jobs with less pay than the national minimum wage, down from the 1.41 million jobs in 1998. Of these, 220,000 were carried by workers over the age of 22. The worst paid jobs were in hotel and kitchen work, waitressing and bar staff.

The minimum wage debate still continues with some employers trying to avoid paying higher wages.

Arguments For a National Minimum Wage

♦ protects the poorest workers from poverty

♦ the government pays out less state benefits if people are paid more

♦ every other European country has a minimum wage

♦ the government will get more money in tax if people have higher wages.

Arguments Against a National Minimum Wage

♦ people may lose their jobs if wages are too high

♦ prices may increase as costs for businesses increase

♦ Britain will be less attractive to foreign companies who may not set up their businesses due to high wage bills.

Activities

1 Give two reasons why there has been an increase in the number of low-paid jobs in the UK?   *(2 marks)*

2 Why do some people feel that they would be better off on state benefits than working?   *(2 marks)*

3 What was the government's response to low pay?   *(2 marks)*

4 Has low pay disappeared from the UK? *(2 marks)*

5 Which types of work are the lowest paid? *(3 marks)*

6 List the arguments for and against the national minimum wage.   *(4 marks)*

FOUNDATION/GENERAL

Helping the Unemployed

We live in a **welfare state**, which means that the government gives support to those in British society that require it. This may mean state benefits or medical or other help as required. The unemployed are one group that needs to be given support by the government. The kind of support available to the unemployed can be separated into three areas:

1 financial benefits – this involves providing money for people to live on

2 help in searching for a job

3 training to provide the skills to help the unemployed get a job.

Financial Benefits – the Job Seekers Allowance (JSA)

This is a complicated type of benefit which is made up of different parts and is paid to people who are unemployed but are capable of and are seeking work. People also need to be under retirement age and not working or working less than 16 hours per week.

Contributions-based JSA

If you have paid National Insurance contributions you will be able to get contribution-based JSA. You cannot normally get JSA if you are aged under 18. It is paid at a fixed rate, based on your age, for up to 26 weeks

Income-based JSA

It is a means tested benefit and more conditions apply. Savings of over £8000 usually mean that you cannot get income based JSA. Savings of over £3000 usually affect how much JSA you can get. If a partner works, even part time, it might affect the amount of income-based JSA you can get.

But income-based JSA may allow a person to claim other income support related benefits such as:

- housing costs
- housing benefit
- council tax rebates
- clothing grant for school age children
- free NHS prescriptions, dental treatment and eye glasses
- free school meals.

People aged under 18 years

If you are aged 16 or 17 you are unlikely to qualify for contribution-based JSA, unless you are an unemployed person in special circumstances. For example:

- you live away from your parents
- you are a parent
- you will suffer severe hardship.

If you are under 18 years and unable to work you may be able to get income support, or you

Contribution-based	
Aged 16–17	£33.85
Aged 18–24	£44.50
Aged 25 +	£56.20
Income-based	
Single aged 16–17	£33.85
Single aged 18–24	£44.50
Single aged 25+	£56.20
Couple both 18+	£88.15
Lone parents aged 16–17	£33.85
Lone parents 18+	£56.20
Addition for dependent children under 19	£43.88

Figure 3.24 JSA benefits January 2005
Source DWP

may be given training. Before a person would receive JSA, it is likely that they would have a Job Seeker Interview and sign a Jobseekers Agreement.

Activities

1 What is the role of the government in a welfare state? *(2 marks)*

2 How can the government support the unemployed? *(3 marks)*

3 What is the main type of financial support offered to the unemployed? *(2 marks)*

4 If you are unemployed what conditions must be met to be able to claim JSA benefits? *(4 marks)*

5 List the other benefits that a person may be able to claim if they are getting income-based JSA. *(3 marks)*

6 What are the circumstances that allow a 16 or 17 year old to receive JSA? *(3 marks)*

7 From Figure 3.24:
   a) What is the rate for lone parents aged 16 or 17 years? *(2 marks)*
   b) How much does a person aged 25 years or over receive each week from contribution-based JSA? *(2 marks)*

Help with Finding a Job

Figure 3.25 Jobcentre Plus logo

Jobcentre Plus is a modern service for people of working age who are claiming benefits. It is there to give people help and support to find work and become independent. It is at the heart

of the government's strategy for welfare reform and brings together the employment service, which runs job centres, and those parts of the Benefits Agency which provide services to people of working age.

The main role of Jobcentre Plus is to provide a work focus for everyone of working age, who is claiming benefit.

Everyone who makes a claim for a working age benefit will have to take part in a meeting with a personal adviser. Advice is given on how to find work, training or other support such as childcare.

Access to job vacancies is provided through such things as a telephone service, use of the Internet and touch screen job points in the offices.

The **New Deal** is part of the government's strategy to get people into work. It is meant to give unemployed people the skills and experience that employers want to help them find suitable work.

At the same time it aims to improve the overall skills base of the British workforce and provide help to employers who are suffering from shortages of skilled staff. It is compulsory for all those claiming JSA for over 18 months.

Figure 3.26 New Deal logo

Under the New Deal service you are given a personal adviser for the length of the programme. The job of the adviser is to:

◆ get to know you so you can be helped to end up with a suitable job

◆ find out what kind of job you would like

- help you look and apply for jobs
- help you overcome any problems that might be stopping you getting work such as problems with reading and writing or with travel to a job
- find out the support you may need, such as interview technique or searching for work.

FACT FILE: New Deal

- 414,200 people 18–24 years were helped into work between 1999 and 2003.
- 135,900 people aged 25 and over were helped into work between 2001 and 2003.
- 98,040 people aged 50 plus were helped into work between April 2000 and 2003.
- 12,449 people with disabilities were helped into work between 2001 and 2003.
- 186,260 lone parents were helped into work between 2001 and 2003.

New Deal 50 Plus

This is for people over 50 years, who are unemployed and have been claiming benefits for at least six months.

It helps people by providing personal support and advice to find a job, a £1,500 in-work training grant, access to financial support when in work (the amount depends on your income and circumstances) and help to start up your own business.

Activities

1   What is the government's New Deal?
    (2 marks)

2   How are people able to join the New Deal programme?   *(2 marks)*

3   What is the job of the New Deal adviser?
    (3 marks)

4   From the fact file answer the following questions:
    a) How successful has the New Deal been for people with disabilities?   *(2 marks)*
    b) How many persons over the age of 25 has the New Deal helped into work between 2001 and 2003?   *(2 marks)*
    c) Between 2001 and 2003 how many lone parents did the New Deal help?
        (2 marks)

5   Describe the ways in which the New Deal helps the over-50s.   *(2 marks)*

6   How do the over-50s qualify for the New Deal?   *(2 marks)*

Another way in which the Government helps to create jobs in Scotland is through Scottish Enterprise, an economic development agency, funded by the Scottish Executive. Its headquarters are in Glasgow.

Figure 3.27 Scottish Enterprise logo

Figure 3.28 Scottish Enterprise headquarters, Atlantic Quay in Glasgow

FOUNDATION/GENERAL

Scottish Enterprise covers 93 per cent of the population of Scotland, from Grampian to the Borders. Its job is to help the people and businesses of Scotland be successful, by creating jobs and improving skills and training.

The main stated aim is to build a world-class economy. To help to achieve, this Scottish Enterprise has four main areas where it tries to provide support:

◆ helping new businesses get started

◆ providing help and support to develop existing businesses

◆ helping people gain the knowledge and skills for the jobs of the future

◆ helping Scottish businesses compete in the world economy by promoting Scotland as a good place to live, work and do business.

As well as companies, Scottish Enterprise works with individuals, universities, colleges, local government and other public bodies to achieve its main targets.

Regional Selective Assistance (RSA)

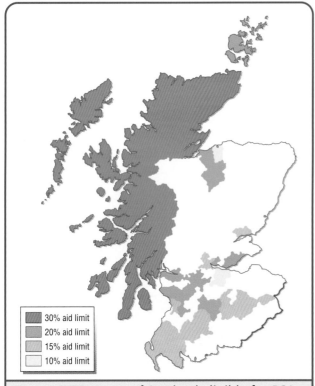

▨	30% aid limit
▧	20% aid limit
▩	15% aid limit
☐	10% aid limit

Figure 3.29 Areas of Scotland eligible for RSA

Figure 3.29 shows the areas eligible for **regional aid** under the RSA scheme and under the scheme for the Highlands and Islands Enterprise scheme. The code tells you how much a project could qualify for in each area. These **assisted areas** have been agreed by the EU and remain assisted areas until the end of 2006.

Regional Selective Assistance (RSA) is a national grant scheme which encourages investment and job creation in the areas of Scotland which have high unemployment and which have been recognised as needing aid under European Union law.

These areas are called assisted areas and businesses of all sizes can apply for aid, whether they are Scottish owned or not. The levels of grants depend on the size of the project and the area's need for assistance.

In the five years to the end of March 2003, businesses in Scotland have gained almost 1000 grants worth £430 million.

'The Scottish Parliament's European Committee has called for the protection of regional aid and warned that major reductions in the scheme could hit Scotland's most deprived areas.

Scotland currently benefits from £1.1 billion of funds. The committee highlights the possible impact on Scotland with the planned entry to the EU of underdeveloped countries from central and Eastern Europe. The Committee has accepted the need to bring the economies of these countries up to the level of other EU members but has also called for reforms to make sure our own less well off regions do not suffer.

Such funds are aimed at helping the most deprived regions of the EU to improve their economies. In Scotland, areas such as the Highlands and Islands, cities such as Glasgow and Edinburgh, parts of Fife, Lanarkshire and many rural areas have benefitted from these funds'

Source: Scottish Parliament news release, July 2003

Case Study

Two grants have been given to motor and home insurer Esure, part of a large British company. The first grant of £1million was made in 2001 to establish a centre in Glasgow. The grant help create 400 jobs. In July 2002 a second grant of £250,000 was given to create a further 175 jobs.

Source: RSA website

Activities

1　What is Scottish Enterprise?　*(2 marks)*

2　How does Scottish Enterprise try to help Scottish businesses?　*(3 marks)*

3　What is Regional Selective Assistance? *(2 marks)*

4　What are assisted areas?　*(2 marks)*

5　How successful has RSA been in providing grants to Scottish companies?　*(2 marks)*

6　Looking at the case study and describe how one British company has benefited from RSA.　*(3 marks)*

7　How many jobs, in total, were created by Esure?　*(2 marks)*

8　Using the Scottish Parliament news release, answer the following questions:
　a)　How much does Scotland receive from EU regional aid?　*(2 marks)*
　b)　What is the threat to Scotland's share of regional aid?　*(2 marks)*
　c)　Which areas of Scotland are the most deprived?　*(3 marks)*

FOUNDATION/GENERAL

Employment and Unemployment

'Everyone has the right to work, to free choice of employment, to just and free favourable conditions of work, and to protection against unemployment.
         Source: UN Declaration of Human Rights

The census of 2001 showed that the UK population was 58,789,194. Of these, 28,581,233 were males and 30,207,961 were females. The number of people available for work was 29.1 million. This means that almost half the population of the UK is not available for work.

Mainly the non-working part of the population are too old or too young to work. This would include children under 16 years of age, students who are in full time education, men over 65 years and women over 60 years.

It also includes people who are disabled or are unable to work because of illness. Many women are not counted as part of the working population because they work at home as housewives. Some have to stay at home to look after their children and others may be caring for a sick relative.

Not all of the available population is in employment. Many are unemployed, while others are participating in some form of training scheme.

The Labour Force

Figure 3.1 shows the age structure of the British labour force. When you look at it you can see how it has changed in the last 20 years. The main change is that the number of people in the working population who are under the age of 24 has fallen. This is mainly due to the increased numbers of young people continuing in some form of education after they leave school. The current Labour government has a target of 50 per cent of school leavers continuing in education. The situation has also been made worse due to a significant decrease in the birth rate in the country.

Who are the Unemployed?

There are two official ways of counting the number of unemployed. The first is the **claimant count** which only counts the number of people unemployed and in receipt of benefit. The second way is the **Labour Force Survey** (LFS) which counts the number of people who want a job, have looked for a job in the last four weeks and who are ready to start work in two weeks. The government regards this as a more reliable measure of real unemployment.

Year	16–24	25–44	45+	Total
1981	5832	11,358	9052	26,242
1991	5536	13,879	8714	28,129
2001	4206	14,678	9951	28,835
Estimate				
2006	4434	14,389	10,586	29,409

Figure 3.1 Age structure of the labour force in 000's
Source Department of Employment

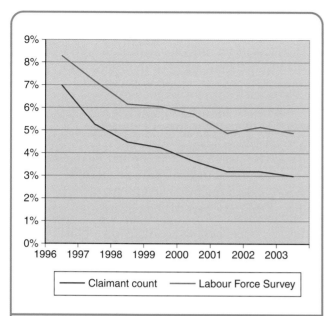

Figure 3.2 UK unemployment from 1996–2003
Source Office for National Statistics

Legend: Claimant count — Labour Force Survey

in Scotland, has now completely disappeared and shipbuilding has virtually disappeared, with only a few working shipyards remaining.

The reasons why these industries have declined is the same in all their cases, **costs**. Compared with other countries, it became expensive to manufacture these products in Scotland. High wage costs meant that many manufacturers have moved to areas where wages and costs are far cheaper, mainly in the Far East. The unemployment caused by this decline in traditional industries is called structural unemployment.

Types of Unemployment

Structural Unemployment

This is unemployed caused by a main change in the structure of jobs available in a country. It usually happens when the traditional industries of a country are lost. These types of jobs do not generally return to a country and workers have to find employment in other fields.

Cyclical Unemployment

The economy of every country goes through periods of ups and downs or booms and slumps. During a slump there is less demand for goods and services and unemployment rises. This is generally because there is less money around in the economy and the result is that unemployment among these workers increases.

Seasonal Unemployment

This type of unemployment is usually found in areas which rely on the tourist industry or farming for employment. For instance, there will be work during the summer tourist season and little or no work during the winter.

Growth in Employment

However, many thousands of new jobs have been created in the service sector. One of the biggest areas of job creation is in call centres. As a result of this there has actually been a rise in the numbers in employment. Employment in Scotland actually grew by 2.4 per cent during the 1990s.

Activities

1 What are the main reasons which prevent people from working?

2 In what way has the age structure of the UK labour force changed in the last 20 years?

3 How is the age structure of the labour force projected to change in the future?

4 Explain the two ways of counting the number of people unemployed

5 Explain in your own words the trends in UK unemployment from 1996–2003.

Changing Patterns of Employment

During the 1980s, the UK experienced a decline in its industrial and manufacturing jobs and a rise in employment in the service sector.

The greatest job losses have been in what are called the traditional industries of shipbuilding, mining, steel, car production and textiles. At one time, coal mining was the main industry in Scotland, with hundreds of coalmines all over Scotland employing thousands of workers. The last deep mine at Longannet in Fife closed in April 2002. Today there are no deep coalmines operating in Scotland. Car manufacturing, which was a thriving industry

GENERAL CREDIT

GENERAL / CREDIT

Activities

1 Describe the three types of industry to be found in Scotland.

2 Why has there been a decline in certain types of industry?

3 Give three examples of industries in decline.

4 Explain the different types of unemployment.

5 Give examples of jobs that would be lost in each type of unemployment.

6 Why would a slump in the economy lead to unemployment?

The North–South Divide

Traditionally there have been large differences in unemployment levels in different parts of the UK. It has become obvious that it is easier to find jobs in some areas of the country than others.

Unemployment is generally higher in areas such as Scotland, the north of England and Northern Ireland than it is in the Midlands and the South of England.

In 2004 Scotland had an unemployment rate of 5.8 per cent, while in the East of England it was 3.5 per cent. In some Scottish areas unemployment rates are 30 per cent and over. This situation has led many people to believe that a North–South divide exists in employment in the UK.

Many people disagree with the point of view that a North-South divide exists in the UK. They point to the increases in unemployment in London, West Midlands and some parts of the south disprove the argument.

The regions in the south of Britain experience lower unemployment than the north of the country. Critics of the North–South divide idea point to the fact that not every part of the south experiences lower unemployment. In 2004, London had an unemployment rate of 7 per cent, higher than every part of the country.

However, if we were to examine unemployment rates for UK cities we would see that the North–South divide still exists, some parts of Glasgow have unemployment rates of 30 per cent and other cities in the north of England have rates almost as high.

In general, unemployment figures are at the lowest they have been for since the 1980s. Unemployment is falling, but this does not tell the whole story.

Brendan Barbour (General Secretary of the TUC), when commenting on the above figures, said 'The further fall in unemployment and increase in total employment is welcome but the labour market is weaker than it looks. The number of full-time and permanent employees went down and the number of less secure temporary jobs and self-employment went up.'

Source: LRD

Region	Claimant count	%	Labour force survey	%
North East	49, 200	4.4	75, 000	6.4
North West	103, 100	3.1	156, 000	4.8
Yorkshire and Humberside	77, 300	3.2	124, 000	5.1
East Midlands	55, 800	2.7	94, 000	4.4
West Midlands	92, 600	3.5	149, 000	5.8
East	56, 200	2.1	98, 000	3.5
London	167, 600	3.6	267, 000	7.0
South East	74, 600	1.7	161, 000	3.8
South West	44, 700	1.7	76, 000	3.1
Wales	41, 500	3.2	65, 000	4.8
Scotland	96, 000	3.6	147, 000	5.8
Northern Ireland	33, 500	4.2	48, 000	6.3
UK Total	**892, 000**	**2.9**	**1, 459, 000**	**4.9**

Figure 3.3 Unemployment by region January 2004
Source Office for National Statistics

Employment is expected to increase by 22,000 jobs a year. This is less than a 1 per cent growth in the number of jobs, despite annual GDP growth of 3.5 per cent. In other words the recovery in the economy is not matched by a similar increase in the number of jobs.

Manufacturing jobs continued to fall. The sector lost 116,000 jobs compared to a year ago, with the number of people employed in the sector down to 3.47 million in the three months to November. Derek Simpson (General Secretary of manufacturing union Amicus) has warned that the decline of manufacturing must be stopped, for the sake of our industrial heartlands. He said 'These figures are a tragedy for the skilled workers thrown on to the scrapheap or forced to take menial and low paid jobs to support their families and bad news for the whole UK economy.'

Source: LRD

Firms and employees are becoming much more efficient – firms are producing 3.5 per cent more output but employing only 1 per cent more workers. It is also likely that the decrease in unemployment also has something to do with population decreases rather than much improved economic prospects.

The reality behind Scottish employment statistics looks like a move away from male employment and a shift towards female part-time, low grade jobs, rather than an increase in the number of jobs available. Scotland alone will see no growth in its labour force during this decade. The Scottish labour force is forecast to fall by 0.2 per cent by the year 2006 in contrast to a projected 5.9 per cent increase for the UK.

This is in line with the forecasted drop in the Scottish population as a whole. This means that Scotland is facing a future with a decreasing number of young people and an increasing number of elderly people. It is doubtful whether the decreasing workforce will be able to support the increasing elderly population. The implications for future generations are that Scotland will need fewer teachers, schools and nurseries, but more care facilities for its increasing elderly population.

The only way out of this situation is by increased immigration into Scotland or to encourage people to have more babies. The Scottish executive has already announced plans to try and encourage people who have emigrated from Scotland to return to their home country and bring their skills with them.

Figure 3.4 Scotland is actively trying to encourage more people to settle in the country

Source www.scotland.gov.uk

Activities

1 Explain what is meant by the North–South divide?

2 'All areas of the UK suffer equally from unemployment, there is no such thing as a North–South divide in employment.' From Figure 3.3, outline the four top and four bottom areas of unemployment

3 Outline the arguments put forward by those who do not believe in the North–South divide?

4 How does Brendan Barbour suggest that changes in employment may not benefit the individuals concerned?

5 In what ways do Derek Simpson's comments support Brendan Barbour's views?

6 How does the passage claim that workers are becoming more efficient?

7 List the problems that a declining labour force will bring for Scotland in the future?

8 Identify the three main solutions to the declining working population.

9 Give one advantage and one disadvantage for each of the three solutions put forward.

New Technology

Advances in new technology are making continual changes to the way that we live our everyday lives all around us – in our homes, our free leisure time, shopping, working or using transport.

At Home

In our homes there are many household appliances as well as advanced computers with broadband Internet access, computer games and electronic toys which are all the result of new technology. The use of e-mail and the Internet in particular has changed the way that many of us lead our lives and spend our leisure time.

It is claimed that these developments have turned the world into a global village were you can communicate with people on the other side of the world and receive almost instant replies. As a result of these advances in computer technology many people now find it easier to work part-time or even full-time from home. Many types of jobs can be performed from home, with access to suitable technology. Telephones, answering machines, fax lines and video conferencing facilities are now in common use. Even away from home a mobile phone and a palm or laptop computer will enable you to carry on your work.

However, income also has an affect on access to new technology.

The government has adopted the slogan 'net access for everyone'. Its aim is for everyone – young and old, regardless of wealth, to be able to access the Internet. Already, 48 per cent of households in the UK can access the Internet from home, compared with just 9 per cent five years ago.

James Crabtree, the research director of iSociety says this is a good idea from the government, 'I think the Internet will eventually become like running water – the idea that someone does not have running water is seen as bad.'

A survey carried out by the Oxford Internet Institute shows that the aim of universal access has broadly been achieved – the majority of the population is able to get online at home, work, school or in a local library.

Activities

1   Describe some of the ways in which new technology affects everyday life.

2   Give two other examples of new technology.

3   How do advances in technology assist the growth of home working?

4   Study Figure 3.5 and answer the following:

'Advances in technology make the government's target of "net access for everyone" easily achievable.' How could the person making this statement be accused of being selective in their use of the facts?

Out of Home

The introduction of bar codes and scanners in shops helps lessen the queues at the checkout and also tells the shop when certain items of stock are running low and have to be reordered. In factories the use of robots and other machines are now commonplace. Banks are also very highly computerised. Cash dispensers allow customers to have a range of services other than just withdrawing cash, and the widespread use of debit and credit cards could eventually lead to cashless shopping. Similarly the big increase in telephone and especially Internet banking means that people do not even have to visit a bank to carry out any transactions.

In hospitals and doctor's surgeries new technology can help doctors diagnose and treat illness. Doctors in city hospitals can use video and other advanced technology to treat people in rural or island communities.

The use of computers, word processors and photocopiers in offices has also made great changes in the ways that traditional office jobs are done.

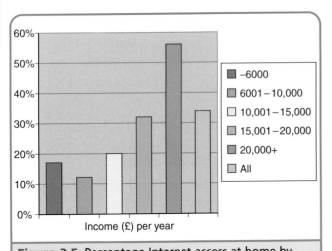

Figure 3.5 Percentage Internet access at home by annual family income

Source Scottish Household Survey 2001–2002
www.scotland.gov.uk

However, one result of the introduction of new technology is that many workers' jobs have been lost. The development of the technology itself has meant that other types of new jobs have been created to replace those lost.

New Technology and Productivity

Case Study: the Office

New technology has completely changed office work. Even the smallest office has the ability to be very efficient and to communicate worldwide.

Typewriters have been replaced by word processors, which can alter mistakes very easily. They can print hundreds of letters to different people simply by changing the names. A great deal of time and effort is saved.

Files and information are now kept on computers or CDs. This saves time and space. No need for filing cabinets or for staff to take up as much time for filing and retrieving. E-mail allows communications between people to be answered quickly. The Internet allows access to large amounts of current information. It can be used for passing information, advertising or other specialised data.

Fax machines also allows copies of documents to be sent to other areas of the world instantly.

Modern phone network systems can 'queue' calls, divert calls and tell you online to take calls.

Individuals wanting face-to-face meetings can 'video conference'. This allows them to see and speak to each other while seeing reactions and facial expressions.

Activity

Describe in your own words how new technology has changed the way a modern day office operates.

Case Study: cake decorating

The Problem

A large commercial bakery decorates cakes with written messages iced on the top – a task generally undertaken by skilled staff, trained to maintain a consistent high standard of work.

During seasonal holiday periods, such as Christmas, consumer demand for these decorated cakes increases fourfold. Training of additional staff to cope with the expanded demand while still maintaining high levels of quality takes a significant period of time and so volume planning is critical.

Solution

Design and build a robotic cake-decorating machine that solved the problem. Cakes are fed to the robot via a conveyor. A simple system ensures that the cakes are presented to the robot in a consistent position.

A computer file of the decoration shape is downloaded to the robot. Because individual cake heights may vary, a laser range finder tells the robot the height of each cake and writes the decorative inscription.

Benefits

◆ **Ability to boost production during peak seasonal demand periods**

◆ **Consistently high product quality due to reduced variability on decorations**

◆ **Reduced employment and training costs**

Activity

Examine the cake-decorating case study and explain what benefits new technology would bring to this firm.

New Technology and Employment

Case Study: Motorola Shocks Workers

Motorola, the world's second biggest maker of mobile phones, has today announced plans to cut 7000 jobs. Management blame the job losses on a reduced demand for their larger chip phones as consumers increasingly demand the new, more fashionable mini phones. The Scottish factory's technology cannot produce such phones. Shocked workers left the factory devastated after today's announcement knowing they would soon be jobless

Source: BBC News Online

Case Study: Jobs Down the Tubes

Electronics company Chunghwa Tubes has confirmed that it plans to axe 600 jobs in Scotland in 2003. The plant was built to manufacture cathode ray tubes for computer monitors and televisions and was hailed as the most technologically advanced factory of its kind in the world. But as the demand for modern flat screen technology has increased, the Scottish factory has quickly grown out of date as it continues to use the same manufacturing techniques it used when it opened five years ago. So the demand for TVs and monitors has decreased.

Source: BBC News Online

New Technology, Jobs and Globalisation

Call centres have developed throughout Scotland in the last ten years. Companies set up in Scotland because they see it as an ideal location for this type of employment with low wages and access to well-equipped office space. Research also showed that people liked the Scottish accent and trusted the person speaking compared with people from other areas in the UK. In 1998, there were over 150 call centres operating in Scotland.

Jobs which are based on the use of new technology, particularly when 'the product' or service can be transferred electronically, are increasingly affected by 'the global market' in jobs, goods and services – globalisation.

Trade Unions are now increasingly concerned about this affect of globalisation and that further developments in telephone technology can lead to call centre jobs being 'off-shored' to countries like India where wage cost are lower than the UK.

The call centre industry could be drying up as a source of jobs. Major employers like BT, Prudential and Aviva are leading the pack in outsourcing (off-shoring) call centre and business processing work to, in particular, India, but also to other locations such as South Africa, the Philippines and Malaysia. The Chief Executive of BT said 'We expect the initiative to generate 30 per cent cost savings during the first five years. As many as 52 large scale call centres in Scotland – 22 per cent of the total- could close by the end of the year.'

Source: Labour Research (abridged)

Activities

1. In what ways were job losses at Motorola and Chunghwa the result of not keeping up with fashion or technological advances?

2. What were the main reasons companies set up call centres in Scotland?

3. Why do you think it is easier to 'off-shore' new technology call centre and business processing work than jobs such as cake production?

4. What evidence is there that globalisation is also a threat to jobs which rely on new technology?

FACT FILE

Arguments for New technology

New technology can lead to increased production of cheaper, better quality goods. Far less goods will be sub-standard more will be sold. This will increase the firm's profits.

Workers will be needed to produce the new technology, from household electrical appliances to home and office computers, from robots to personal mobile phones and the miniaturised chips that they use.

Jobs, which are repetitive, boring or dangerous will be taken over by machines. This may mean that many work related problems such as days lost due to ill health or strikes are likely to be reduced.

➤

GENERAL/CREDIT

FACTFILE continued

Employee costs will be reduced. Fewer workers will be needed. This means that firms will make savings on their wages bill.

An increasing number of people are able to work from home as a result of advances in computer and phone technology.

Arguments against New Technology

Unemployment will increase as machines and robots take over the jobs of working people.

New technology will change jobs so much that a great amount of retraining will be needed. This may not be a problem for younger workers, but the fast pace of working with new technology may cause problems for older workers.

More jobs using new technology leads to the de-skilling of formerly skilled jobs. This means that many of the old skilled jobs will disappear. Skilled workers may become machine minders.

It will be harder for trade unions to recruit new members and protect their interests. This could lead to a worsening of pay and conditions among workers.

Technology can cause job losses and employers prefer to cut jobs rather than reduce the working week.

Activities

1   'The increasing use of new technology has been beneficial for the entire population. No one could complain about the benefits that it brings.'

    Why could the person making this statement be accused of being selective in there use the facts?

2   Look at the factfile on new technology. Choose two points from each argument which you consider to be the strongest points. Copy them out and explain why you consider them to be the strongest points.

3   What challenges face trade unions in the introduction of new technology?

4   Describe all of the features you would expect to find in a new high tech house.

Unemployment in Europe

Unemployment is not only a problem for Britain, it is also a European problem. The European Union has a population of 380.8 million. On 1 May 2004, ten more countries with a combined population of 74 million joined the European Union.

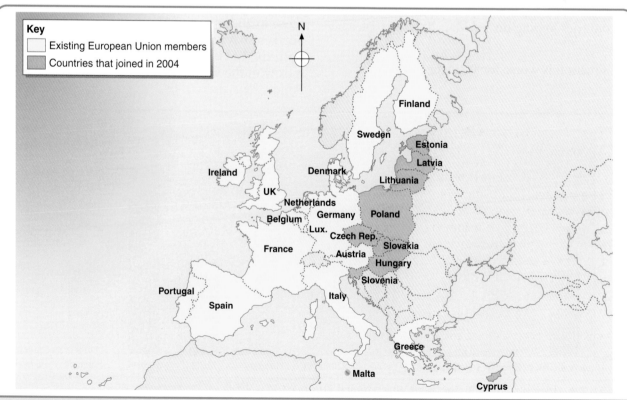

Figure 3.6 Old and new EU members

Key
☐ Existing European Union members
▨ Countries that joined in 2004

Finland
Sweden
Estonia
Latvia
Lithuania
Ireland
Denmark
UK
Netherlands
Germany   Poland
Belgium
Lux.
Czech Rep.
France   Slovakia
Austria   Hungary
Slovenia
Portugal   Italy
Spain
Greece
Malta
Cyprus

Employment and Unemployment

Country	% Labour force unemployed
Spain	11.3
Greece	9.6
France	9.5
Germany	9.3
Finland	8.9
Italy	8.4
Belgium	8.1
Portugal	6.9
Denmark	6.0
Sweden	6.0
UK	4.9
Ireland	4.6
Austria	4.5
Netherlands	4.0
Luxembourg	3.9

Figure 3.7 Unemployment rates, December 2003
Source www.europa.eu.int/comm/eurostat (abridged)

Country	% Labour force unemployed
Spain	22.4
Greece	26.1
France	20.7
Germany	9.6
Finland	22.4
Italy	26.5
Belgium	22.1
Portugal	15.7
Denmark	11.1
Sweden	14.1
UK	11.8
Ireland	8.2
Austria	7.4
Netherlands	7
Luxembourg	11

Figure 3.8 16–25 year old unemployment rates December 2003
Source www.europa.eu.int/comm/eurostat (abridged)

In December 2003, 8 per cent of all EU citizens were out of work. In the Eurozone, unemployment was higher at 8.8 per cent. Unemployment in the 10 countries joining on 1st May 2004 was 14.1 per cent.

The situation is worse for younger people.

European Action on Unemployment

The European Union (EU) has specific policies for those in and out of work. It is estimated that Scotland has received some £1.3 billion in grants from the EU in the last ten years. This comes mostly in the form of European Structural Funds.

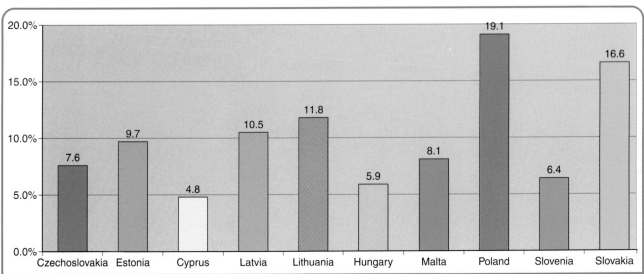

Figure 3.9 Unemployment in the states which joined EU on 1st May 2004
Source www.europa.eu.int/comm/eurostat (abridged)

The most important of these funds are:

European Social Fund

Helps communities where there is a high rate of unemployment

European Regional Development Fund

Supports specific projects such as building roads to improve Scotland's links with other parts of the EU.

Rechar and Reneval

Funds to help communities where coal mining or shipbuilding industries have declined.

Not all of the funds to help unemployment are taken up. This is becaue the rules say that the government must match the sums from the European Union, for example, if the EU gives £5 million then the government or local government most also spent £5 million.

Type of industry	1984	2004
Agriculture and fishing	2.6	1.4
Energy and water	2.9	1.1
Manufacturing	24.9	16.6
Construction	7.7	7.1
Distribution, hotels and restaurants	20.3	19.6
Transport and communications	6.3	7.1
Banking, finance and insurance	9.3	15.6
Public administration, education and health	20.9	25.4
Other services	5.1	6

Figure 3.10 Percentage of all employees by industry
Source National Office of Statistics

Type of industry	1984	2004
Agriculture and fishing	3.5	1.9
Energy and water	4.3	1.5
Manufacturing	30.3	18.5
Construction	12	13.4
Distribution, hotels and restaurants	15.8	17.8
Transport and communications	8.5	9.5
Banking, finance and insurance	8.4	16.1
Public administration, education and health	13.1	16
Other services	4	5.2

Figure 3.11 Percentage of male employees by industry
Source National Office of Statistics

Activities

1 In what ways is unemployment a European problem?

2 'Youth unemployment in the UK in 1999 was amongst the worst in Europe.' Community youth worker

   In what way is the youth worker being selective with their use of the facts?

3 What are the main European Structural funds?

4 In what ways are they aimed at helping Scotland's unemployed?

5 Explain why Scotland does not take advantage of all the funds available.

6 For what reasons might the new countries joining the EU in May 2004 have a better claim to EU assistance than Scotland?

Employment by Industry

Industry in a country can generally be divided into three different types:

Primary Industries

This is an industry which deals mainly with a country's natural resources. It would include jobs in coalmining, fishing or farming.

Secondary Industries

This refers to manufacturing industries which make products. It would include jobs such as making furniture or engineering.

Tertiary Industries

This includes jobs such as working for the government, working for banks or insurance firms, leisure and tourism and service industries.

Since the beginning of the 1990s, the communications sector has been growing with many new jobs being created because of advances in cable, satellite and mobile phone 'blue tooth' technology. This has meant that new jobs have been created for the manufacturing of these products. These new jobs tend to employ mostly women. One problem of traditional sector jobs being replaced by jobs in the service sector is that many are part-time, lower paid and less secure jobs.

Type of industry	1984	2004
Agriculture and fishing	1.3	0.7
Energy and water	1	0.5
Manufacturing	17.3	7.2
Construction	1.6	1.8
Distribution, hotels and restaurants	26.5	22
Transport and communications	3.1	3.5
Banking, finance and insurance	10.6	14.9
Public administration, education and health	31.9	42.4
Other services	6.6	6.9

Figure 3.12 Percentage of female employees by industry

Source National Office of Statistics

Activities

Answer the following questions by giving detailed answers using the figures from Figures 3.10–12.

1. In what ways has employment in the UK changed in the years shows?

2. Explain the differences between changes in numbers working in traditional industries and in the service sector.

3. Which jobs have experienced the biggest changes during the period shown?

4. Which jobs saw the biggest rise in female employees?

Inequality in the Workplace

Women make up 52 per cent of the Scottish population and a large proportion of the workforce. Despite this many women experience problems in relation to employment matters.

Britain has laws that make it illegal for employers to discriminate against women in relation to jobs and pay. The Equal Pay Act 1970 and the Sex Discrimination Act 1975 mean that women can expect to be treated equally with men when in employment or when seeking employment.

Despite these laws and the fact that women now account for 50 per cent of the entire workforce, women are much more likely to experience employment problems and be employed in part time jobs where pay is low and the working conditions are not as good as those for full time employees. There are several reasons why so many women are in part time employment. They may have to care for a dependent child or relative or part-time work may be the only type of employment available.

Nationally, the typical cost of a nursery place for a child under two is £128 per week or more than £6650 a year. There are few subsidised nurseries and only a third of three year olds are at a nursery or primary school – many of these will only qualify for a half day attendance.

The typical cost for a childminder for a child under two is £118 a week and £34 a week for an after school club. Consequently lower paid workers have little incentive to stay in work.

Source: Labour Research (abridged)

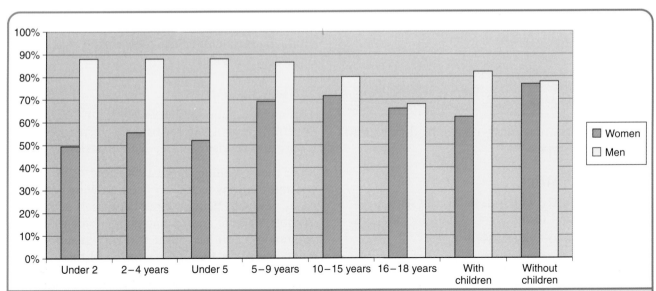

Figure 3.13 Employment rates of men and women by age of youngest child
Source www.womenandequalityunit.gov.uk

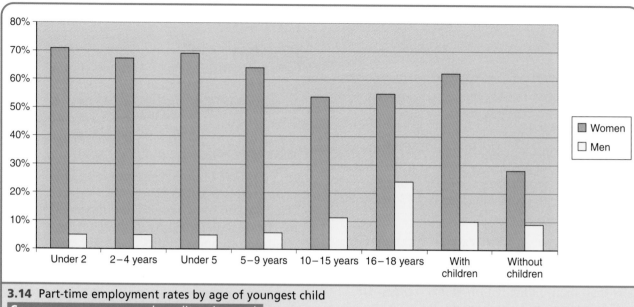

3.14 Part-time employment rates by age of youngest child
Source www.womenandequalityunit.gov.uk

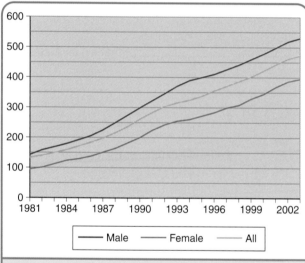

Figure 3.15 Average gross earnings of workers by gender 1981 – January 2003
Source www.statistics.gov.uk

Many more women work nowadays because there are jobs available and they need the income.

However, many jobs women do tend to be part-time, unskilled and low paid. Part-time workers are extremely vulnerable to low pay. Only a quarter of them earn more than half the average male full-time earnings.

For the UK as whole, the Office of National Statistics estimate that the national minimum wage of £3.60 for those over 22 will affect 4.1 per cent of men and 11.9 per cent of women. In October 2003, the minimum wage was increased to £4.50 for over 22s. In 2005 it goes up to £5.05.

In January 2004, the average wages of a full-time male worker was £536.60 per week compared with the average wage of £404.70 per week for a woman. with a high proportion of woman workers such as sales had average wages of only £295.30 per week.

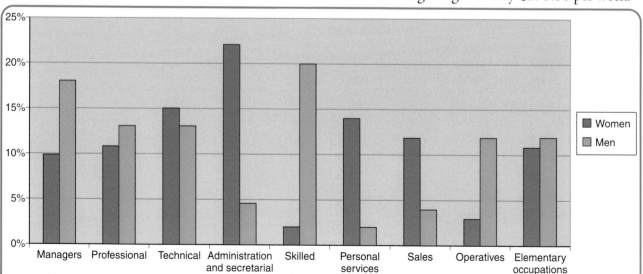

Figure 3.16 Per cent of all in employment by gender and occupational group
Source www.statistics.gov.uk

GENERAL/CREDIT

Employment and Unemployment

There is a continuing pay gap between even full time workers and a variation between the genders in occupation.

FACT FILE

Employment

Women workers are concentrated in a relatively small number of areas of employment, in particular the service sector. 57 per cent of working women work full time and 43 per cent work part-time.

Full time women workers earn an average of 72 per cent of male wages. Although in general wages have risen steadily women's wages are still less than men's. One reason is that women are still in a minority in high paid jobs.

There are considerable variations in female average earnings in Scottish regions, with women in Lothian having the highest level and women in Fife the lowest. Three quarters of women working in manual jobs and 40 per cent of women in non-manual jobs are low paid.

75 per cent of secretarial and clerical workers are women, and there are only three women in the boards of the top 20 Scottish companies. Secretaries, sales people and hairdressers are still mostly women and plumbers, machinists and senior managers are still mostly men.

FACT FILE

Education

Girls in Scottish secondary schools continue to achieve better results than boys. A smaller proportion of girls with the necessary qualifications go on to university compared with boys. However a higher proportion of girls enter teacher training.

Over a period of time the segregation of boys and girls in terms of subject choice has lessened. There are still some significant differences with girls being in the majority of those taking modern languages, business studies and home economics, and boys the majority of those taking physics, computer studies and technological subjects.

At university women form the majority of those taking social studies, business administration and languages, with men in the majority in mathematics and computing, sciences and engineering and technology.

FACT FILE

Law

There is under-representation of women at all levels of the Scottish legal profession.

The proportion of female lawyers is increasing, but the rate at which it is increasing is very slow.

Latest figures show that women form about a third of all solicitors in Scotland. Women have recently increased their representation at the very top of the legal profession and amongst advocates and Queen's Council. Scotland now has one permanent woman judge and the top law officials in the country, The Advocate General and Solicitor General are women. The Advocate General is principal legal adviser to the Government on Scots Law

Activities

1 What evidence is there that childcare costs are a major impediment in women taking full time work?

2 How has the national minimum wage helped women?

3 How might the raising of the national minimum wage be of particular benefit to women?

4 'Having children has nothing to do with women working or not working. Women only go out to work to earn money to buy luxuries.' What evidence is there to suggest the speaker is being selective with the facts?

5 What evidence is there that wages are different for women in different parts of Scotland?

6 Describe, in your own words, the differences in occupations by gender.

Figure 3.17 Dr Lynda Clark QC MP – The Advocate General

Figure 3.18 Elish Angiolini QC – The Solicitor General for Scotland

'The number of women currently serving as police officers in Scotland stands at 2723, and is equivalent to 17.8 per cent of all police officers. This is an increase of 123 officers on last year (or 4.7 per cent) and continues the steady increase in the ratio of female to male police officers of recent years.

Equal opportunities feature as a key issue in the regular inspection programme of all forces and we must acknowledge the positive progress that has been made over the past decade by forces.

Nevertheless women officers remain a minority group and are disproportionately under-represented

Type of member	Women	Men	Women as % of total
Solicitors	2667	5321	33.4
Judges (permanent)	1	26	3.7
Judges (temporary)	0	8	0
Sheriffs (full-time)	8	94	7.8
Sheriffs (part-time)	10	102	8.9
Advocates	74	306	19.5
Queen's Councils	8	75	9.6

Figure 3.19 Scottish legal profession by gender, 1998
Source Faculty of Advocates

Constabulary	Women 2002	Men 2002	Women 2002 (% of total)	Women 1996 (% of total)
Central	107	612	14.8	11.9
Dumfries and Galloway	94	388	19.5	13.2
Fife	159	753	17.4	12.0
Grampian	254	1004	20	13.8
Lothian and Borders	470	2230	17.4	12.4
Northern	113	570	16.5	10.5
Strathclyde	1302	6025	17.7	11.1
Tayside	239	931	20.4	13.1

Figure 3.20 Police strength in Scotland by gender, 2002 and 1996
Source www.scotland.gov.uk

within promoted posts and specialisms. This year the percentage of promoted posts held by female officers was 7 per cent. Last year the figure stood at 6.5 per cent. Despite this increase the numbers of female officers in promoted posts are relatively low, especially in the most senior posts.

As more women enter the service it is not unreasonable to expect a concomitant increase in those occupying promoted posts. Forces must critically examine their procedures for the selection of staff for specialist and promoted posts to ensure that it is fair and reflects equal opportunities legislation and policy.'

Source: April 2004 report of HMCI of Constabulary for Scotland

Activities

1 'Despite the passing of laws and the fact that girls do better than boys at school, women still fail to get appointed to the top jobs in our society.'
   a) In what ways does the factfile on employment support this statement?
   b) How is the person making this statement being selective with the facts?

2 'There is now very little difference in the results that boys and girls achieve in schools. This is mainly because they now study the same subjects as each other.'

   Use the factfile on education to show how the person making this statement is being selective with the facts.

3 'Women are under-represented at every level of the Scottish legal profession. Recently the situation has shown signs of improvement.'

   Do you agree or disagree with this statement? Give evidence to support your point of view.

4 Look at the numbers of female police officers in the different forces in Scotland. What conclusions can you come to about the numbers of female police officers?

5 'Women are represented well in promoted positions within the Scottish police force.'

   How could the person making this statement be accused of exaggeration?

6 Would the police be keen to recruit more female officers?

   Give reasons for your answer.

Race and Employment

Approximately 2 per cent of Scotland's population are from ethnic minorities. Race relations laws make it illegal to discriminate on the grounds of colour, race or religion. Nevertheless, members of ethnic minority groups still continue to encounter different treatment in employment.

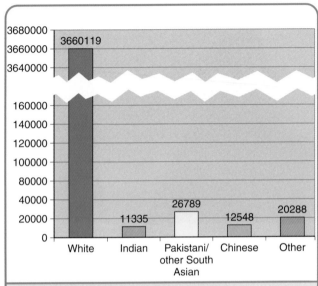

Figure 3.21 Population of Scotland 16–74 by ethnic group (Census 2001)
Source www.scrol.gov.uk (abridged)

The type of jobs people do can relate to the ethnic group one belongs to.

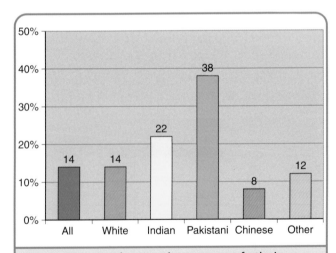

Figure 3.22 Employment by per cent of ethnic group in wholesale and retail trade and repairs (Census 2001)

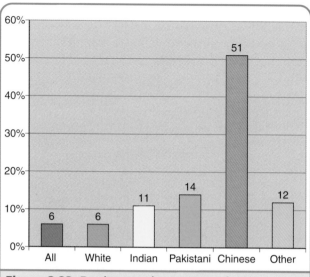

Figure 3.23 Employment by per cent of ethnic group in hotels and restaurants (Census 2001)
Source www.scrol.gov.uk (abridged)

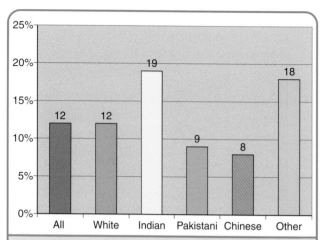

Figure 3.24 Employment by per cent of ethnic group in health and social work (Census 2001)
Source www.scrol.gov.uk (abridged)

Occupation	All	White Scottish	Other white British	Indian	Pakistani	Bangladeshi	Chinese
Managers	12	11	18	20	28	16	14
Professionals	11	10	19	30	10	16	15
Technical	14	13	19	9	7	7	7
Administration and secretarial	13	13	10	8	7	4	6
Skilled	12	13	8	6	7	19	28
Personal services	7	7	6	3	3	2	3
Sales	9	9	6	12	25	9	9
Plant operatives	10	10	5	4	4	3	2
Elementary occupations (unskilled)	13	13	9	8	8	24	17

Figure 3.25 Scottish employment by occupation, percentages of each ethnic group (Census 2001)
Source www.scrol.gov.uk (abridged)

FACT FILE

The age profile of the ethnic minority population is younger than the white population. 57 per cent of the ethnic minority population were under 30 years old compared with 38 per cent of the white population.

46 per cent of non-whites living in Scotland were born in the United Kingdom.

In Scotland 25 per cent of non-whites work more than the legal number of hours per week (over 48 hours), compared with 16 per cent of whites.

Just under 0.5 per cent of police officers in Scotland are non-white. However, over the last five years the number of non-white officers has increased by 71 per cent

50 per cent of employed ethnic minority young people work in hotels, catering and repairs.

One in 6 of the Indian community is in social class 1, compared with one in 20 in the white community.

12 per cent of ethnic minority employed males and 34 per cent of females work in a family business as compared to 3 per cent and 1 per cent white males and females.

Employment and Unemployment

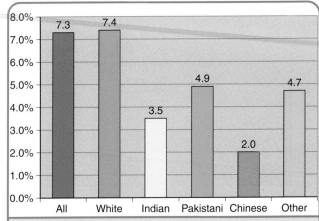

Figure 3.26 Employment by per cent of ethnic group in manufacturing (Census 2001)

Source www.scrol.gov.uk (abridged)

Ethnic minority unemployment is much higher than white unemployment in the UK as a whole. In Scotland the situation is more complex.

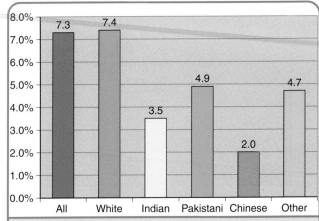

Figure 3.27 Unemployment amongst 16–24 year olds, percentage of each ethnic group (Census 2001)

Source www.scrol.gov.uk (abridged)

Activities

1   Look at Figures 3.23–26. Describe in your own words the major employment areas by ethnic group for:
   a) whites
   b) Indians
   c) Pakistanis and other South Asians
   d) Chinese.

2   Look at Figure 3.23.
   a) What evidence is there that other white British people brought high levels of qualifications with them when they settled in Scotland?
   b) What evidence is there that a high number of Pakistanis run their own businesses?
   c) What evidence is there that Indians have a higher level of educational qualifications and income than other ethnic groups?
   d) 'The Bangladeshi community is the poorest and most likely to be unemployed.' Suggest reasons why the speaker could be accused of exaggeration.

3   Using the information from the Figures and the factfile, discuss the statement 'Immigrant communities have brought high levels of skills to Scotland, tend to work harder and have become successful'.

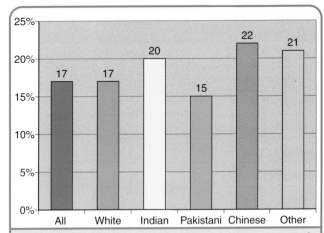

Figure 3.28 Students aged 16–24 as a percentage of each ethnic group (Census 2001)

Source www.scrol.gov.uk (abridged)

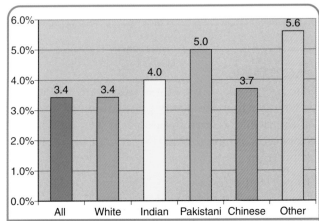

Figure 3.29 Unemployment amongst those aged 25 and over as a percentage of each ethnic group (Census 2001)

Source www.scrol.gov.uk (abridged)

Activities

1 Discuss the relationship between 16 to 25 year old unemployment and studying full time for the ethnic groups listed.

2 What evidence is there that younger members of minority ethnic groups may have better employment prospects than their older generations.

Age and Employment

Many unemployed middle-aged and older people have severe problems in finding employment regardless of the skills they have or how well qualified they are. Long-term unemployment is more heavily concentrated among older people. Employers also appear to provide less job-related training to those over 50.

Employers often point out that younger people can be hired for lower wages and that older workers lack the skills needed for today's modern workplace and that training takes too long and is uneconomic.

There are around 19 million people aged 50 and over in the UK, 40 per cent of the adult population. The proportion of older people in the population is growing. The report 'Winning the Generation Game' published in April 2000 states that by 2020 the 50 plus age group will have increased by a further three million.

Employment Rate

Currently just over six million people aged between 50 and state pension age are in employment, an employment rate of 69 per cent. The employment rate for men aged 50–64 is 71 per cent and for women aged 50–59 is 66 per cent.

Since 1997 the employment rate of older people has risen faster than that of the working population as a whole. The average length of time in current employment is much higher for older workers, 13 years compared with seven years for those aged 25–49. Older workers are more likely to work part time and be self-employed. People aged between 50 and state retirement age has less qualifications than those aged 25–49. They are more than twice as likely to have no formal qualifications.

However many older people want to work and are prepared to work beyond normal retirement age. A survey by 50 Connect found that 59 per cent of those surveyed were in favour of working beyond state pension age. They say that younger workers can bring enthusiasm and willingness to the workplace, while older workers bring experience and reliability. Employers need both.

> 'People who enjoy their work should have the option of continuing in employment until they feel ready to retire, rather than the current trend of being forced out of work before they're ready. People should be allowed to be flexible to do what they want or need to do with their later years.'
>
> David Appledore, Executive Director at 50 Connect
> Source: Age Positive, July 2003

Age Legislation

The UK government has adopted the EU proposals on age and employment, the Employment Directive on Equal Treatment. This requires all 15 members of the EU to introduce laws banning discrimination at work on the grounds of age, sexual orientation, religious belief and disability.

The government will introduce age legislation by 2006. The time taken will allow the government to consult with individuals, employers and expert groups in order to try and pass the most appropriate legislation for this area.

But it may be quite a while before everyone can expect their age to be no barrier to getting a job, being promoted or staying in their job. Governments may pass laws, but it is very difficult to change people's attitudes.

Emma Parry, of the Cranfield School of Management, Human Resource Research Centre, points out that currently 43 per cent of all UK organisations have no plans for an anti-ageism policy and 65 per cent have no plans for flexible retirement options.

She thinks that 'policies are just the first step, changing attitudes is the bigger challenge'. She also says that demographics, and not legislation, will force a change in attitudes. With the number of young people falling, and the overall population aging it does not make business sense to discard those over 50, along with all their experience and skill. (Source: *Sunday Times* 2 November 2003)

What the Government Says

Andrew Smith, former Secretary of State for Work and Pensions, said:

'We need to make sure we put in place options for people to work longer if they choose. Working a few years longer can make a huge difference to retirement income. For business it promises a more experienced skilled workforce.

We believe people should have greater choice over how long they work, and when they retire. But people won't be able to exercise this choice unless we tackle the discrimination that all too often affects employment opportunities for older people. We need to challenge stereotypes and discrimination and show the benefits of an age diverse workforce.

New legislation will highlight the need for all of us to change culture and attitudes to older workers. Discrimination is unfair and it is bad for business.'

Source: TUC Conference 2003

Case Study: B&Q

B&Q is a company which has taken positive steps to recognise the skills and experience older employees bring with them. Today B&Q's older employees enjoy working with younger people as part of a team, while younger employees appreciate the extra skills and life experience, which mature workers bring to the job.

'As a business which attracts DIY-ers and gardeners of all ages, it's common sense to make sure that we have people of all ages to serve them. We find that our customers associate older people with having DIY knowledge and they feel comfortable asking them for advice.'

Bill Whitting, Chief Executive
Source: B&Q Newsletter

Activities

1 Why do many older people face problems in finding employment?

2 What reasons do employers give for not employing older people?

3 'The large and increasing numbers of elderly people means that it is a complete waste of resources not to employ them.'

What evidence would you use to support the above statement?

4 'Very few people are interested in working beyond retirement age. It is a myth that many do.' Why could the person making this statement be accused of being selective with the facts?

5 What part is the EU playing in combating age discrimination?

6 'Policies are just the first step, changing attitudes is the bigger challenge.'

What does Emma Parry mean by this statement and why would it be considered important?

7 'The government does not really care about older people finding jobs. Their real concern is creating employment for young people.'

In what way does Andrew Smith's statement show this to be selective in its use of the facts?

8 What benefits do older workers bring to B&Q and how could they improve profits?

Disability and Employment

Another group of people who often face employment problems are those with disabilities. Workers with disabilities often face prejudice from employers and fellow workers.

To try and combat this, the government passed the Disability Discrimination Act 1995. This law aims to protect disabled people against discrimination in employment, when using a service or facility, buying or renting property and in the use of public transport.

The government introduced this law in three separate stages:

◆ in 1996, it was made illegal to treat disabled people less favourably because of their disability

◆ in 1999, businesses had to make reasonable adjustments for disabled staff, like providing additional support or equipment. They also had to start making changes to the way they provided their services to customers, for example providing gas or electricity bills in large print

- from October 2004, businesses have to make physical alterations to their premises to overcome access barriers.

The example most people think of is installing ramps or special toilets for wheelchair users.

The law will apply to all businesses, no matter how many or how few employees they have. It is also irrelevant whether a service is paid for or free of charge. The law is not only problematic for employers. However, many employers recognise the advantages of employing a more diverse workforce. These advantages include:

- companies employing staff from all sections of society will get a balance between staff and customers that creates a better atmosphere. With disabled people contributing an estimated £40 billion spending each year this is too large a market to ignore.
- with disabled people making up 18 per cent of the British working population, it makes sense to tap into the pool of skills, expertise and resources on offer from disabled employees. With the current shortage in skilled employees it would be wasteful not to consider the potential of disabled staff.

FACT FILE

There are almost 9 million disabled people in the UK.

6.8 million disabled people are of working age. This represents 18 per cent of the workforce.

Only 42 per cent of working age disabled people have paid employment. The average for non-disabled people is approximately 80 per cent.

Disabled people are six times more likely to be unemployed.

Almost half the 2.4 million disabled people on benefits and out of work would like to work.

Almost 70 per cent of disabled people in Scotland live in households where their annual income is less than £10,000.

13.7 per cent of the population of Scotland have a long term health problem or disability, equal to one in every six adults.

8 per cent of Income Support Claimants in Scotland are disabled compared to 14 per cent in Britain as a whole.

Source: Scottish Executive website

Popular Myths

Disabled people:

- can only work in factories or as cleaners
- are not as clever or as useful as non-disabled people
- won't be able to cope with the stress of work and won't be able to deal with everyday problems that arise
- don't stay in jobs for long
- will always be off sick
- are a danger to their fellow workers and the workplace – their wheelchairs will block fire exits thus creating a health and safety hazard.

Reality:

Disabled employees:

- prefer to work within the same range of jobs as non-disabled people
- have the same range of skills as non-disabled people
- have additional problem solving, organisational and coping skills developed through living everyday life situations
- are in fact more loyal than non-disabled employees
- have fewer days off sick and less non-illness related absence than non-disabled employees
- have a better than average health and safety record
- less than 5 per cent of the disabled use a wheelchair, this is contrary to popular beliefs held by many employers.

Source: Employers Forum on Disability website

Activities

1 Why did the government introduce the Disability Discrimination Act?

2 What benefits does this law bring for disabled people?

3 'Employers can gain benefits from employing disabled people.'

Outline the benefit which employers could gain.

4 'Finding a job is not difficult for those disabled people who want to work. The situation is that most disabled are unable to work and have to rely on benefits.' In what ways does the

information contained in the fact file show this statement to be an exaggeration?

5 'It is unfair to force an employer to hire someone who will miss work because of illness.'

Why could the person making this statement be accused of being selective in their use of the facts?

6 An employer has asked you to provide reasons why they should hire disabled workers. Write a short report outlining the case for hiring disabled workers.

Your report should also answer any negative points, which an employer may make.

Low Pay

With the loss of so many manufacturing jobs and the increase of various forms of casual work, the number of low paid workers in Scotland has risen. Many people try to avoid unemployment as a way of avoiding poverty.

Being in employment is no guarantee of escaping poverty. People often complain that wages are so low, for some jobs that they would be better off on benefits. In order to deal with this, in 1999 the government introduced a national minimum wage for those in employment.

Despite the minimum wage recent research has shown that almost a third of full-time workers in

	18–21 year olds	22+ year olds
April 1999	£3.00/hour	£3.60/hour
June 2000	£3.20/hour	£3.60/hour
October 2000	£3.20/hour	£3.70/hour
October 2001	£3.50/hour	£4.10/hour
October 2002	£3.60/hour	£4.20/hour
October 2003	£3.80/hour	£4.50/hour
October 2004	£4.10/hour	£4.85/hour
October 2005 (proposed rate)	£4.25/hour	£5.05/hour
October 2006 (proposed rate)	£4.45/hour	£5.35/hour

Figure 3.30 National minimum wage rates 1999–2006
Source Office for National Statistics

Scotland are paid below the national average. Research by the Scottish Low Pay Unit found that many workers earn less than two-thirds of the average male weekly wage. It also found that the number of women who fall into the full-time low pay category is double that of men.

Year	000's of jobs	% of total
1998	1410	6.0
1999	530	2.2
2000	240	1.0
2001	270	1.1
2002	360	1.4
2003	260	1.0

Figure 3.31 Jobs below the national minimum wage
Source Office for National Statistics

Poorly Paid Jobs

In April 2003 there were 260,000 jobs with pay less than the national minimum wage. 18–21 year olds held 40,000 of these jobs and 220,000 were held by those aged over 22. Kitchen and hotel porters, waitresses and bar staff are among the worst paid jobs in the country.

Worst paid jobs for women:

1 Waitress

2 Launderers

3 Bar staff

4 Kitchen porters

5 Retail check-out operators

6 Bakery workers

7 Shelf fillers

8 Cleaners and domestics

9 Catering assistants

10 Food preparation workers

FACT FILE

Part-time jobs are about five times as likely to be low paid as full-time jobs, while women's jobs are three times as likely to be low paid as men's.

Full-time jobs held by women are twice as likely to be low paid as those held by men.

Employers are twice as likely to pay those aged 18–21 below the adult minimum wage.

The proportion of women's jobs to men's paying below £5 per hour is at its greatest for workers between the ages of 35 and 49.

There are very large differences in low pay between different occupations, jobs in the hotel and restaurant sector are particularly low paid.

Arguments for a national minimum wage:

- **protects the poorest workers from poverty**
- **the government may have to pay out less in benefits if people are paid more**
- **every other European country has a minimum wage, so Britain should have one too**
- **the government will get more money in tax if people have higher incomes.**

Arguments against a national minimum wage:

- **some people may lose their jobs if businesses have to pay out more in wages**
- **other workers might want more if they see others being paid more**
- **prices may increase as costs for businesses increase**
- **makes Britain less attractive to foreign companies who may not set up their businesses due to high wage bills.**

Activities

1 Why did the government introduce the national minimum wage?

2 'Very low paid jobs have almost disappeared since the minimum wage was introduced.'

   How does Figure 3.24 both prove and disprove this statement?

3 Say which jobs tend to be the lowest paid in British society and explain why you think this is the case.

4 What are the main arguments for and against a national minimum wage?

FACT FILE

Poverty in the UK

One in four people in the UK live in poverty.

One in three children in the UK live in poverty.

6.5 million adults go without essential clothing, such as a warm coat because of lack of money.

9.5 million people can't afford adequate housing, free from damp.

Children from poor homes are more likely to die as a baby, and have lower life expectancy.

Children from poorer backgrounds do less well in school.

Children raised in poverty are, as adults, more likely to be unemployed, in low paid work and to get into trouble with the police.

One in four women lived in poverty in 2000 compared with one in five men.

1.2 million people live in low income households in Scotland.

30 per cent of Scottish children live in low income households.

Most people consider £53.95 per week for everything except housing costs and council tax is not enough even for a single person.

Death rates in the 10 per cent most deprived areas in Scotland are double those of the least disadvantaged 50 per cent.

Source: Oxfam 'The facts about poverty'

Activity

1 Use the information in the fact file to write a report describing the effects of living in poverty on a family.

Helping the Unemployed

The United Kingdom is called a **welfare state**. This means that the government provides help and support for those less fortunate in our society. Being unemployed most definitely decreases the life chances of those who experience it, and the government provides different forms of help to try and meet the needs of unemployed people.

The needs of the unemployed are separated into several different areas:

- financial benefits to help unemployed people cope with a loss of income and to provide enough money to support them and their families
- help with finding a job
- training programmes to help people find work and to provide training to equip them with new and modern skills.

Jobseekers Allowance

Jobseekers allowance (JSA) is paid if you are unemployed but are capable of work and are actively seeking work. You also need to be under retirement age, not working or working less than 16 hours per week.

Contribution Based JSA

If you have paid National Insurance contributions you will be able to get contribution based JSA. You cannot normally get JSA if you are aged under 18 and any redundancy payments and other money you get when a job ends may affect your JSA. Contribution based JSA is paid at a fixed rate based on your age for up to 26 weeks.

Income Based JSA

The amount of money that you receive with income based JSA is less than with contribution JSA. It is a means tested benefit and more conditions apply. Those with savings of over £8000 usually cannot get income based JSA, and savings of over £3000 usually affect how much JSA you can get.

If you have a partner who works even part time their earnings will affect the amount of income based JSA you can get.

Receiving this type of JSA will, however, allow you to access other income support related benefits such as:

- help with housing costs and housing benefit
- help with council tax
- extra money for your family, such as a clothing grant for school age children
- free NHS prescriptions, dental treatment and eye glasses
- free school meals
- free milk and vitamins for pregnant women and those with children under five
- Social Fund Crisis Loan to help with emergency expenditure, such as buying a new cooker.

16 and 17 Year Olds

If you are aged 16 or 17 you are unlikely to have worked long enough to qualify for contribution based JSA.

If you are an unemployed person of this age you may be able to get income based JSA for a short period in special circumstances. For example:

- you are forced to live away from your parents
- you are a member of a couple who has a child
- you will suffer severe hardship if you do not get JSA.

If you are 16 or 17 and unable to work you may be able to get income support, but would be more likely to be placed on a training scheme.

Jobseekers Interviews

If you claim JSA you will be given a New Jobseekers Interview. At the interview, an adviser will:

- make sure you understand the rules for JSA
- discuss the types of work you may be looking for and the best ways to find a job
- give you any help you may need to fill in forms.

To get JSA you must have a Jobseekers Agreement. You and your adviser will make the agreement and you will both sign it. You must report or sign on at the Jobcentre every two weeks and must attend for other interviews to look at your situation.

Jobseekers Agreement

The agreement will include details of:

- your availability for work
- the kind of work you are looking for
- what you will do to look for work and improve your chances of finding work
- how the jobcentre will help you.

If you are under 18, your agreement will cover areas such as training courses you may need to attend as well as finding work. You will not be able to get JSA if you do not have this Jobseekers Agreement. If you are receiving contribution based JSA you may reject offers of work, for the first six months, on the basis of pay or suitability.

After six months you will have to sign a new agreement to get income based JSA. Under this agreement you will not be able to refuse a job on the basis of pay or suitability. If you do you may lose your benefits. This means that people can be forced into jobs they do not want to do.

Contribution-based	
Aged 16–17	£33.85
Aged 18–24	£44.50
Aged 25 plus	£56.20
Income-based	
Single aged 16–17	£33.85
Single aged 18–24	£44.50
Couple aged 25+	£56.20
Couple both 18+	£88.15
Lone parents aged 16–17	£33.85
Lone parents 18+	£56.20
Addition for dependent children under 19	£43.88

Figure 3.32 JSA benefits in January 2005

Jobcentre Plus

Jobcentre Plus is a modern service for people of working age who are claiming benefits. It's there to give people help and support to find work and become independent. It is at the heart of the Government's strategy for welfare reform and brings together the Employment service, which runs Jobcentres, and those parts of the Benefits Agency which provide services to people of working age. The main role of Jobcentre Plus is to provide a work focus for everyone of working age, who is claiming benefit.

Everyone who makes a claim for a working age benefit will have to take part in a meeting with a personal adviser. Advice is given on how to find work, training or other support such as childcare.

Access to job vacancies is provided through such things as a telephone service, use of the Internet and touch screen job points in the offices.

Source: Jobcentre plus leaflet

New Deal

New Deal is part of the government's strategy to get people off benefits and into work. It is meant to give unemployed people the chance to develop the skills and experience that employers want so that they can find suitable work.

At the same time it aims to improve the overall skills base of the British workforce and provide help to employers who are suffering from skilled staff shortages. It is compulsory for all those claiming JSA for 18 months or more.

Under the New Deal service you are given a personal adviser, who will remain with through the programme. The job of the adviser is to:

- **get to know you so you end up with a suitable job**
- **discuss with you what kind of job you would like**
- **help you look and apply for jobs**
- **help you overcome anything that might be stopping you getting work. This could anything from a problem with reading and writing to problems with travelling to a job**
- **identify any extra support you may need, such as interview technique or searching for work.**

Activities

1 What are the main needs of unemployed people?

2 In what ways does the government attempt to meet these needs?

3 Explain what jobseekers allowance is.

4 In what ways does JSA open the door to other benefits?

5 What is the situation with 16 and 17 year olds?

6 Why do you think that the Government forces 16 and 17 year olds into paid training schemes rather than give them any benefits?

7 Why is the Jobseekers Agreement considered to be so important?

8 'JSA weekly benefits are more than enough for a person to live on. Poverty is due to laziness.'

'Poverty is due to injustice in our society. Benefit levels are too low for people to live on.'

Which of these statements do you agree with?

Employment and Unemployment

Use the information from the sources to argue your point of view.

9 What are the main features of the Government's New Deal?

10 How do people qualify to join the New Deal programme?

11 'New Deal is simply a way to force long-term unemployed people into jobs, no matter whether these jobs are suitable or not.'

'New Deal is a new concept that put the needs of the unemployed first. The main focus is to get to know the unemployed person and decide what is best for them.'

Which of these two statements is closest to your own opinion of the New Deal. You must give reasons to justify your decision.

Case Study 1: the unemployed person

'My name is Rambai. I worked as machinist until my factory closed down. There is not much work for machinists in my area as most factories are closing down. I went to the jobcentre and was put on a new deal programme, and given a personal adviser to help me. We talked about what sort of job I wanted and I said that I had always wanted to work in retailing, but because I had a steady job, I'd kept putting it off.

After meeting with my adviser I went on some exercise courses, learning about filling in application forms and helping with going to interviews, with advice on what to wear and things like that. My adviser also put me on a temporary placement to let me get experience of working in shops, as this is what most employers were looking for. While on my placement I saw an advert for a new DIY store that was ➤

opening. My adviser phoned for me and I went for an interview and got the job.

I've found New Deal very easy. They gave me bus fares for getting to interviews and money for coffee and meals. I did one interview quite a distance from my home and they gave me money for the train. They even helped me save on my phone bill, some of my interviews were on the phone, and they let me do them from their offices.'

Figure 3.33 Rambai's story

Case Study 2: New Deal personal adviser

Minal has been involved with New Deal since the programme was launched.

'I'd been working in a job centre for about a year before New Deal started, and I could see that a lot of the time, when we were trying to help someone looking for work, we could only take them so far. You never developed a close relationship with your customers and you couldn't follow their progress.

Our interviews with New Deal customers are quite casual, because we want to put people at their ease when we meet them. We try to get them to talk about themselves, so that we understand what they need from us. The best part of the job is trying something you've not tried before. I had one person who wanted to be an environmental adviser. I knew nothing about it, so I went to find out more about the job and managed to get him a placement with the council.

We can also use special funding to try different ways of overcoming barriers. For example, ➤

we recently bought a bike for a customer, because he wouldn't have been able to get to work on time by public transport.

New Deal has definitely been a big step forward. Now, with one adviser taking them through all the different stages, we can actually see how people are progressing and provide the support they need.'

Figure 3.34 Minal's story

FACT FILE
New Deal
- 414,2000 people aged between 18–24 into work between 1999 and March 2003
- 135,900 people aged 25 plus into work between 2001 and March 2003
- 98,040 people aged 50 plus into work between April 2000 and March 2003
- 12,449 people with disabilities into work between July 2001 and March 2003
- 186,260 lone parents into work between September 2001 and March 2003

New Deal 50 plus

This is a programme for people aged over 50 who have been out of work and claiming benefits for at least six months. It helps people by providing:

- **personal support and advice to find a job**
- **a £1,500 in-work training grant**
- **access to financial support when in work**
- **the amount depends on your income and circumstances**
- **help to start up your own business,**

Activities

1 'The case of Rambai shows that New Deal forces people to take low paid jobs such as those in DIY stores.'

2 In what ways does Minal's story highlight the positive aspects of the New Deal programme?

3 In what ways does the factfile show New Deal in a very positive light?

4 In what ways is New Deal 50 plus different from the other New Deal programmes?

5 What is your own opinion of the New Deal programme?

Figure 3.35 Logo of Scottish Enterprise

Figure 3.36 Scottish Enterprise Headquarters, Atlantic Quay in Glasgow

Scottish Enterprise

Scottish Enterprise is Scotland's main economic development agency, funded by the Scottish Executive, with its headquarters in Glasgow. It covers 93 per cent of the population, from Grampian to the Borders. Its job is to help the people and businesses of Scotland succeed, by creating jobs and improving skills and training. The main stated aim is to build a world-class economy. In order to achieve this, Scottish Enterprise has identified four main areas where it tries to provide support:

- **to help new businesses get started**
- **to help support and develop existing businesses**
- **to help people gain the knowledge and skills for the jobs of the future**
- **to help Scottish businesses compete in the world economy by highlighting Scotland's reputation as a good place to live, work and do business.**

Employment and Unemployment

As well as companies, Scottish Enterprise also works with individuals, universities, colleges, local authorities and other public bodies to achieve its main targets.

Regional Selective Assistance

Regional Selective Assistance (RSA) is a national grant scheme, aimed at encouraging investment and job creation in the areas of Scotland, which have high unemployment and which are classified as needing aid under European Union law.

These areas are called Assisted Areas and businesses of all sizes can apply for RSA, whether they are Scottish owned or owned outside Scotland. Levels of grants depend on the size of the project and the area's need for assistance. In the five years to the end of March 2003, businesses in Scotland have gained almost 1000 grants worth £430 million.

Case Study 1

Fluid Creative is a Glasgow based creative and Internet agency, specialising in consultancy, graphic design, web development, advertising and marketing. Since its establishment it has worked with a host of well-known companies including Scottish Enterprise, EMI, Virgin Records and Simple Minds.

The company received a grant of £80,000 in April 2002 to expand the business. At that time the company had 9 employees and the money was used to fund a further 12 new jobs.

Case Study 2

Two grants have been given to motor and home insurer Esure, which is part of the HBOS group. The first grant of £1 million was made in 2001 to establish a centre in Glasgow. The grant helped create 400 jobs. In July 2002 a second grant of £250,000 was given to create a further 175 jobs.

Committee Calls For Retention of Regional Funding in Scotland

The Scottish Parliament's European Committee has called for the protection of regional aid and warned that major reductions in the scheme could hit Scotland's most deprived areas.

Scotland currently benefits from £1.1 billion of funds. The committee highlights the possible impact on Scotland with the planned entry to the EU of underdeveloped countries from central and Eastern Europe. The committee has accepted the need to bring the economies of these countries up to a level of other EU members but has also called for reforms to make sure our own less well off regions do not suffer.

Such funds are aimed at helping the most deprived regions of the EU to improve their economies. In Scotland, areas such as the Highlands and Islands, cities such as Glasgow and Edinburgh, parts of Fife, Lanarkshire and many rural areas have benefited from these funds.

Source: Scottish Parliament News Release, July 2003

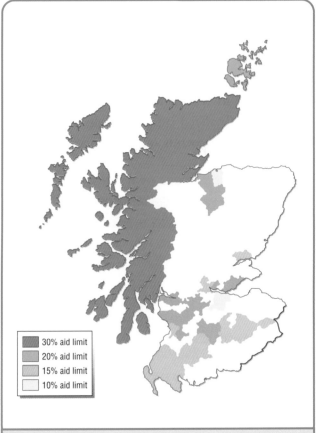

30% aid limit
20% aid limit
15% aid limit
10% aid limit

Figure 3.37 Map of assisted areas

GENERAL/CREDIT

Figure 3.37 shows the areas eligible for regional aid under the RSA and Highlands and Islands Enterprise schemes. The code tells you how much a project could qualify for in each area.

These assisted areas have been agreed by the EU and remain assisted areas until the end of 2006.

Activities

1 In what ways does Scottish Enterprise attempt to help Scottish businesses?

2 What is Regional Selective Assistance?

3 'RSA has largely been a failure. It spends large amounts of money to bring foreign firms to Scotland only to see them close and leave the workers unemployed after a few years.' How do the two case studies show that the person making this statement is being selective in their use of the facts?

4 'Scotland receives a large amount of funding from the EU to help with job creation, in areas of deprivation. These areas can be very grateful that this funding will be received for many years to come.' Explain how the person making this statement could be accused of exaggeration.

5 Which areas of Scotland are named as being the most deprived?

6 Figure 3.37 shows the level of aid, which is available to different parts of Scotland. Say which areas receive the most aid and explain why you think this is the case.

Families with Dependent Children

The Family

Most people in the UK live in a family. Some families are large and some are small, with possibly only two people in them. Nowadays people are more likely to marry in their late 20s or 30s and have fewer children. For example, in 1991 the average age of a first marriage was 25 years of age for a female and 27 years for a male, in 2002 this had risen to 29 years for females and 31 years for males.

There are three main family types:

◆ the nuclear family
◆ the extended family
◆ the lone parent family.

The Nuclear Family

Figure 4.1 A nuclear family

This family type is one where a married couple lives in the same house as their children. This type of family is often also called a traditional family. Although this is the traditional family in Scotland it is one that is becoming less popular – only 23 per cent of families in 2003 were traditional families.

The Extended Family

An extended family is one where different generations of the same family live together in the same house. This could be:

◆ **parents, their children and the grandparents**
◆ **parents, grown up children and their children**
◆ **a couple who are both married for the second time who live with children from previous marriages.**

Extended families are most often of the type that include grandparents.

Extended families are more likely to be supported in the Scottish Asian community than the white community. This is because many Asian families feel they have a traditional duty to support elderly relatives in their own homes. In addition, fewer Asian women work because they are looking after children or an elderly relative.

This tradition has died out amongst many of the white community because many people feel they do not have a big enough house, do not have the time or believe the welfare state should look after the elderly.

Figure 4.2 An extended family

Having a grandparent live in the same house can be very useful when it comes to child minding to allow both parents to go out to work.

Activities

1 Name three types of family. *(3 marks)*

2 Describe a nuclear family. *(2 marks)*

3 Describe the differences between a nuclear family and an extended family. *(2 marks)*

4 Why are extended families more common amongst the Scottish Asian community? *(2 marks)*

5 List an advantage and disadvantage of living in an extended family. *(4 marks)*

Lone Parents

A lone parent family is one where a single adult is bringing up children on their own. Some of these families are single mothers who have never married. Most become lone parent families because of divorce, death or separation.

Figure 4.3 A single parent family

An increasing number of families consist of couples living together and raising children, without being married. In recent years divorce, separation and births outside marriage have been growing at a very high rate.

According to the 2001 census, lone parents headed just under 20 per cent of families in Scotland and 91.5 per cent of these lone parents were women as Figure 4.4 shows.

Scotland in total	151,426
Male	12,756
Female	138,696

Figure 4.4 Lone parents in Scotland 2001
Source GROS

The number of lone mothers has grown so much that by 2001, 20 per cent of mothers with dependant children were lone mothers. Teenage mothers make up only about 3–4 per cent of this total.

Families with Dependent Children

Activities

1 What is a lone parent family?   *(2 marks)*

2 List the four possible reasons how a family may become a single parent one. *(2 marks)*

3 What does the 2001 census tell us about lone parent families?   *(4 marks)*

4 What percentage of lone parents are teenage mothers?   *(2 marks)*

Divorce

The two most common types of households in Scotland in 2003 were:

1 a couple in a first marriage (the most common type)

2 single people who had never married.

Until the 1980s, the gradual increase in the numbers of lone mothers was mainly due to the growing number of divorces in Scotland.

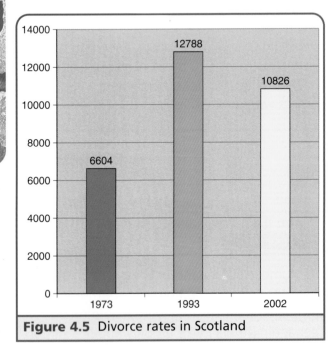

Figure 4.5 Divorce rates in Scotland

Nowadays divorce is less common because more people are living together instead of marrying and a breakdown in this type of relationship does not require a divorce.

The Divorce Act 1976 (Scotland) introduced a new set of rules for divorce. This meant that couples who had not lived together for two to five years could file for divorce simply on the grounds of being separated and not living together. This meant that no one had to blame the other for the break-up of the marriage.

In 2002, separation was the most frequent reason for divorce, accounting for 80 per cent of all divorces. 30 per cent of all divorces were for couples aged 20 or under. This is a fall from 60 per cent in 1981 but it is not unexpected since the number of marriages where the couples were under 20 has fallen from 36 per cent in 1981 to just 4 per cent in 2002. The explanation for this fall may be due to more couples living together rather than getting married.

Since the high rates of the 1980s and 1990s, the number of divorces has not increased significantly, but the number of single mothers has more than doubled. Despite this increase in single mothers, marriage breakdown and death are still the most common reasons for lone parents.

Family type	1981	1991	2001
Married couple with one dependent child	18%	17%	17%
Married couple with two or more dependent children	70%	66%	60%
Lone mother with one dependent child	3%	5%	6%
Lone mother with two or more dependent children	7%	12%	15%
Lone father with one dependent child	1%	0%	1%
Lone father with two or more dependent children	1%	1%	1%

Figure 4.6 Family type and number of dependent children: 1981 to 2001, percentage of dependent children in each family type
Source Office for National Statistics

Activities

1   What were the two most common types of households in Scotland in 2003?   *(2 marks)*

2   Up to the 1980s what was the major reason for lone parent families?   *(2 marks)*

3   Why is divorce less common nowadays?   *(2 marks)*

4   What new set of rules did the Divorce Act 1976 (Scotland) introduce?   *(2 marks)*

5   In 2002, what was the most common reason for divorce?   *(2 marks)*

6   What is the percentage fall in divorces in the under–20 age group between 1981 and 2002?   *(2 marks)*

7   Since the 1990s, what has happened to the number of single mothers?   *(2 marks)*

8   From Figure 4.6 explain what has happened to the number of single mothers compared to single fathers.   *(4 marks)*

Income

About 70 per cent of families received some sort of social security benefit in 2003. Some benefits like child benefit are universally available – almost all families with dependent children receive child benefit.

A large number of lone parent families also receive income-related benefits such as housing benefit, council tax benefit and income support. Lone parents are more likely to be women who also have no job and live in poor housing. 75 per cent of lone parents live on income support.

Many lone parents do not have to rely on benefits. Some are divorced or separated and receive money from ex-partners. The majority do rely on benefits.

Lone parents tend to remain on benefits for longer periods of time than other families. This means that their children experience disadvantage over a longer period of time. For example, the number of children in poverty in Scotland has trebled in the last 15 years. Poverty is not simply about lack of income. It adversely affects:

◆   health

◆   education

◆   housing.

Figure 4.8   Poor housing

Family type	% Income support	% Housing benefit	% Council tax benefit
All family types	17	17	21
Couples with dependent children	10	10	12
Couples with no children	6	5	8
Single with dependent children	63	60	61
Single with no children	18	13	14

Figure 4.7   Percentages of family types on different low-income benefits
Source   Office for National Statistics

Families with Dependent Children

Family situation	Under 6 Months	1 Year to 2 Years	2 Years and over
Unemployed	21	15	8
Sick/Disabled	3	10	78
Lone parents	5	15	63

Figure 4.9 Families and length of time on benefits May 2003

Source Office for National Statistics

Case Study

Anne Gray is a lone parent. She stays in a two-room council flat in Glasgow with her four-year old son Thomas.

She receives child benefit, income support and housing benefit. Her weekly income is £90.90, out of which she has to pay £15 towards housing costs such as electricity and gas, and money to a catalogue company.

Figure 4.10 Anne Gray

She has very little money left to buy other things. She does not drink, smoke or go out socialising. She buys all of her food at the cheapest shops and uses the cheapest brands.

Before Thomas was born, Anne worked in a call centre. She would love to get back to work. The cost of childcare and the long hours prevent her from doing this.

She feels she is caught in a poverty trap and there is no escape.

Activities

1 What percentage of families were receiving social security benefits in 2003? *(1 mark)*

2 List three types of income-related benefits? *(3 marks)*

3 What percentage of lone parents receive income support? *(1 mark)*

4 From Figure 4.7, what do we learn from comparing couples with dependent children with lone parents with dependent children? *(4 marks)*

5 What link can be made between lone parent families and poverty? *(3 marks)*

6 Apart from income, what other parts of life are affected by poverty? *(3 marks)*

7 From Figure 4.9, what is the percentage of lone parents who have been on benefits for two years or more? *(2 marks)*

8 From the case study, which benefits does Anne Gray receive? *(2 marks)*

9 How much has Anne left from her income after paying out weekly amounts? *(2 marks)*

10 What problems does Anne face in going back to work? *(2 marks)*

11 Why is the term 'poverty trap' a good description of Anne's situation? *(2 marks)*

Childcare and Employment

Lone parents face many problems in finding a job. Often single parents need to pay for childcare to allow them to go out to work. Many cannot afford to pay for this.

The choice of work is often limited because of caring for young children. This may mean that they could only work during school or nursery hours. Many young single mothers have not completed their education. This means that they do not have the educational qualifications that employers are looking for.

Groups	Under 5	5 to 11	11 to 16
Unemployed	50	21	12
Sick/disabled	96	88	82
Lone parents	403	274	141

Figure 4.11 Families on benefits by group and age of youngest child: May 2003 (figures in thousands)

Source Office for National Statistics

Housing

Only 15 per cent of lone parents own their home compared with 60 per cent of the population as a whole. 86 per cent live in rented accommodation.

Lone parents find it difficult to buy a home because of unemployment and a reliance on benefits. They tend to be more concentrated in poorer areas with lower quality council houses. According to Scottish Homes 70 per cent of all lone parents live in council housing and of this 40 per cent live in the poorest areas in the country.

'We cannot go out to work because of the high costs of childcare. This makes us second-class citizens who have to live on benefits. We also have live in the poorest houses in the worst areas. On top of everything, we have to put up with people looking down on us all the time.'

a single parent

Health and Education

There is a great deal of research, which shows that people living on low incomes experienced greater health problems. This has been shown to be the result of a combination of factors such as stress, diet, housing and environment.

There is also increasing evidence, which shows that many children from lone parent families do less well and display more behavioural problems in school.

Activities

1 Why is childcare a major problem for lone parents who want to work? *(2 marks)*

2 What other problem do younger lone parents have in getting a good job? *(2 marks)*

3 Look at Figure 4.11. Which group is receiving the most benefits? *(2 marks)*

4 Which type of families by the age group of children receive most benefits? *(2 marks)*

5 What housing problems do lone parents face? *(2 marks)*

6 Explain the link between low income and poor health. *(2 marks)*

7 What effect does poverty have on the education of children? *(2 marks)*

Benefits

The government provides a range of help and benefits to people who are not in work or on low incomes. The range of benefits includes:

◆ income support
◆ housing benefit
◆ council tax rebate
◆ jobseekers allowance
◆ the social fund
◆ child tax credit
◆ working tax credit.

Many of the benefits mentioned above have been covered in previous sections and will not be discussed here.

Child Tax Credit

Child tax credit is a new system of support for children that began in 2003 but was not fully running until April 2004. It replaces the children's tax credit and parts of the income support and jobseekers allowance.

Families with Dependent Children

Child tax credit is paid directly to the person mainly responsible for the care of a child, usually the mother. This is a big change because in the past it was paid in the wage packet to the main earner, usually the father.

To be eligible for a child tax credit the person applying must be a single person, a married couple or a man and woman living together as husband and wife, be over 16 years and have a child under 16 or have a young person aged 16 to 19 who is in full time education.

Working Tax Credit

This benefit was introduced in April 2003. It is paid to workers without children who have a low income, and to couples or single parents with children who are in work. It also includes an amount to help pay for childcare. Working tax credits are available to people who have a child, if they are over 16 years and work at least 16 hours a week. Or if they are over 25 years old and work at least 30 hours a week. Also if they have a disability that hinders them getting a job and are 16. Finally, if a person is over 50 and returning to work after being on benefits

The purpose of this benefit is to help people to go out to work and to make sure that they will receive at least as much as they would if on benefits.

Part of the benefit is aimed at helping with the costs of childcare and will pay for up to 70 per cent of childminding costs while the parent goes to work.

Activities

1 What is child tax credit? *(3 marks)*

2 How is child tax credit paid? *(2 marks)*

3 Why has there been a big change from the past with child tax credit? *(2 marks)*

4 Who is eligible for child tax credit? *(3 marks)*

5 What are the rules which allow a person to claim working tax credit? *(4 marks)*

6 What is the purpose of working tax credit? *(2 marks)*

7 Looking at Figure 4.12 and list the main benefits that a person on a low income can expect to receive. *(3 marks)*

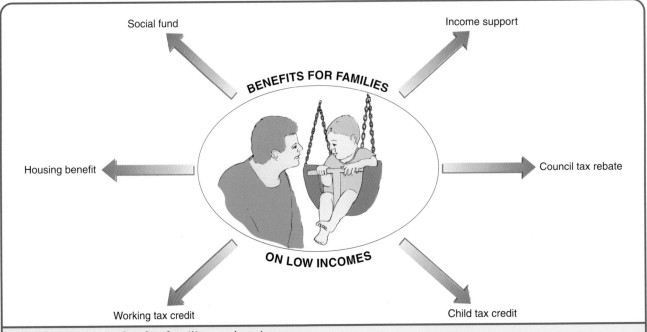

Figure 4.12 Benefits for families on low incomes

The Child Support Agency

The Child Support Agency (CSA) was set up in 1993. One of its aims was to save £500 million per year by removing income support from some lone parent families. It does this by trying to make sure that absent parents, mostly fathers, contribute money to help support their children. 90 per cent of lone parents are women.

The CSA looks at the needs of both the child and the absent parent. Safeguards have been put in place to make sure that absent parents do not pay more than 30 per cent of their income in maintenance payments. If an absent parent cannot be tracked down then the level of maintenance payable will increase over time.

Criticisms of the CSA

The CSA is controversial and has attracted criticism from absent parents, women's groups and children's organisations:

◆ some lone parents feel forced to give the name of absent parents with whom they do not wish to have any contact, possibly fearing violence from them

◆ parents who do not help track down such partners may lose benefits

◆ financial demands on the absent parents may affect a good relationship

◆ some parents may actually be worse off as they might lose some benefits which come with income support such as free school meals, clothing grants and housing benefit

◆ absent fathers complain that the money left after paying maintenance is not enough to live on.

Activities

1 Why was the CSA set up? *(2 marks)*

2 Give four reasons to explain why the CSA has come in for criticism. *(4 marks)*

Pressure Groups

The 2001 census figures show a 66 per cent increase in lone parent families in Scotland over the last 10 years. About 50 per cent of all families in Glasgow are lone parent families, mainly headed by single mothers.

Pressure groups offer support and look after the interests of lone parents. These groups include:

◆ **lone parents' forums**

◆ **women's groups**

◆ **One Plus.**

Many lone parents need childcare support such as nurseries and crèches to let them look for work or take part in opportunities for training and education.

One Plus was set up in 1986 and it has offices throughout Scotland. It is Europe's largest lone parent organisation and helps deliver a variety of support in childcare, health education, counselling, financial advice, education and training.

'One plus works with a range of partners to provide training and employment within local communities to help tackle the poverty facing so many one parent families.

Their aim is to provide training for work and access to support for travel and childcare, improving lone parents' incomes as well as allowing a balance between work and family commitments.

The work is "family focused" and the needs of children are at the centre of this work.'

Source: One Plus Newsletter

FOUNDATION/GENERAL

173

Families with Dependent Children

One Plus, together with other groups like the children's charity NCH, also lobbies the government for policies and changes to the law which affect the lives of lone parents.

'We need policies that offer a lot more support to make lone parents family lives easier and not harder.'

Source: Maggie Mellon, NCH

Activities

1 What is the level of one-parent families in Glasgow? *(2 marks)*

2 How do women's pressure groups look after the interests of women? *(3 marks)*

3 Describe the work of the pressure group One Plus. *(3 marks)*

4 Why would the support being offered by One Plus be important to lone parents? *(3 marks)*

5 The work is 'family focused.' What does this mean? *(2 marks)*

6 What does Maggie Mellon want the government to do for lone parent families? *(3 marks)*

Families with Dependent Children

The Family

Not everyone one in Scotland lives in the same type of family. Families come in all different shapes and sizes, from very large to very small. The trend nowadays is for people to marry later and to have fewer children.

In 1991, the average age of a first marriage was 25 years of age for a female and 27 years for a male. By 2002 this had risen to 29 years for females and 31 years for males. This trend to marry later in life means that families generally have fewer children today.

Family Types

The **traditional** family is one where a married couple lives in the same house as their children. This type of family is often also called a nuclear family. Although this is the traditional type of family in Scotland, it is one which is becoming less and less popular. Only 23 per cent of families fit this model in 2003.

An **extended family** is one where different generations live together in the same house. This could be parents, children and grandparents. It could also be mum, dad, grown up children with their own children, or it could be a couple married for the second time who live together with sets of children from their previous marriages.

Extended families are generally ones which includes grandparents. This is especially true amongst Asian families in Scotland. Having a grandparent live in the same house can be very useful when it comes to childminding, allowing both parents to go out to work.

Lone parent families are where one adult is bringing up children on their own. Some of these families are single mums who have never married. Most have, however become lone parent families as a result of divorce, death or separation.

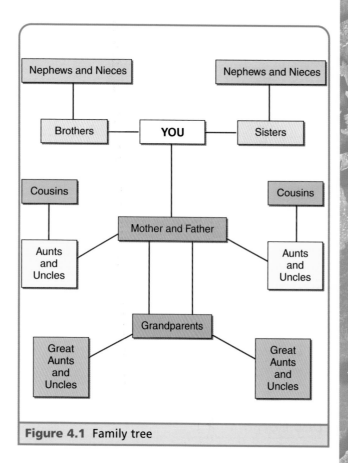

Figure 4.1 Family tree

An increasing number of families consist of cohabiting couples. This is when couples live together, often raising children, without being married.

Families with Dependent Children

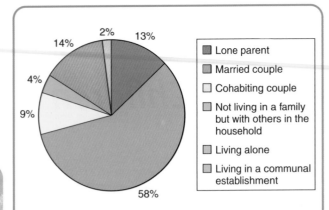

Figure 4.2 Types of family in Scotland 2001 (Census)
Source www.scrol.gov.uk

Scotland in total	151,426
Male	12,756
Female	138,696

Figure 4.3 Lone parents in Scotland 2001
Source 2001 Census Scotland

Activities

1 'Traditional families are the most common type of family structure in Scotland.'

What points would you put forward in order to disprove this statement?

2 Describe the main differences between nuclear families and extended families.

3 Draw your own family tree, using the same format as the one shown in Figure 4.1.

4 What would be the main advantages and disadvantages of living in an extended family situation?

Lone Parents

There have been many changes to the patterns of family life and to the types of families that are to be found living in Scotland today. Certain changes have meant that some sections of the population are much more vulnerable to poverty and all the problems that it brings.

Divorce, separation and births outside marriage have been increasing at a very high rate.

According to the 2001 Census, lone parents headed 13 per cent of families in Scotland, and 91.5 per cent of these lone parents were women. Teenage mothers make up only about 3–4 per cent of lone parent families.

Divorce

The most common type of household in Scotland in 2003 was a couple in a first marriage. The next most common type was single people who had never married.

Until the 1980s, the gradual increase in the numbers of lone mothers was mainly the result of the increasing rate of divorce in the country. In 1973, 6604 marriages ended in divorce. By 1993, this had risen to 12,788. In 2002 the number had fallen back to 10,826. The reason for this may be that there is now a move away from divorce, but it is more likely that more people are cohabiting instead of marrying and the breakdown of cohabiting relationships is not the subject of divorce proceedings.

The Divorce Act 1976 (Scotland) introduced new grounds for divorce, mainly non-cohabitation. This meant that couples who had not lived together for two to five years could file for divorce simply on the grounds of non-cohabitation (being separated and not living together).

In 2002. separation was the most frequent reason for divorce, accounting for 80 per cent of all divorces. Separation (2 years) increased from 25 per cent of all divorces in 1981 to over 50 per cent of all divorces in 2002. Separation (5 years) increased from 14 per cent to 24 per cent.

The other reasons for divorce, mainly adultery, desertion and unreasonable behaviour have all fallen. For example, divorces on the grounds of adultery have fallen from 17 per cent in 1981 to four per cent in 2002.

In 2002, 30 per cent of all divorces were to couples aged 20 or under. This is a fall from 60 per cent in 1981, but is not unexpected since the proportion of marriages where the couples were under 20 has fallen from 36 per cent in 1981 to just four per cent in 2002. The changing balance between cohabiting relationships, and marriage may affect this fall.

Since the high rates of the 1980s and 1990s the number of divorces has not increased significantly, but the number of single mothers has more than doubled. Despite this increase in single mothers, marriage breakdown and death of the husband/wife are still the most common reasons for lone parents.

Status of parent	% in 1981	% in 1991	% in 2001
Married/cohabiting couple	87	81	75
Lone mother	11	18	22
Single	2	6	10
Widowed	2	1	1
Divorced	4	6	7
Separated	2	4	4
Lone father	2	1	3
All lone parents	13	19	25

Figure 4.6 Marital status and dependent children, 1981 to 2001 (%)
Source 2001 Census

Activities

1 Describe the main causes for the changes in family life in Scotland today.

2 'The increases in lone parents is a myth. The balance of families is the same as it has always been.'

   Use the statistics from this page to disprove this statement.

3 Explain why has divorce become much more common in recent years.

4 What changes have there been in the reasons for divorce?

Activities

1 Study Figure 4.4.

   'Marriage as a way of life is finished.'

   How does the table disprove this statement?

2 'Lone fathers are just as likely to be bringing up their children as lone mothers.'

   In what way does Figure 4.6 show this statement to be exaggerated?

3 Outline the changes in family life shown in Figure 4.5.

4 'The main reasons for lone parents in this country is the death rate among men. Most lone parents are widows.' Study Figure 4.6 and give a detailed explanation as to why this statement is an exaggeration.

5 What picture of family life today do the tables give you?

Status	% Population
Single (never married)	30.55
Married (first marriage)	44.27
Remarried	5.52
Separated	3.57
Divorced	7.02
Widowed	9.06

Figure 4.4 Marital status 2003
Source www.gro-scotland.gov.uk (abridged)

Family type	1981	1991	2001
Married couple with one dependent child	18%	17%	17%
Married couple with two or more dependent children	70%	66%	60%
Lone mother with one dependent child	3%	5%	6%
Lone mother with two or more dependent children	7%	12%	15%
Lone father with one dependent child	1%	0%	1%
Lone father with two or more dependent children	1%	1%	1%

Figure 4.5 Percentage of dependent children in each family type 1981 to 2001
Source 2001 Census

Families with Dependent Children

Family type	% Income support	% Housing benefit	% Council tax benefit
All family types	17	17	21
Couples with dependent children	10	10	12
Couples with no children	6	5	8
Single with dependent children	63	60	61
Single with no children	18	13	14

Figure 4.7 Benefits by family type 2003
Source www.gov.uk

Income

Some 70 per cent of families receive some sort of social security benefit in 2003. Some benefits like child benefit are universally available. Almost all families with dependent children receive child benefit. A very high proportion of lone parent families also receive income-related benefits such as housing benefit, council tax benefit and income support.

Lone parents are most likely to be women who have no job. They are more likely to live in poor housing and some 75 per cent of lone parents live on income support.

Not all lone parents have to rely on benefits. Many are divorced or separated people who are well provided for by affluent partners. The majority do, however, rely on benefits. They also remain on benefits for longer periods of time than other families. This means that their children experience a wide range of disadvantage and over a longer period of time.

The number of children in poverty in Scotland has trebled in the last 15 years. Poverty is not simply about lack of income: it adversely affects health, education and housing choice and damages children's chances for the future. (Source: Child Poverty Resource Unit.)

Family situation	Under 6 months	1 Year to 2 years	2 Years and over
Unemployed	21	15	8
Sick/Disabled	3	10	78
Lone parents	5	15	63

Figure 4.8 Families and length of time on benefits May 2003
Source Office for National Statistics

Case Study

Anne Gray is 24. She shares her two-room council flat in Glasgow with her four-year old son Thomas.

She receives income support and housing benefit. Her weekly income is £90.90 out of which she has to pay £15 towards housing costs such as electricity and fuel and a debt to a catalogue company for clothes for her son.

She tries very hard to budget her spending, but finds it very difficult. She does not drink, smoke or go out socialising. She buys all of her food at the cheapest shops and uses the cheapest brands.

Before Thomas was born, Anne worked as a customer services operative in a call centre. She would love to get back to work. Her problem however is the cost of childcare and the hours she would have to work.

She feels she is caught in a trap, which keeps her in poverty and does not know how to break free of it.

Childcare and Employment

Lone parents face many problems in finding a job. Often single parents need to pay for childcare to allow them to go out to work. Many cannot afford to pay for this. The choice of work is often limited because of caring for their children. This may mean that they could only work during school or nursery hours. Young single mothers have often failed to complete their education. This means that they will have no educational qualifications that employers may be looking for.

Groups	Under 5	5 to 11	11 to 16
Unemployed	50	21	12
Sick/disabled	96	88	82
Lone parents	403	274	141

Figure 4.9 Families on benefits by group and age of youngest child: May 2003 (figures in thousands)
Source Office for National Statistics

Housing

Only 15 per cent of lone parents live in owner occupation compared with 60 per cent of the population as a whole. 86 per cent live in rented accommodation. Many lone parents find it impossible to own a home because of unemployment and a reliance on benefits.

Lone parents tend to be more concentrated in poorer areas, with lower quality council houses. According to Scottish Homes, 70 per cent of all lone parents live in council housing and, of this, 40 per cent live in areas which have been designated as the poorest areas in the country.

> 'We cannot go out to work because of the high costs of childcare. This makes us second-class citizens who have to live on benefits. We also have live in the poorest houses in the worst areas. On top of everything, we have to put up with people looking down on us all the time.'
>
> A single parent

Health and Education

There is a great deal of research, which shows that people living on low incomes experienced greater health problems. This has been shown to be the result of a combination of factors such as stress, diet, housing and environment.

There is also increasing evidence, which shows that many children from lone parent families do less well and display more behavioural problems in school.

Activities

1 What evidence is there that most lone parents are on a low income?

2 Study Figure 4.7. What does it tell you about families and benefits?

3 How would being on benefits affect children?

4 'Lone parents are the group which rely most on benefits. They are also the group which stays on benefits the longest.' How does Figure 4.8 show this statement to be exaggerated?

5 What problems would Anne Gray have in bringing up her son?

6 Outline the problems that Anne would have if she wanted to get back to work.

7 'It does not matter what age your child is. If a person really wants to work they will find a way.' In what way does Figure 4.9 refute this statement?

8 What housing and social problems do lone parents experience?

9 What evidence is there that lone parents are concentrated in the worst off areas?

10 In what ways other than financial can being part of a lone parent family affect children?

Benefits

The UK government provides a range of help and benefits to people who are unemployed or on low incomes. These benefits have been looked at in detail in the section on the unemployed and the help that they receive.

The range of benefits includes:

◆ **income support**
◆ **housing benefit**
◆ **council tax rebate**
◆ **jobseekers allowance**
◆ **the social fund**
◆ **family tax credit**
◆ **child tax credit.**

Working Tax Credit

This is the one benefit that is specific to low paid workers and families. It is a weekly benefit paid to people who have at least one dependent child

GENERAL CREDIT

Families with Dependent Children

under the age of 16 and who work for at least 16 hours per week.

The purpose of this benefit is to help people to go out to work and to ensure that, if they are working, they will receive at least as much as they would if they were on benefits.

It also includes a benefit aimed at specifically helping with the costs of childcare. The child care tax credit will pay for up to 70 per cent of childminding costs if the child is looked after by an approved childminder while the parent goes out to work.

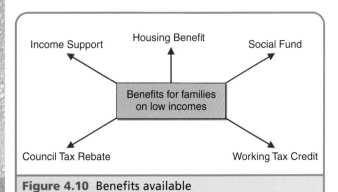

Figure 4.10 Benefits available

Group	Average annual income
Single-parent family	£9,600
Two-parent family	£20,550

Figure 4.11 Annual income of families

Family Type	Wages	Savings	Benefits
Single-parent family	32%	13%	55%
Two-parent family	88%	4%	8%

Figure 4.12 Source of family income

Activities

1   What is the Working Tax Credit?

2   In what way could this benefit help Anne Grey?

3   Copy Figure 4.10 into your workbook. Write a paragraph on each of the benefits shown on your diagram.

4   Study Figure 4.11 and 4.12. Using the sources, what conclusions can be reached about the incomes of single parent families compared to two parent families?

    Comment on at least two differences in your answer.

5   Study Figure 4.13.

    'The benefits system tries to help poor families bring up their children. Benefits are only given to families when the adults are unemployed. Only a very small amount of families with children receive any financial help from the government.'

    Use Figure 4.13 to explain why this statement is an exaggeration.

The Child Support Agency

The Child Support Agency (CSA) was set up in 1993 as part of the Child Support Act.

One of the aims of the Child Support Act was to save £500 million per year by removing income support from some lone parent families. It does this by trying to ensure that absent parents, mostly fathers (90 per cent of lone parents are women), make some contribution towards the support of their children.

The CSA assesses the needs of both the child and the absent parent. Safeguards have been out in place to make sure that absent parents do not pay more than 30 per cent of their income in maintenance payments.

Benefit	Recipients	Number of families in receipt
Child Benefit	All families with children under 16	6.9 million
Working Tax Credit	Low-income workers, including families	0.5 million
Child Tax Credit	Low-income families and families without jobs	Not known
Income Support	Low-income families without jobs	1.0 million

Figure 4.13 Recipients of benefits by different family types

If an absent parent cannot be tracked down then the level of maintenance payable will increase over time.

How Payments Are Calculated

Stage 1

Lone parents receiving or applying for income support are required to give the DSS the name(s) of the absent parent(s) of their children. If the lone parent does not do this then their income support payments may be reduced.

Stage 2

The CSA assesses the needs of the lone parent family. It decides on an amount which the absent parent will make, taking into account their needs and current situation. If the absent parent is unemployed and receiving income support they will not have to pay any contributions.

Stage 3

The parent bringing up the family has the amount, which the absent parent has to pay, deducted from their benefits. If a lone parent received £100 a week in benefit and the absent parent is told to pay £70, this is then deducted from the lone parent's benefit, so they are no better off.

Stage 4

The government has saved £70 per week in benefit payments.

Criticisms of The CSA

The CSA has been very controversial and has attracted criticism from absent parents, women's groups and children's organisations. These include:

- many lone parents feel forced to give the name of absent partners, who may have been violent, with whom they do not wish to have any further contact
- benefits may be withdrawn from parents who do not help track down such partners
- good relationships between both parents can be put under strain because of increased financial demands on the absent parent
- some parents may actually be worse off when they count the loss of certain benefits which come with income support, such as free school meals, clothing grants and housing benefit

- absent fathers complain that the income they are allowed to keep after paying the maintenance decided by the CSA is not enough to live on
- if the absent parent has a second family, the income of their new partner is taken into consideration. This could mean the new partner is paying for the other family
- any good relations between parents are affected because of the CSA activities, making relations more difficult for the family as a whole
- the CSA just goes after the easy targets parents who keep in contact with their children and whose addresses are known – it does not target those who wish to pay nothing and who do not wish to keep in contact with their children
- many also argue that the CSA is just the government's way of saving money.

Activities

1. What is the main aim of the Child Support Agency?

2. What is the overall effect on the amount of money the lone parent may receive?

3. Describe the overall effect on the finances of the absent parent.

4. Which benefits might the lone parent lose if they stopped receiving income support?

5. Explain how many lone parents could find themselves worse off since the setting up of CSA.

6. In what ways can it be said that the CSA makes absent parents face up to their responsibilities?

7. 'The CSA is hated by absent fathers and feared by lone mothers.'

   John Findlay, Director of One Plus.

   Explain what John Findlay means by this statement.

8. Look at the list of criticisms of the CSA. Chose the four criticisms that you consider to be the worst. Explain the reasons for your choice.

FACTFILE

The CSA

The CSA has tracked down over 66,000 absent parents, a success rate of 73 per cent.

More absent fathers that ever before are paying maintenance directly from earnings.

The CSA made mistakes, like sending maintenance demands to the wrong people, to begin with but the number of errors has now been drastically reduced.

The CSA is now responsible for some £130 million being transferred between parents each year.

Activity

Use the information from the fact file and the list of criticisms to write a balanced report on the success or failure of the CSA.

Pressure Groups

Latest census figures show that there has been an increase of lone parent families in Scotland of over 66 per cent in the last 10 years.

Half of all families in Glasgow are currently lone parent families mainly headed by single mothers.

Pressure groups have developed to provide support and champion the cause of these increasing numbers of lone parents.

These groups include lone parents forums, women's groups and One Plus.

Many lone parents need childcare support such as nurseries and creche facilities to allow them to look for work or take part in opportunities for training and education.

One Plus was set up in 1986 and works throughout Scotland. It is Europe's largest lone parent organisation and helps deliver a variety of support in the form of childcare, health education, counselling, financial advice as well as education and training.

'One plus collaborates with a range of partners to create training and employment within local communities to help tackle the poverty facing so many one parent families.

The aim is to provide vocational training and employment, as well as access to a range of support travel and childcare, and thus increase lone parents' incomes as well as enabling a balance between work and family commitments. The work is 'family focused' and the needs of children are at the centre of this work.'

Source: One Plus Newsletter

One Plus, together with other groups like the children's charity NCH, also lobbies the government for policies and changes to the law which affect the lives of lone parents.

'We need policies that offer a lot more support to make lone parents family lives easier and not harder.'

Maggie Mellon, NCH

Activities

1 Describe the work of the pressure group One Plus.

2 Why would the support being offered by One Plus be important to lone parents?

3 'The work is family focused.' What do you understand this statement to mean?

4 Look at the quote from Maggie Mellon. What type of policies do you think that she is looking for the government to introduce?

The Elderly

There are one million elderly people in Scotland – 18 per cent of the population.

It is important to note about the elderly that:

◆ the number of older people will rise by 2051 to over 20 per cent of the entire population

◆ older people own 40 per cent of the country's wealth, so they have spending power

◆ large numbers of older people can use their vote to influence the result of elections.

Population Changes

A country's population changes as a result of deaths, births, emigration and immigration. For most of the twentieth century there were falling death rates and rising birth rates, so the population got bigger. More recently things have changed – Scotland now has a falling birth rate and an increase in the lifespan of its ageing population.

As can be seen by Figure 5.1, in 1993 17.8 per cent of the population was 65 years of age or over. This number is expected to rise to 24.1 per cent by 2051, meaning that about a quarter of the population will be 'pensioners' by that time.

Why are People Living Longer?

A main reason for the increase in numbers of the elderly is that people are living longer because of the National Health Service that provides good healthcare in the UK. Advances in medicine have also wiped out many diseases. People are living longer and have a better quality of life. Better housing and welfare state benefits have also helped people to live longer.

Problems for the Government

The very large increase in the number of elderly people in Scotland and the rest of the UK has brought extra problems for the government in trying to meet the needs of elderly people. This has led to strains on social services such as pensions, housing and medical services.

Government spending on the elderly will have to increase as more people live longer. More state pensions will have to be paid out and spending on benefits such as income support will also have to increase.

At the moment 50 per cent of all NHS beds are taken up by elderly people, and 40 per cent of

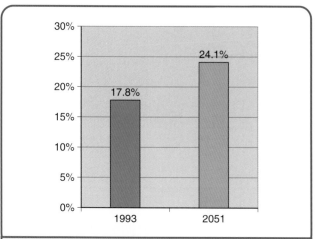

Figure 5.1 Percentage of the population aged 65+ in 1993 and 2051

The Elderly

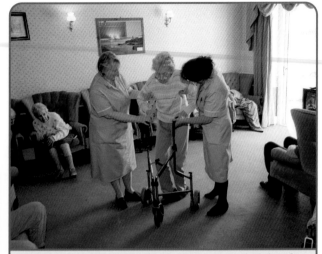

Figure 5.2 The elderly require many kinds of nursing care

all spending on the NHS is taken up by the elderly.

This amount of spending is set to rise as demands for specialist elderly health services increases. Services such as home helps, meals on wheels, community nurses, GPs and carers will be placed under greater strain.

The increases in the numbers of elderly people will also see a large increase in demand for things such as specialised geriatric care, sheltered housing as well as other care housing and nursing homes.

Activities

1. Why is the number of elderly people in Scotland increasing?   *(2 marks)*

2. What percentage of the Scottish population will be elderly by 2051?   *(2 marks)*

3. Describe the improvements that have led to people living longer?   *(4 marks)*

4. In what ways will the increasing numbers of elderly people have an impact on social security spending?   *(4 marks)*

The Elderly in Scotland

The population of Scotland is 5,062,011 (Census 2001). There are almost one million elderly people in Scotland, that's 18.6 per cent of the population. The number of older people is set to rise over the next 50 years to about a quarter of the population.

Officially, men are classed as OAPs (Old Age Pensioners) when they reach 65 years of age and women at 60 years – this is how the elderly are classified.

However, many people live well beyond this age. The average person today can live well over the age of 70, and people reaching 100 years is not uncommon in today's society.

Figure 5.3 Celebrating 100 years

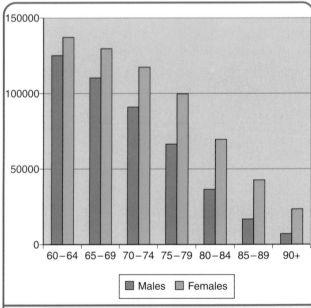

Figure 5.4 Scotland's elderly population by gender 2001

Source Registrar General for Scotland www.gro-scotland.gov.uk

Many more women than men are elderly as women tend to live longer. In Scotland in 2001 there were 325,361 male pensioners (over the age of 65) and 616,621 female pensioners (over the age of 60).

Scotland's Changing Population

Scotland's population will change over the next 20 years, with fewer young people and an increase in the number of older Scots.

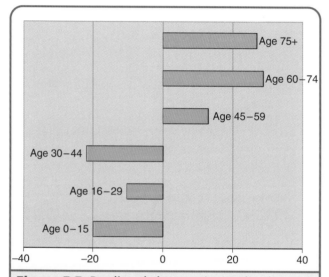

Figure 5.5 Predicted changes in Scotland's population by age group 2000 – 2021
Source Registrar General for Scotland www. gro-scotland.gov.uk

The growing number of elderly people in Britain means that more will have to be paid in pensions as more people live longer.

Following a European Union decision that pension ages should be the same for men and women, the government decided to raise the retirement age of women to 65. This will take effect from 2010.

Activities

1 What is the expected rise in the number of elderly people by 2051? *(2 marks)*

2 Define the term 'OAP'. *(2 marks)*

3 What is the size of the elderly female group in the Scottish population? *(2 marks)*

4 Look at the charts and explain in your own words why some elderly women in particular might suffer from loneliness? *(2 marks)*

5 Look at Figure 5.5, which age groups are going to grow the most in the period 2000–2021? *(2 marks)*

6 Which age groups are going to decline in the same period? *(2 marks)*

7 Why might women complain about the way the government equalised the retirement age? *(2 marks)*

Scottish Factfiles

Standards of Living

◆ Only 12 per cent of pensioners receive income from work.

◆ Single women pensioners are the worst off.

◆ 41 per cent of single pensioners have an income of less than £6,000 per year

◆ 13 per cent of single pensioners have an income of less than £4,000 per year

◆ 16 per cent of single pensioners have an annual income of over £10,000 per year

◆ Pensioners who live in rented accommodation pay 30 per cent of their income on rent

◆ 9 per cent of pensioners living in urban areas have incomes over £15,000 compared with 18 per cent living in rural areas

◆ Poorer and older pensioners spend less money on food and fuel

The Elderly

- 15 per cent of pensioners' houses are in a bad state of repair
- 25 per cent of the worst housing is occupied by pensioners

Health

- The most common diseases of old age are arthritis, heart disease and strokes.
- Eye and ear impairments are more common in older than younger people.

Source Older People in Scotland: Scottish Household Survey
www.scotland.gov.uk/cru

Problems Facing the Elderly – the Needs of the Elderly

One of the most important needs of elderly people is good quality housing that meets their specific requirements. Good quality housing will greatly improve their quality of life of older people.

Activities

Look at the Scottish Factfiles and answer the following questions:

1. Which type of pensioner is the poorest? *(2 marks)*

2. What percentage of pensioners has income of less than £6,000 per year? *(2 marks)*

3. Where do most of the richer pensioners stay? *(2 marks)*

4. How much of their income do pensioners who live in rented accommodation pay on rent? *(2 marks)*

5. Do most pensioners stay in good quality housing? *(2 marks)*

6. From the Figures can we assume that most pensioners have good health? Explain your answer. *(6 marks)*

7. What type of problems faces the elderly who live in disadvantaged areas? *(3 marks)*

8. What are the most common ailments that old people face? *(2 marks)*

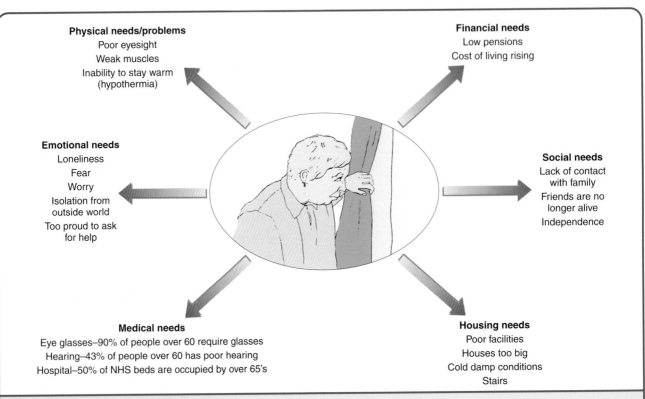

Physical needs/problems
Poor eyesight
Weak muscles
Inability to stay warm (hypothermia)

Financial needs
Low pensions
Cost of living rising

Emotional needs
Loneliness
Fear
Worry
Isolation from outside world
Too proud to ask for help

Social needs
Lack of contact with family
Friends are no longer alive
Independence

Medical needs
Eye glasses–90% of people over 60 require glasses
Hearing–43% of people over 60 has poor hearing
Hospital–50% of NHS beds are occupied by over 65's

Housing needs
Poor facilities
Houses too big
Cold damp conditions
Stairs

Figure 5.6 Needs of the elderly

High-rise flats are totally unsuitable for the following reasons:

◆ lifts may be out of order – the elderly struggle with flights of stairs and may become prisoners in their own homes

◆ being up high, or feeling the wind swaying the building, may increase the anxieties experienced by the elderly

◆ lack of contact with neighbours – social exclusion.

In Scotland, housing has traditionally been provided by local authorities – they currently provide homes for 41 per cent of those aged between 60–75.

In recent years housing associations, voluntary groups and private property companies have provided more housing specifically for elderly people. There is also an increasing variety of different types of housing for the elderly. These include sheltered housing, retirement homes, residential homes, care housing and nursing homes.

Sheltered Housing

Sheltered Housing allows elderly people to be independent within a secure environment. This type of housing is specifically designed to meet the needs of elderly people. It is usually set up as a complex of houses, where the elderly live in their own house with their own facilities. This helps the residents to feel that they have kept their independence, but also to feel safe, as, whenever they need help they can call for it from the warden in the complex.

This is possible as the houses come equipped with special facilities linked to the warden's office. This type of housing also comes with specific features and facilities designed to make life easier for elderly people.

The following features are usually found within a sheltered housing complex:

◆ **warden service provided 24-hours a day** – the warden is there to take care of any

problems and also to provide the residents with a sense of security

◆ community lounge where tenants can meet and socialise while still in the safety of the complex – suitable for activities such as bingo or card games

◆ corridors allow tenants to go for a walk, or visit a friend living there, whilst still feeling safe – many corridors have non-slip surfaces and railings to help mobility

◆ guest rooms allow the occupants to have friends and relatives stay on visits if they do not stay in the area or if a person is ill

◆ laundry room so that residents do not need to pay for their own machines or the cost of using them as heating and power bills are included in the costs of the rent

◆ a TV licence is held by the complex so no individual has to pay for their own licence

◆ ramps and railings are installed to help those with physical disabilities

◆ pressure pads are installed under carpets and linked to the warden's office so that they know when the residents are moving around

◆ pull cords and alarms are positioned so that the warden can be summoned in emergencies.

Case Study

A partnership between Scottish Homes and Kirkcare Housing Association will provide kitchen and dining facilities for 18 sheltered housing tenants.

The £220,000 investment will also create an assisted bathroom and sleep over room. Meals will also be provided with tenants able to benefit from a service that provides one meal a day and 24-hour staff support.

Ewan Johnston, Managing Director for Scottish Homes Glasgow and North Clyde, said, 'It is vital that we provide facilities of a high standard to satisfy the varying needs of the older members of our communities.'

Source: Press Release, 4 May 2000

Year	Houses
1992	32,192
1993	32,267
1994	33,100
1995	33,687
1996	34,976
1997	35,484
1998	36,069
1999	34,752
2000	35,342
2001	34,615
2002	34,247

Figure 5.7 Number of sheltered houses available in Scotland
Source Housing Trends in Scotland

Residential Homes

Residential homes are usually run by a local authorities or private companies as well as voluntary groups. Residents have a higher level of care but do not have as much freedom as in sheltered housing. They usually have the following features:

◆ more one to one care

◆ meals are cooked for the residents and a choice of menu is given

◆ entertainment is usually available

◆ hairdressers usually visit once per week

◆ lounges for family and friends are provided

◆ help is available 24-hours a day.

Residential homes can be an expensive option for elderly people. The cost of staying in one of these homes can be as much as £500 per week. Many private companies have opened private nursing homes and these are run as private businesses. This is a cause of concern to the authorities and the families of elderly residents.

Many homes are well run and provide an excellent standard of care. Others have been accused of putting profit before the welfare of their elderly residents.

The worst homes have been found to be overcrowded, under-staffed and staffed with people with no proper qualifications. Some staff have been accused of cruelty to elderly residents in some of these homes.

Nursing Homes

Nursing homes are very similar to residential homes in many of the facilities they provide. Private companies run many of them but they usually cater for older people with greater needs. This means that they have to provide a greater level of care such as 24-hour care from trained nursing staff. This means that they are also more expensive to stay in than residential homes.

Activities

1 Why are high-rise flats unsuitable for the elderly?   *(3 marks)*

2 How important are local authorities in providing housing for the elderly?   *(2 marks)*

3 List the groups who in recent years have provided more housing for the elderly. *(3 marks)*

4 Describe the typical sheltered housing. *(4 marks)*

5 Identify five important features of sheltered housing.   *(5 marks)*

6 Looking at Figure 5.7, how impressive has the growth in sheltered housing been between 1992 and 2002?   *(2 marks)*

7 From the case study, what are the two organisations going to provide for the elderly?   *(2 marks)*

8 Describe the main differences between sheltered housing and residential nursing homes.   *(4 marks)*

9 What is the major disadvantage of residential homes and nursing homes?   *(2 marks)*

Needs and Problems

An important need for elderly people is health care. The elderly need much more medical help than younger people. In cold countries like Scotland, hypothermia (when body temperature drops due to the cold) can easily affect the elderly.

Common ailments affecting the elderly are those concerning hearing, sight and mobility. Arthritis, fragile bones and bronchitis can also create problems for older people. This is where the system of **primary care** is designed to help the elderly.

Primary care takes place outside of hospitals, in the community. A specific care team, normally located in the local health centre, carries out the primary care of elderly people. The care team would include people such as GPs, community nurses, physiotherapists, chiropodists, occupational therapists, speech therapists and dieticians.

These people often visit elderly people in their own homes making it even easier to receive care. Primary care also helps hospitals to reduce the numbers of elderly people in hospital, thus helping with the problem of bed blocking.

Bed-blocking occurs when patients cannot be admitted to hospital because there are no beds available, due to them being taken up by elderly people. It is estimated that the elderly take up 40 per cent of all hospital beds.

Meeting the Health Care Needs of the Elderly

Many of the health problems of the elderly are looked after by the National Health Service (NHS). It is the job of the NHS to provide health care for those who need it regardless of whether they can pay for it.

NHS Services for the Elderly

Community Nurse: checks blood pressure, changes bandages and checks general health of elderly in their own home.

Optician: sight tests and glasses. Examines eyes for signs of disease.

Dentist: teeth and gum care, but this is means tested.

GP: prescribes medication free of charge and can recommend operations or any further health care.

Health Centres: provides a wide range of services. Doctors and many other health services all under one roof.

Physiotherapist: provides assistance after operations and help elderly people with movement if they suffer from diseases such as arthritis.

Daycare Hospital Units: help carers of the elderly to have a short break. They are taken into hospital and looked after by trained staff who understands their needs.

Geriatric Wards: Hospital wards that are specifically for the needs of elderly hospital patients. Many elderly people end up staying in this ward for long periods of time because they cannot take care of themselves and have no family to help take care of them.

No end to bed-block crisis

A scheme to eliminate bed-blocking has failed to cut the number of elderly people waiting in hospital, mostly due to a shortage of nursing home places and funding problems.

After some initial success, figures out yesterday showed that last October 1,356 patients were waiting for more than six weeks to leave hospital, an 8 per cent rise from April 2003.

Dozens of private care homes now face closure because of a lack of funding despite ministers last year giving £30million to NHS health boards and councils to deal with bed-blocking. Scottish Care, which represents private care homes, claims they are being underfunded by councils.

Deputy Health Minister Tom McCabe said yesterday the scheme would succeed in the long term, with more patients being treated at home.

But David Davidson, Scots Tory health spokesman, said: 'Preferential treatment is given to council-run homes, which leaves private homes with less money. When that ends, the bed-blocking figures will come down.'

Figure 5.8 News report on bed-blocking
Source *Daily Mail*, 17 January 2004

FOUNDATION/GENERAL

Activities

1 What is hypothermia? *(2 marks)*

2 Why is hypothermia especially a threat to the elderly in Scotland? *(2 marks)*

3 List the more common ailments affecting the elderly. *(3 marks)*

4 Describe the system of primary care. *(4 marks)*

5 Why is 'bed-blocking' a major problem in the UK? *(2 marks)*

6 How does primary care help with the problem of 'bed-blocking'? *(2 marks)*

7 List four services that the NHS provides for the elderly. *(4 marks)*

Case Study: Dementia

A common illness which affects the elderly and is also one of the most worrying for older people is dementia.

Dementia is when the brain deteriorates and memories, even recent ones, are lost. It becomes very difficult for an individual to cope with everyday life. In advanced stages of the illness simple tasks can be very difficult and eventually sufferers will have to go into care.

At the moment 50,000 people over the age of 65 suffer from dementia, 1 per cent of those are in the 65–74 years bracket and 10 per cent are those aged 75+ years. Age Concern estimates that 800,000 people will suffer from the illness by the year 2005.

In Scotland, 50,000 people suffer from senile dementia – 5 per cent of Scotland's elderly population. 96 per cent of sufferers are over 65. 50 per cent of sufferers are over 80.

FACT FILE

A person suffering from dementia can have many problems. Some of the possible symptoms are that the person:

◆ does not recognise their friends and relatives

◆ forgets to turn off fires and cookers

◆ forgets to feed themselves

◆ feels lonely and frightened

◆ becomes violent to their carers

◆ can be untidy and does not wash.

Figure 5.9 shows the types of accommodation dementia sufferers live in.

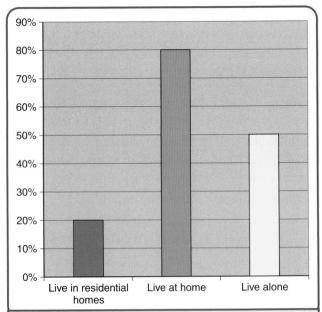

Figure 5.9 Accommodation for dementia sufferers

Activities

1 Describe how dementia affects the elderly? *(3 marks)*

2 How many over-65s in Scotland suffer from dementia? *(2 marks)*

3 Describe the symptoms of dementia in the elderly. *(4 marks)*

4 Where do most people with dementia live? *(2 marks)*

5 Using the factfile, describe in your own words why this might be a problem. *(4 marks)*

Care in the Community

Since April 1993 certain needs of elderly people are looked after under the policy of **community care**.

Community care tries to get people who had been looked after in geriatric or psychiatric hospitals to be cared for within the local community. It was felt that many people would have a fuller life. Only those with very serious conditions would have to stay in hospitals.

Under care in the community, GPs, health visitors, community nurses and other specialised health professionals provide medical help. The housing needs of people are met by sheltered housing, residential homes, nursing homes and other specific housing provided by specialised housing associations.

Area social work departments are the main organisers of community care. Their job is to make sure that people's needs are met to as high a standard as possible.

The needs of each person are assessed and a personal care plan is drawn up to try and make sure that these are catered for. This could range from:

◆ providing 'home-help' for someone

◆ adapting an elderly person's home by installing special waist high electrical sockets

◆ adapting their toilets to make them easier to use

◆ installing special alarms if they need help

◆ finding a place in nursing home for someone who can no longer look after him or herself

◆ anything else which lets a person to live as full and easy a life as possible in their local community and to prevent people being placed in long term care if it is not absolutely necessary.

Care in the Community Services

Home helps:

◆ keep the house clean and tidy

◆ clean the bathroom to prevent disease

◆ go shopping for their patients.

Community nurses:

◆ dress wounds

◆ give necessary injections

◆ prevent people from having to go into hospital or a nursing home.

Figure 5.10 A meals on wheels delivery

The Elderly

Meals on wheels:

◆ helps people to stay in their own homes and stay independent

◆ provides hot meals

◆ daily visits mean company for the elderly person.

Occupational therapists provide a range of home adaptations including:

◆ stair lifts

◆ special plugs and sockets

◆ special baths, toilets and showers

◆ lower kitchen work surfaces and cupboards

◆ special alarms.

Day centres provide a range of services including:

◆ day trips

◆ classes on how to avoid hypothermia

◆ hot lunches

◆ games and social events such as bingo or sing-along sessions

Figure 5.11 Pensioners enjoying day centre facilities

Figure 5.12 gives a step-by-step guide to care in the community.

Government gives up to 50% of costs to local authority.
The needs of individual elderly people assessed by social work departments (Patients means tested)
Needs met by, or by a mixture of, local authorities, private companies or voluntary agencies.

Local authorities and Health Boards (Community Health Partnerships)	Private companies	Voluntary agencies e.g. Age Concern
Health visitors Home helps Social workers Health professionals such as chiropodists	Sheltered housing Residential Homes Nursing homes	Meals on wheels Help the Aged Lunch clubs Support groups Respite care House adaptations

Figure 5.12 Care in the community

Activities

1 What is community care? *(2 marks)*

2 How does community care work? *(3 marks)*

3 Who are the main organisers of community care? *(2 marks)*

4 What type of information is included in a personal care plan? *(3 marks)*

5 What are the major services provided by care in the community? *(3 marks)*

6 From Figure 5.12, list the three types of organisation involved in providing community care. *(3 marks)*

Criticisms of Community Care

Although it has many positive features, the policy of care in the community also comes in for criticisms, such as the belief that some people are released from psychiatric hospitals when they cannot look after themselves. Critics say that community care was introduced because the government was worried about the costs of care for the elderly (a residential home can cost as much as £500 per week and a geriatric hospital place can cost about £800 per week).

Some owners of private residential and nursing homes are more concerned with profits than the care of the elderly. Untrained people can often be employed in private homes.

Many elderly people do not receive proper assessments and do not get the level of care that they really need. People with a certain level of savings or owners of certain homes have to pay towards their care.

Activity

List the main criticisms of community care. *(6 marks)*

Meeting the Elderly's Financial Needs

The Westminster government deals mainly with the financial needs of the elderly, whilst leaving health and social needs to the NHS or local government. The financial needs of elderly people are met in a number of different ways, the main ones are listed below:

State retirement pension is still the main form of financial help for the elderly. Women receive it at 60 years old and men at 65. In 2005 the state retirement pension was £82.05 for a single person and £131.20 for a married couple.

Second state pension based on contributions.

Pension credits top up the pension or other earnings for those over 60 to £109.45 if single and £167.05 if a couple.

Winter fuel allowance of £200 per household given out at the start of the British winter. Around 700,000 households benefit in Scotland.

Christmas bonuses of £10 are given to every pensioner during the month of December.

Invalidity allowances are given depending on the type of disability that a person has and the amount of extra care that they need.

Attendance allowance is another benefit given to those who cannot look after themselves. The amount given depends on the amount of care that a person needs, for example, daytime care or 24-hour care.

Free TV licence for people aged over 75.

Income support is a means tested benefit (pension credit). It is given to those who have been unable to invest or save enough for their retirement. Receiving income support also opens the door to gaining some or all of the other financial benefits, which are listed below:

◆ council tax rebates are one benefit the elderly may receive if they get income support (depending on any savings an elderly person has, they can receive up to 100 per cent rebate on council tax bills. However, four out of ten elderly people do not claim this benefit)

◆ housing benefit helps people with the cost of their rent

◆ cold weather payments are given out when the temperature falls below zero over a 7-day period – this is currently a one off payment of £8.50 for every continuous seven-day spell of cold weather.

Activities

1   Which level of government deals with the financial needs of the elderly?   *(2 marks)*

2   What is the main form of financial help available to the elderly?   *(2 marks)*

3   List four other types of financial help that an older person could get?   *(2 marks)*

4   Which benefit is means-tested?   *(2 marks)*

5   What financial help does the government give to elderly people with disabilities?   *(2 marks)*

6   What is the level of up-take for council tax rebates?   *(2 marks)*

7   When are the cold weather payments given out?   *(2 marks)*

Council Tax and Housing Benefits

For many older people, council tax is a financial burden as many of them live on a tight budget. Council tax benefit, which can reduce your council tax, is the benefit pensioners are most likely to miss out on. It is reported on the government's own website that 40 per cent of pensioners do not receive a rebate.

Council tax rebates can be claimed by homeowners as well as tenants, the value of your home is not taken into account.

> 'Currently up to 1.4m eligible older people miss out on Council tax benefit, resulting in up to £580m remaining unclaimed each year. The average amount unclaimed is £7.50 a week, or £390 a year. Up to 270,000 eligible older people are not claiming housing benefit, resulting in up £400m remaining unclaimed each year.'
>
> Source: BBC News Service, September 2003

Housing benefit helps with rent and some other charges. These benefits are based on your income and savings and in general you must have less than £16,000 in savings.

The government currently provides cold weather payments of £8.50 to pensioners on income support when the average temperature falls below 0 degrees Celsius for seven consecutive days.

Age Concern has been fighting for many years to bring attention to the issue of pensioners who die of hypothermia because they cannot afford winter fuel bills. It says up to 48,000 more people die in winter than summer in the UK, 94 per cent of whom are elderly. 'It is a simple fact that the cold kills' said Age Concern director Sally Green.

Figure 5.13 The costs of winter fuel can be a struggle for the elderly

'Elderly people often have to make a choice between eating and heating. They either turn off their heating or cut down on food. The cold and hunger makes them more likely to become ill. The longer they are ill, the weaker they become and they can't cope. It's a vicious circle.'

Help the Aged Spokesperson

Activities

1. Why do many older people view council tax as a burden? *(2 marks)*

2. What evidence is there to suggest that older people are aware of council tax rebates? *(2 marks)*

3. To qualify for housing benefit, what is the level of savings that an older person must have less than? *(1 mark)*

4. From the article by the BBC, describe the failure of the housing benefit system? *(2 marks)*

5. Why does Age Concern say that many pensioners are in danger from hypothermia? *(2 marks)*

6. A Help the Aged spokesperson says that many older people are faced with a choice. What is this choice? *(2 marks)*

Fight for the 'Grey Vote'

FACT FILE

◆ There are over twice as many voters over 60 than there are aged 18–24. 12 million compared to 5 million.

◆ 87 per cent of people over 60 voted in the 2001 election. Only 44 per cent of 18–24s voted in this election.

◆ Only 4 per cent of over 65s agree with the statement 'it's not really worth voting.'

◆ 13 per cent of 18–24 year olds agree with the statement 'it's not really worth voting.'

All the main political parties are targeting older people with promises of more money in their pocket in return for their vote.

The Conservatives launched a manifesto for pensioners, claiming that a pensioner couple would be more than £8 a week better off under their proposals. Labour says it has spent an extra £4.5 billion a year on pensioners. The Liberal Democrats want to spend another £4 billion a year for the state pension for older people.

All the political parties hope that by helping the 'grey vote', they will win the support of the UK's most reliable voters and secure public support.

Activities

1. What is the 'grey vote'? *(2 marks)*

2. How many over 60s voters are there in the UK? *(1 mark)*

3. What percentage of the over 60s voted in the 2001 general election? *(2 marks)*

4. List the ways that the main political parties are trying to win the votes of the elderly? *(4 marks)*

Voluntary Organisations/ Pressure Groups

There are a range of voluntary organisations that exist to help elderly people and to promote their interests. The best known of these groups are Age Concern and Help the Aged.

These organisations act as pressure groups as well as voluntary agencies for older people. The money to run these voluntary groups comes mainly from donations, fundraising, charity shops and some grants.

Help the Aged is Britain's leading charity working for older people.

Figure 5.14 Help the Aged's logo

The Elderly

Help the Aged is dedicated to reducing poverty, neglect and isolation among older people in the UK and overseas, to defeating age discrimination and preventing future deprivation. It does this through campaigning, carrying out or funding research and providing services, advice and information to support independent living.

Its main aim is to try to help elderly people to lead as happy and secure a life as possible. The organisation has four main priorities:

◆ **to fight poverty**

◆ **to reduce loneliness**

◆ **to ensure older people receive good care**

◆ **to fight against negative ideas about elderly people.**

Age Concern Scotland works throughout Scotland to help make the lives of older people more secure, comfortable, dignified and enjoyable. Their aims are to ensure that older people in Scotland have:

◆ **their rights upheld**

◆ **their needs addressed**

◆ **their voices heard**

◆ **choice and control over all aspects of their lives.**

They support a wide network of older people and older people's groups, which in turn provide local services to older people in their own communities.

Age Concern Scotland offers a range of services. They work with members to develop locally-based services which focus on local needs. They provide information to meet the needs of older people living in the community, to bring attention to issues relevant to older people, and to inform them of their rights.

Age Concern Scotland also campaigns with older people for:

◆ **an adequate income for retirement**

◆ **improved housing**

◆ **better health and care services for older people**

◆ **an end to age discrimination.**

Inequality in Retirement

Many people believe that elderly people are all poor. Not all pensioners are short of money. Some may have savings of their own, a pension from their previous jobs, investments or even a part time job, as well as their state pensions. This group of elderly people have more money and a better lifestyle than others with only their state pension to rely on each week.

A lot of people prepare for retirement by contributing to an occupational pension. Workers pay money into their company pension scheme each week and when they retire they get money back each week in addition to their state pension. This means that they should be able to buy necessities, pay bills and still have money left over for things that other pensioners may consider luxuries.

Occupational pensions vary in amount based on the job that a person did before retiring. Most lower paid workers don't have occupational pension schemes.

A better-paid job would probably mean a better pension in retirement because of the occupational pension scheme. The higher paid the worker is the more that is paid in and the more money from the pension on retirement.

Pensioners who are relatively well off in retirement have been called many different names. The most common nicknames are 'whoopies' and 'glams' or 'SKIing pensioners'.

Figure 5.15 Not all pensioners are struggling financially

Whoopies stands for Well Off Older People. Glams for Greying Leisured Affluent Married. The newer term 'SKIing' stands for Spending the Kids Inheritance. Many older people now believe they should enjoy their retirement properly instead of continuing to save so that their money will go to their children when they die.

The over-55s have over 43 per cent of the net wealth of the country. Many firms now focus on these older people who have money to spend. Building firms and holiday companies are especially interested in this group and there is now a large market for retirement property and off-peak holidays for older people.

Activities

1 For what reasons do some elderly people enjoy a higher standard of living than others?   *(2 marks)*

2 Explain how some elderly people have an occupational pension but some others do not have one.   *(3 marks)*

3 Explain the terms whoopies, glams and SKIing pensioners.   *(3 marks)*

4 Why would holiday companies and building firms be interested in these groups of people?   *(3 marks)*

Ageing Europe

Britain is not the only European country to have an increasing number of elderly people. Other European nations such as Italy, Belgium and Greece have a higher proportion of people over 60 years of age than in the UK. The number of people over 60 is expected to increase in all the countries of the EU.

British pensioners do not think that all European pensioners are treated the same. Pensioners in other EU countries receive more money in their state pensions and often receive extra benefits which UK pensioners would like to have.

It is difficult to compare pensions in the different EU member states as each country operates a different pension scheme, gives different benefits and has different costs of living.

In purely financial terms, UK pensioners are the poor relations when it comes to direct comparisons. The UK government could point to the fact that the cost of living is different in each of the EU countries. The cost of living in Germany is 15 per cent higher and prices in France are 7 per cent higher than those in the UK.

One way is to look at the amount that people get for their state pension compared with what they received when they were in work.

In Scotland a pensioner receives a pension worth on average 46 per cent of his/her former wage. In Germany a pensioner would receive 82 per cent of their former wage. In France a pensioner would receive 92 per cent of their former wage.

Indeed the governments of large industrial countries of the EU such France, Germany are thinking about changing their pension shemes and there has been a great deal of protest from pensioners and workers because of this.

The Elderly

1 Why do UK pensioners feel that they are the 'poor relations of Europe'? *(2 marks)*

2 How does the UK government explain the differing amounts of money that pensioners in EU countries receive? *(2 marks)*

3 Why would a Scottish pensioner have a complaint about the state pension in the UK if he compares it to pensions in other European Union countries? *(2 marks)*

4 What idea is causing protests in France and Germany? *(2 marks)*

Pensioners' Benefits in Selected EU States

British pensioners claim that it is not only in the amount of cash that they receive in their state pensions that puts them at a disadvantage. Pensioner groups claim that other EU countries actually give their pensioners much more in the way of general benefits. Figure 5.16 shows the range of benefits available in some EU countries. These should help you make up your own mind.

Activities

Look at Figure 5.16 and answer the following questions.

1 In which of the EU countries are pensioners better-off than UK pensioners? Explain your answer. *(2 marks)*

2 In which country are pensioners worst off? Explain your answer. *(2 marks)*

3 Could the UK learn any lessons from other EU countries in the way that pensioners are treated? Explain your answer. *(2 marks)*

United Kingdom

Christmas bonus of £10

Winter fuel payment of £200

Cold weather payments

Free TV licences for over 75s

Travel reductions in regions they live in

France

Free telephone installation

Cheap telephone calls

Free TV licence for all pensioners

Cheap nationwide travel

Free travel on Paris Metro

Denmark

Half price TV licence for all pensioners

Half price nationwide travel

Reductions on telephone bills

Germany

Reduced TV licence fee

Reduced travel costs

Reduced telephone calls

Ireland

Free nationwide travel

Free electricity

Free telephone installation

Extra pension for living alone

Holland

Reduced TV licence

Half-price nationwide travel

One week's free nationwide travel per year

An extra month's pension every year

Extra pension for holiday allowance

Belgium

Free TV licence

Half-price telephone charges

Half-price travel nationwide

Extra pensions for holidays

A extra month's pension per year

Figure 5.16 Benefits for pensioners in various EU countries
Source Glaswegian Newspaper

FOUNDATION/GENERAL

5

The Elderly

Why study the elderly? There are millions of them – well, actually, 1million in Scotland, that's 18 per cent of the population. The number of older people is set to increase over the next 50 years to a quarter of the entire population.

Older people own 40 per cent of the country's wealth, so they have spending power. Older people can have a significant effect on the outcome of elections too, this voting power is sometimes called 'grey power'.

We will all be old one day.

Population Changes

A country's population changes as a result of deaths, births, emigration and immigration. During the first half of the twentieth century there were declining death rates and increasing birth rates, so the population grew. In more recent times these trends have changed. Scotland now has a falling birth rate and an increase in the lifespan of its ageing population.

In 1993, 17.8 per cent of the population was 65 years of age or over. This number is expected to rise to 24.1 per cent by 2051. This means that by 2051 almost a quarter of the population will be old age pensioners.

A Longer Life

One of the main reasons for the increase in the elderly population is that people are living longer because of the health care provided by the National Health Service. Medical advances have managed to wipe out many diseases and also prolonged the length of people's lives and improved the quality of those lives.

The better quality of modern day housing and welfare state benefits have also helped people to live longer lives.

The very large increase in the number of elderly people in Scotland and the rest of the UK has also brought extra problems for the government in trying to meet the needs of elderly people.

Problems for the Government

The large increase in the numbers of elderly people has led to strains on social services such as pensions, housing and medical services.

◆ **Government spending on the elderly will have to increase as more people live longer. More state pensions will have to be paid out and spending on benefits such as income support will also have to increase.**

◆ **At the moment, 50 per cent of all NHS beds are taken up by elderly people and 40 per cent of all spending on the NHS is taken up by the elderly. This amount of spending is set to increase as demands for specialist elderly health services increases.**

◆ **Services such as home helps, meals on wheels, community nurses, GP's and carers will all be placed under greater strain.**

◆ **The increases in the numbers of elderly people will also see a large increase in demand for facilities such as specialised geriatric care, sheltered housing as well as other care housing and nursing homes.**

Activities

1 Explain why the number of elderly people in Scotland is increasing.

2 In what ways will the increasing numbers of elderly people have an impact on government spending?

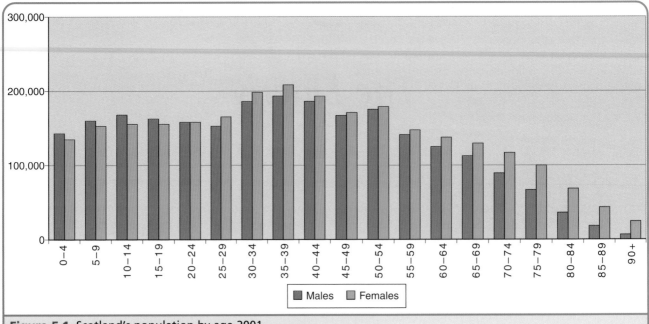

Figure 5.1 Scotland's population by age 2001

Source Registrar General for Scotland www.gro-scotland.gov.uk

The Elderly in Scotland

The population of Scotland is 5,062,011 (Census 2001). There are almost 1 million elderly people in Scotland, that's 18.6 per cent of the population (up from 17.8 per cent in 1993). The number of older people is set to increase over the next 50 years to a quarter of the population.

What Do We Mean by The Elderly?

Officially, men are classed as OAPs (Old Age Pensioners) when they reach 65 years of age, while women are OAPs at 60 years.

However the changing nature of the world today means that people live well beyond this age. The average person today can live well over the age of 70, and people reaching 100 years is not uncommon in today's society. Many more women than men are elderly as women tend to live longer.

In Scotland in 2001 there were 325,361 male pensioners (over the age of 65) and 616,621 female pensioners (over the age of 60).

Scotland's Changing Population

Scotland's population will change over the next 20 years. There will be fewer young people and an increase in the number of older Scots.

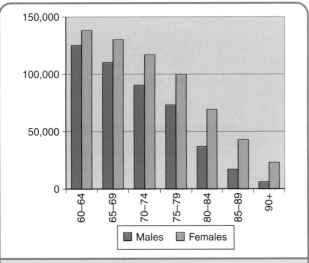

Figure 5.2 Scotland's elderly population by gender 2001

Source Registrar General for Scotland www.gro-scotland.gov.uk

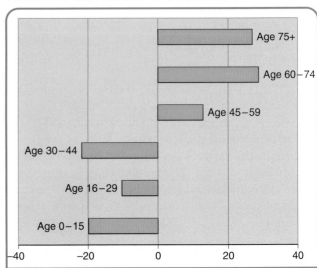

Figure 5.3 Changes in Scotland's population by age group 2000–2021

Source Registrar General for Scotland www.gro-scotland.gov.uk

The growing number of elderly people in Britain means that more will have to be paid in pensions as more people live longer. Following a European Union decision that pension ages should be the same for men and women, the government decided to raise the retirement age of women to 65. This will take effect from 2010.

Activities

1 What evidence is there that the number of elderly people is rising?

2 Look at Figures 5.1 and 5.2. Explain in your own words, why some elderly women in particular might suffer from loneliness.

3 Look at Figure 5.3. Which age groups are going to grow the most?

4 Which age groups are going to decline?

5 Why might women complain about the way the government equalised the retirement age?

Facts About Scotland

Standards of Living

◆ Only 12 per cent of pensioners receive income from employment.

◆ Only 42 per cent of single pensioners and 49 per cent of pensioner couples receive an occupational pension.

◆ Women pensioners are less likely to have an occupational pension than men and are more likely to have a lower pension

◆ Single women pensioners are the worst off.

◆ 41 per cent of single pensioners have an income of less than £6000 per year.

◆ 13 per cent of single pensioners have an income of less than £4000 per year.

◆ 16 per cent single pensioners have an annual income of over £10,000 per year.

◆ 9 per cent of pensioner couples have incomes of more than £20,000 per year.

◆ 9 per cent of pensioners living in urban areas have incomes over £15,000 compared with 18 per cent living in rural areas.

◆ Poorer older people spend a greater part of their income (24 per cent) on food than better off pensioners (16 per cent).

◆ Poorer and older pensioners spend less money on food and fuel.

◆ Pensioners who live in rented accommodation pay 30 per cent of their income on rent.

◆ 15 per cent of pensioners' houses are in a bad state of repair.

◆ 25 per cent of the worst housing is occupied by pensioners.

◆ Single pensioners are more likely than others to live in houses which are expensive to heat.

Health

◆ 25 per cent of the 85+ age group are in long term care.

◆ 34 per cent of men and 33 per cent of women aged 65–74 have longstanding illnesses.

◆ 41 per cent of pensioners living in disadvantaged areas have longstanding illnesses.

◆ 30 per cent of pensioners in high income areas have long standing illnesses.

◆ Older people living in disadvantaged areas have more difficulty coping with every day activities, such as walking, using public transport and household tasks.

◆ Those living in high income areas have less difficulty.

◆ The most common diseases of old age are arthritis, heart disease and stroke. Eye and ear impairments are more common in older than younger people.

Source: Older People in Scotland: Scottish Household Survey www.scotland.gov.uk/cru

Activities

1 Using the facts about Scotland, draw up a table with three headings:
◆ poor pensioners
◆ better off pensioners
◆ all pensioners.

Insert the facts under the correct heading.

2 Write a paragraph comparing the standards of living and health of poorer and better off pensioner.

Problems Facing the Elderly – the Needs of the Elderly

Housing

One of the most important needs of elderly people is good quality housing that meets their specific requirements. It is especially true of the elderly that good quality housing will greatly improve their quality of life.

Good sheltered housing allows elderly people to be independent within a secure environment.

High-rise flats on the other hand are totally unsuitable. The lifts may be out of order, forcing the elderly to struggle up and down flights of stairs or to become prisoners in their own homes. Being up high, or feeling the wind swaying the building, may also increase the fear experienced by the elderly.

In Scotland, housing has traditionally been provided by local authorities. Local authorities currently provide homes for 41 per cent of those between 60–75 years of age.

Recent years have seen much greater involvement of housing associations, voluntary groups and private property companies in providing housing specifically for elderly people. There is also an increasing variety of different types of housing for the elderly. These include sheltered housing, very sheltered housing, retirement homes, residential homes, care housing and nursing homes.

Sheltered Housing

Sheltered housing is specifically designed to meet the needs of elderly people. It is usually set up as a complex of houses, where the elderly live in their own house with their own facilities.

This helps the residents to feel that they have their independence, but also to feel safe, as, whenever they need help they can call for it, as there is a warden in the complex. This is possible as the houses come equipped with special facilities linked to the warden's office.

Very sheltered housing provides a higher level of support for elderly people with greater levels of need. Although there is sufficient sheltered housing in Scotland, there is a shortage of very sheltered housing. The demand for very sheltered housing will increase as people live longer.

This type of housing also comes with specific

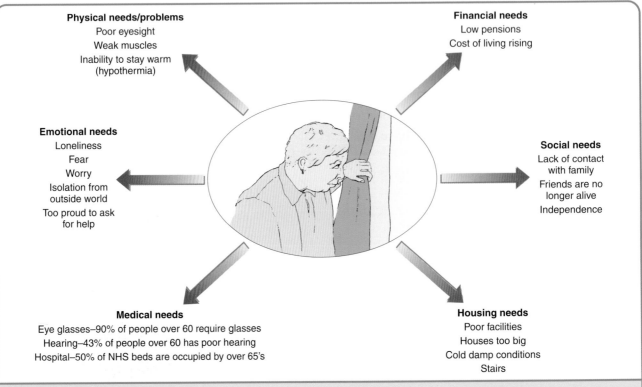

Physical needs/problems
Poor eyesight
Weak muscles
Inability to stay warm
(hypothermia)

Financial needs
Low pensions
Cost of living rising

Emotional needs
Loneliness
Fear
Worry
Isolation from
outside world
Too proud to ask
for help

Social needs
Lack of contact
with family
Friends are no
longer alive
Independence

Medical needs
Eye glasses–90% of people over 60 require glasses
Hearing–43% of people over 60 has poor hearing
Hospital–50% of NHS beds are occupied by over 65's

Housing needs
Poor facilities
Houses too big
Cold damp conditions
Stairs

Figure 5.4 Needs of the elderly
Source www.helptheaged.org.uk

features and facilities designed to make life easier for elderly people. Depending on the level of need of residents, most sheltered and very sheltered housing has the following features:

◆ warden service provided 24 hours a day, the warden is there to take care of any problems and also to provide the residents with a sense of security

◆ community lounge where tenants can meet and socialise while still in the safety of the complex, it also provides for activities such as bingo or card games

◆ corridors allow tenants to go for a walk, or visit a friend living there, whilst still feeling safe, and many corridors have non slip surfaces and railings to help mobility

◆ guest rooms allow the occupants to have friends and relatives stay on visits if they do not stay in the area or if a person is ill

◆ laundry rooms so that residents do not need to pay for their own machines or the cost of using them as heating and power bills are included in the costs of the rent

◆ a TV licence is held by the complex so no individual has to pay for their own

◆ ramps and railings are installed to help those with physical disabilities

◆ pressure pads are installed under carpets and linked to the wardens office so that they know when the residents are moving around

◆ pull cords and alarms, positioned so that the warden can be summoned in emergencies

◆ very sheltered housing also has much higher levels of adaptations and care staff to meet the needs of the elderly residents.

Activities

1 In what ways do sheltered and very sheltered housing meet the physical and social needs of elderly people?

2 Why will demand for very sheltered accommodation increase?

3 In what ways do the household aids in Figure 5.5 contribute to meeting the elderly's housing needs?

Figure 5.5 Some household aids for the elderly

Case Study

A partnership between Scottish Homes and Kirkcare Housing Association will provide kitchen and dining facilities for 18 sheltered housing tenants.

The £220,000 investment will also create an assisted bathroom and sleep over room. Meals will also be provided with tenants able to benefit from a service which provides one meal a day and 24-hour staff support.

Ewan Johnston, Managing Director for Scottish Homes Glasgow and North Clyde, said 'It is vital that we provide facilities of a high standard to satisfy the varying needs of the older members of our communities.'

Source: Scottish Homes Press Release, 4 May 2000

Case Study

It is quite likely that many children in Scotland will never experience the satisfaction, not to mention the health benefits, of serving up a pot of soup. Their Mums find it impossible to fit in time in the kitchen teaching children to cook.

People in their 70s and 80s have the skills and the leisure time to pass on these life skills

Residents at Hanover's sheltered housing complex in Glasgow offered baking, cooking, knitting and even history classes to the children of neighbouring Blackfriars Primary.

Eight years ago the children named the sheltered housing development around the corner from their school and, since then, the school and the development have enjoyed a close relationship.

After a term of weekly sessions with the residents, the Primary 7 knitting class were turning out scarves, gloves, baby clothes and Christmas decorations. The Primary 3 chefs were tucking into bowls of broth and tomato soup which they had helped to make. Other residents helped out with the P7's World War Two studies. Residents shared their experiences as wartime evacuees.

'I couldn't believe how interested the children were. The children prompted memories of events and details I hadn't thought about for years. When they asked me about VE Day and what it ➤

felt like – I could remember it like yesterday. I told the children how thousands of people descended on George Square, the brightness of the lights after so many years of darkness and all the dancing and hugging.'

Source: Hanover Housing Association

Year	Houses
1992	32,192
1993	32,267
1994	33,100
1995	33,687
1996	34,976
1997	35,484
1998	36,069
1999	34,752
2000	35,342
2001	34,615
2002	34,247

Figure 5.6 Sheltered housing accommodation
Source *Housing Trends in Scotland* 2002

Residential Homes

These are usually run by a local authorities or private companies as well as voluntary groups, including the churches.

Residential homes usually have the following advantages:

◆ **in residential homes residents are not given as much freedom as in sheltered housing, but they do receive more one to one care**

◆ **meals are cooked for the residents and a choice of menu is given**

◆ **a variety of entertainment is usually available**

◆ **hairdressers usually visit once per week**

◆ **lounges for family and friends are provided**

◆ **help is provided twenty four hours a day as in sheltered housing and nursing homes.**

Residential homes are an expensive option. The cost of staying in one of these homes can be as much as £500 per week.

This helps to explain why so many private companies have opened private nursing homes. The fact that so many nursing homes are run as private businesses has also been a cause of much concern to the authorities and the families of elderly residents.

Many homes are well run and provide an excellent standard of care. Others have been accused of putting profit before the welfare of their elderly residents.

The worst homes have been found to have overcrowding, not enough staff as well as staff without proper qualifications and examples of cruelty by staff to elderly residents have been discovered in some of these homes.

Nursing Homes

Nursing homes are very similar to residential homes in many of the facilities they provide. Many of them are run by private companies but they usually care for people with greater care needs.

This means that they have to provide a greater level of care such as 24-hour care from trained nursing staff. They are even more expensive to stay in than residential homes.

Activities

1 Describe the main differences between Sheltered Housing and Residential Nursing Homes.

2 In what way is very sheltered housing like residential or nursing homes?

3 'The number of Sheltered Houses has continued to increase in the last decade to meet the needs of the elderly population of Scotland'

Housing spokesperson.

Use Figure 5.6 to explain why the housing spokesperson could be accused of exaggeration.

4 'Sheltered housing may help meet the needs of some infirm elderly people, but for most it just simply shuts them off from the rest of the community.'

Local teenager.

In what ways do the case studies contradict the views of the teenager?

5 'Building sheltered and very sheltered housing for the elderly is very expensive and often a waste of money. Residential and nursing homes are there

already for the elderly who need care. The authorities would be better off building new houses for young people so that they could benefit.'

Resident of high rise flat.

Make arguments for and against this statement.

Meeting the Health Care Needs of the Elderly

One important need for elderly people is health care. The elderly can become very susceptible to illnesses such as hypothermia (when body temperature drops due to the cold) especially in this country where it can become very cold and there are great numbers of over 70 year olds.

More commonly treated illnesses in this country are those relating to hearing, seeing and walking. Arthritis, bad eyesight and hearing as well as brittle bones and bronchitis can create problems for older people. This is where the system of primary care (first level of care) is designed to help the elderly.

Primary care takes place outside of hospitals and in the community. The primary care of elderly people is carried out by a specific care team, normally located in the local health centre. The care team would include people such as GP's, community nurses, physiotherapists, chiropodists, occupational therapists, speech therapists and dieticians.

These people often visit elderly people in their own homes making it even easier to receive care. Primary care also helps hospitals to reduce the numbers of elderly people in hospital, thus helping with the problem of bed-blocking.

Bed-blocking occurs when patients cannot be admitted to hospital because there are no beds available due to them being taken up by elderly people. It is estimated that the elderly takes up 40 per cent of all hospital beds.

The Primary Care Team

Community Nurse

Checks blood pressure, changes bandages and checks general health of elderly in their own home.

Optician

Provides sight tests and glasses. Examines eyes for signs of disease.

Dentist

Provides teeth and gum care.

General Practitioner

Prescribes medication free of charge and can recommend operations or any further health care.

Health Centres

Provide a wide range of services. Doctors and many other health services are all under one roof.

Physiotherapist

Provides assistance after operations and helps elderly people with movement if they suffer from diseases such as arthritis.

Short Stay Hospital Beds

Help carers of elderly to have a short break (respite care). Respite care enables elderly people to be taken into hospital and looked after by trained staff who understand their needs.

Geriatric Wards

Hospital wards which are specifically for the needs of elderly hospital patients.

Many elderly people end up staying in this type of ward for long periods of time because:

- they cannot take care of themselves
- they have no family to help take care of them
- there are insufficient numbers of sheltered or very sheltered house available
- there are delays in getting a place in a residential or care home.

Activities

1. Describe how each of the following assist in meeting elderly health needs:
   a) community nurse
   b) optician
   c) general practitioner
   d) dentist
   e) heath centres
   f) physiotherapist
   g) short stay hospital beds
   h) geriatric wards.

2. What other specialists make up the primary care team and how can they help the elderly?

3. How does primary care help reduce bed-blocking?

Diseases of Old Age

One of the more common diseases in Britain, and also one of the most worrying for older people, is senile dementia. Dementia is when the brain deteriorates and memories, even recent ones, are lost.

It becomes very difficult for an individual to cope with everyday life. In advanced stages of the disease simple tasks can be very difficult and eventually sufferers will have to go into institutional care, such as a residential or nursing home, where the illness can be managed.

At the moment 50,000 people over 65 suffer from dementia, one per cent of those are 65–74 years old and 10 per cent of those are aged 75+ years.

Age Concern estimates that 800,000 people will suffer from the illness by the year 2005.

FACT FILE

Senile Dementia

A person suffering from dementia can have many problems, including:

- **forgetting who their friends and relatives are**
- **forgetting to cook or feed themselves**
- **forgetting to turn off fires and cookers**
- **feeling lonely and frightened**
- **becoming violent to those that look after them**
- **forgetting to keep themselves clean and tidy.**

In Scotland 50,000 people suffer from senile dementia. That is five per cent of Scotland's elderly population and the breakdown is:

- **96 per cent of sufferers are over 65**
- **50 per cent of sufferers are over 80**
- **20 per cent of sufferers live in residential homes**
- **80 per cent live at home**
- **50 per cent live alone.**

GENERAL/CREDIT

1 What is senile dementia?

2 Describe four problems that senile dementia may cause.

3 To what extent is senile dementia a problem in Scotland? You must provide evidence from the fact file to support you viewpoint.

4 What evidence is there that not all sufferers are at an advanced stage of dementia?

Elderly Use of the National Health Service

Many of the health problems of the elderly are looked after by the National Health Service (NHS). It is the job of the NHS to provide health care for those who need it regardless of whether they can pay for it.

There is no doubt that the elderly make more use of the NHS than younger people – they occupy over 40 per cent of the beds at any one time.

The NHS provides services specifically for the elderly. These include services such as day care hospital units, community nursing services, physiotherapy rehabilitation units and long stay geriatric wards.

Activity

'The NHS provides services specifically for the elderly.'

Write a paragraph about four of the special services that the NHS provides for elderly people.

Activity

'Age and gender play no part in a person's health.'

In what ways does Figure 5.7 contradict this statement?

Care in the Community

Since April 1993 certain needs of elderly people have been taken care of by the policy of community care. This policy aimed to allow people who had previously been cared for in geriatric hospitals or psychiatric hospitals to be cared for in the local community instead. The idea was that many people would be allowed to live a fuller life and only those with very serious conditions would have to live in hospitals.

Under care in the community help would be provided by GPs, health visitors, community nurses and other specialised health professionals. The housing needs of people would be met by sheltered

| | Age | | | | | | |
	16–24	25–34	35–44	45–54	55–64	65–74	Total
Men							
No longstanding illness	79	70	66	55	40	35	60
Serious longstanding illness	6	15	17	25	42	43	22
Non-serious illness	16	15	16	19	18	22	17
Total with illness	*21*	*30*	*34*	*45*	*60*	*65*	*40*
Women							
No longstanding illness	75	73	68	54	41	38	60
Serious longstanding illness	9	15	19	31	38	43	25
Non-serious illness	15	13	13	15	22	19	16
Total with illness	*25*	*27*	*32*	*46*	*59*	*62*	*40*

Figure 5.7 Health problems affecting the different age groups in Scotland in 2001, percentages of each group affected

Source The Scottish Health Survey 2001

housing, residential homes, nursing homes and other specific housing provided by specialised housing associations.

Area social work departments have the main role to play in running community care and ensuring that peoples needs are met to as high a standard as possible. The needs of each person are assessed and a personal action plan is drawn to try to make sure that each of their needs are catered for.

This care package could range from simply providing a home help for a person to adapting an elderly person's home by installing special waist high electrical sockets, adapting their toilets to make them easier to use and installing special alarms if they need help.

The main aim of community care is to enable a person to live as full and easy a life as possible in their local community and prevent people being placed in long term care unnecessarily.

Finally, it could also involve finding a place in a residential or nursing home for someone who can no longer look after themselves.

Criticisms

Despite its many positive features the policy of care in the community also comes in for criticism. The following points are among the most common criticisms:

◆ some people are released from psychiatric hospitals and they really cannot look after themselves

◆ critics claim that it was introduced because the government was concerned about the increasing costs of care for the elderly in residential and nursing homes and hospital wards

◆ the cost of care in a residential home can be as much as £500 per week and a geriatric bed in a hospital costs an average of £800 per week

◆ some owners of private residential and nursing homes are more concerned with profits than the care of the elderly

◆ untrained people can often be employed in private homes

◆ many elderly people do not receive proper assessments and do not get the level of care that they really need

◆ people with a certain level of savings or owners of certain homes have to pay towards their care.

Care in the Community Services

Home Help:

◆ keeps the house clean and tidy
◆ cleans the bathroom to prevent disease
◆ goes shopping.

Community Nurse:

◆ dresses wounds
◆ gives necessary injections
◆ prevents people from having to go into hospital or a nursing home.

Meals on Wheels:

◆ provides hot meals
◆ helps people to stay in their own homes and stay independent

Government gives up to 50% of costs to local authority.

The needs of individual elderly people assessed by social work departments
(Patients means tested)

Needs met by, or by a mixture of, local authorities, health boards, private companies or voluntary agencies.

Local authorities and Health Boards (Community Health Partnerships)	Private companies	Voluntary agencies e.g. Age Concern
Health visitors Home helps Social workers Health professionals such as chiropodists House adaptations	Sheltered housing Residential Homes Nursing homes	Meals on wheels Help the Aged Lunch clubs Support groups Respite care

Figure 5.8 Care in the community

- daily visits mean company for the elderly person.

Occupational Therapist (provides a range of home adaptations including):

- stair lifts
- special plugs and sockets
- special baths, toilets and showers
- lower kitchen work surfaces and cupboards
- special alarms.

Day Centres (provide a range of services including):

- day trips
- classes on how to avoid hypothermia
- games and social events such as bingo or sing-along sessions
- hot lunches.

Activities

1 In what ways does community care help meet the physical and emotional needs of elderly people?

2 Study Figure 5.8 and explain how community care works in practice.

3 Why do certain people criticise the policy of care in the community?

4 Study the list of care in the community services. Imagine you are a social worker.

Draw up a care package for an elderly woman of 80 years of age. She has just been released from hospital after having a hip replacement and suffers from arthritis in her hands and wrists.

Meeting the Personal Care Needs of the Elderly

Many elderly people rely on personal care services on an every day basis to maintain their health and dignity.

Help with personal care includes:

- personal hygiene such as bathing, showering, hair washing and oral hygiene
- continence management such as help with the toilet and skin care
- food and diet, including assistance with eating and special diets

- help with immobility
- counselling and support services
- simple treatments such as assistance with medication, application of creams and dressings
- personal assistance such as help with dressing and assistance to get up and go to bed.

One of the key early pieces of legislation passed by the Scottish Parliament was the Community Care and Health Act (Scotland) 2002. This introduced universal free personal and nursing care for the elderly from 1st July 2002. The 2002 Act applies to everyone no matter what their income.

Universal free personal and nursing care has not been introduced by the Labour Government in England.

The 2002 Act followed publication of the report from the Royal Commission on Long Term Care (The Sutherland report) and the establishment of the Care Development Group, whose aim was to 'ensure that older people in Scotland have access to high quality and responsive long term care, in the appropriate setting and on a fair and equitable basis'.

The following is an extract from a Scottish Executive question and answer guide on the introduction of universal free personal care.

Care Homes

- My care home costs are already being fully paid from public funds. Will I see any change?

  No. There will be no change.

- I fully fund my own care. What contribution will I be entitled to?

  You will be entitled to a contribution of £145 a week towards the cost of personal care and a further £65 a week if you also require nursing care.

- If you have capital assets of more than £18,500, you will be expected to use them to fund the parts of your care not covered by the new system.

At Home

- My local authority currently charges for my personal care services. Will these be abolished?

  Yes, if you are aged 65 or over.

The Elderly

◆ **What will I still need to pay for?**

You will still need to pay for non-personal care such as day care, lunch-clubs, meals on wheels, community alarms and help with shopping and housework.

◆ **Will the local authority still be able to charge me for my home help?**

Yes. You can still be charged for non-personal care services.

◆ **Although I own my own home, have savings and a private pension, will I still be entitled to free personal care?**

Yes. Free personal care is available regardless of your income, capital assets or marital status.

Source: Age Concern Scotland Bulletin (abridged)

Activities

1 Why is help with personal care important for the elderly?

2 What types of help would an elderly person get through free personal care?

3 What difference did the Community Care and Health Act (Scotland) 2002 make for poorer pensioners in care homes?

4 What difference did the Act make for richer pensioners who manage to pay for their care homes?

5 'Universal free personal care was a Liberal Democrat policy aimed at helping the rich who vote Lib Dem. It wasn't Labour Party policy and it hasn't helped the poor who had it anyway before the Act was passed.'

Sam Galbraith, former Labour MSP.

Say whether you agree or disagree with Sam Galbraith's statement. Give reason for your answer.

Meeting the Elderly's Financial Needs

Elderly people in Britain receive a variety of help in meeting their health and housing needs. There is one more factor, which has a major bearing on how an elderly person lives – finance.

The Westminster government deals mainly with the financial needs of the elderly, whilst leaving health

and social and care needs to Health Boards and local government. The financial needs of elderly people are normally met in a variety of different ways.

Some benefits are 'means tested' – that is, pensioners get the benefits once their income, including savings is taken into account. Others are 'non-means tested' – that is, all pensioners get them as of right, others are contributory and depend on the level of national insurance contributions paid during a person's working life.

Contributory Benefits – State Pensions

The basic state retirement pension is a contributory benefit. This means that it is based on the national insurance that a person has paid throughout their working lives. It is the main form of financial assistance for the elderly. The current state pension is £82.05 per week for a single person and £131.20 per week for a couple (2005).

Women receive it when they are 60 years of age and men when they are 65. To qualify for the full basic pension a man has to have worked and paid full national insurance contributions for 44 years and a woman for 39 years. People who have not paid full national insurance for these periods have their state pensions reduced.

According to 2002 figures from the Department of Work and Pensions, the average amount of pension entitlement was £79.92 a week. But while men receive £88.14 a week on average, women got only £63.90.

For some, the position is not just unfair, but dire – generally because of gaps in their working lives when they paid no national insurance contributions. Around two million women get between £40 and £50 a week state pension, while another half a million receive less than £30.

Source: Labour Research March 2003

Activities

1 What is the difference between, contributory benefits, non-means tested and means tested benefits?

2 From the information on state pensions, why do you think many women do not receive the full or any state pension?

3 What financial impact does this have on these pensioners?

Non-Means Tested Benefits

- winter fuel allowance of £200 per household is paid at the start of the British winter – around 700,000 households benefit in Scotland

- attendance allowance is paid to those who cannot look after themselves – the amount given depends on the amount of care that a person needs (daytime care or 24-hour care)

- carer's allowances is given to carers if they spend over 35 hours per week looking after a pensioner who has qualified for attendance allowance

- people aged over 75 get a free TV licence.

Means Tested Benefits

Income support is a means tested benefit. It is given to those who have been unable to invest or save enough for their retirement. Income support given to pensioners was called the **minimum income guarantee**.

The minimum income guarantee was replaced by the **pension credit** in October 2003.

The pension credit will seek to ensure that single pensioners do not have an income of less than £109.45 per week and pensioner couples have an income of at least £167.05 a week (as of 2005).

Receiving Income support/pension credit also opens the door to gaining some or all of the following financial benefits:

- **council tax benefit** is one of the benefits you can receive if you are in receipt of income support – depending on any savings, an elderly person can receive up to 100 per cent rebate on their council tax bills

- **housing benefit** helps people with the cost of their rent

- **cold weather payments** are given out when the temperature falls below zero over a 7-day period. A one-off payment of £8.50 is made for every continuous seven day spell of cold weather.

Activities

1 In what ways does the government help elderly people with disabilities?

2 What other means tested benefits can be of benefit to elderly people?

   Look at the text box following these Activities and answer the following questions:
   a) What are the main reasons given for the low take up of means tested benefits?
   b) What is the author's solution to pension poverty and what impact would this have on pensioner incomes?
   c) How might his/her solution not bring all women out of pensioner poverty?

3 'Women are disproportionately affected by poverty faced by those in old age. The Labour government has done little to help them.' With reference to the section on the Financial Needs of the Elderly, in what ways can the author be accused of exaggeration. Give reasons for and against in your answer.

Women are disproportionately affected by poverty faced by those in old age. The Labour government has done little to help them.

It has introduced measures to boost pensioners' income, such as the Minimum Income Guarantee (MIG), but these are means tested and so are reliant on a person's circumstances.

In any case, the take up of such benefits is lower among pensioners than in the population as a whole. The Department of Work and Pensions estimated that between 22 per cent and 36 per cent of pensioners entitled to MIG did not claim it from 1999 to 2000. Around a third of pensioners entitled to council tax benefits and one tenth entitled to housing benefit also did not claim such benefits.

Many reasons have been given for the non-take up of such benefits. These include the complexity of the system – the MIG form, for example, once ran to 40 pages and is still very long at 10 pages. Ignorance of the benefits available is also cited.

Pensioners of this generation still have memories of the stigma that used to attach to means tested benefits.

➤

The government could cut the stigma out of means tested benefits and improve the single pensioner's lot if it restored the link between state pensions and earnings, broken by the Conservative government, but it has steadfastly refused to do so.

Had the link between earnings been restored, the basic state pension for a single person would have been almost half as high again as it is – at £112.05 instead of £75.50 – a difference of over £1,900 a year.

Source: Labour Research March 2003

Council Tax and Housing Benefits

Many older people find council tax a major drain on their income. **Council tax benefit**, which can reduce the bill, is the benefit pensioners are most likely to miss out on. It can be claimed by homeowners as well as tenants. The value of the home is not taken into account.

Housing benefit helps with rent and with certain service charges.

These benefits are based on your income and savings and in general you must have no more than £16,000 in savings.

Currently up to 1.4 million eligible older people miss out on council tax benefit, resulting in up to £580 million remaining unclaimed each year. The average amount unclaimed is £7.50 a week, or £390 a year.

Up to 270,000 eligible older people are not claiming housing benefit, resulting in up to £400m remaining unclaimed each year.

Source: BBC News Service,
September 2003

Activities

1 'Receiving income support opens other benefits doors for elderly people.' Explain what this statement means?

2 Why do you think that so many older people fail to claim council tax and housing benefits, which they are entitled to?

3 What could the government and local councils do to try and help older people claim the benefits available to them?

Investigation

Use the website below to investigate and write a more detailed report on some of the financial benefits available to elderly people:

www.thepensionservice.gov.uk

Heating or Eating?

Fuel poverty is estimated to cause thousands of winter deaths.

The government currently provides cold weather payments of £8.50 to pensioners on income support when the average forecast or recorded temperature falls below 0 degrees Celsius for seven consecutive days.

Age Concern has been campaigning for many years to highlight the plight of pensioners who die of hypothermia because they cannot afford winter fuel bills. It says up to 48,000 more people die in winter than summer in the UK, 94 per cent of whom are elderly.

'It is a simple fact that cold kills' said Age Concern director Sally Green.

Source: Age Concern

Figure 5.9 Heating costs can be difficult for the elderly to manage

'Elderly people often have to make a choice between eating and heating. They either turn off their heating or cut down on food. Being constantly cold or hungry makes them more susceptible to illness. The more often they are ill, the weaker they get, and the less able to cope with cold and hunger. It's a vicious circle.'

Help the Aged Spokesperson

'We know that some people have problems meeting fuel bills after prolonged periods of cold weather, and this Government is determined to help those in most difficulty. We are clear: people should not have to choose between heating and eating.'

Helen Liddell, Scottish Secretary of State,
April 2001

Activities

1 What is hypothermia and why is winter a risky time for the elderly?

2 Why does Age Concern say that many pensioners are in danger from hypothermia?

3 Which of the two statements above do you agree with the most? Give reasons for your decision and say why you reject the other statement.

Fight For the Grey Vote

Figure 5.10 John Swinburn, elected as Regional List MSP for the Scottish Senior Citizen's Unity Party 2003

All the main parties are targeting older people – the grey vote – with promises of more money in their pocket in return for their vote.

The Conservatives have now launched a manifesto for pensioners, claiming that a pensioner couple would be more than £8 a week better off under their proposals. Labour says it has spent an extra £4.5bn a year on pensioners, while the Liberal Democrats want to spend another £4bn a year on the state pension for older people.

All the political parties hope that by helping the grey vote, they will win the support of the UK's most reliable voters and secure public support.

The voting population of the UK is approximately 45.9 million. In the 2001 election only 32.8 million people voted. One third of these votes were cast by elderly people. Less than seven per cent were cast by people aged 18–24, 2.2 million. The UK's eleven million pensioners are far more likely to vote than their younger counterparts.

Gordon Lishman, director of Age Concern, says that 'the potential rewards are high for those candidates and parties who show they are genuine in wishing to meet the aspirations of older people'. (Source: BBC News Online, 22.05.2001.)

FACTFILE
The Grey Vote

There are over twice as many people over 60 than there are aged 18–24. Twelve million compared to five million.

The proportion of people over 60 who say they voted in the 2001 election is twice the proportion of 18–24s. 87.5 per cent compared to 44 per cent.

80 per cent of over-65s agree that 'everyone has a duty to vote'.

Only 36 per cent of 18–24 year olds agree that 'everyone has a duty to vote'.

85 per cent of over-65s think that people should vote even if they do not care who wins.

50 per cent of 18–24 year olds think that you should only vote if you care who wins.

96 per cent of over 65s disagree with the statement 'it's not really worth voting'.

13 per cent of 18–24 year olds agree with the statement 'it's not really worth voting'.

Activities

1 'Young people in the 18–24 year age range are the group with the biggest interest in politics. They are just as likely to vote as any other age group.' Use the information in the factfile to explain why the person making the above statement could be accused of exaggeration.

GENERAL/CREDIT

Voluntary Organisations / Pressure Groups

As well as the help provided by national and local government, a range of voluntary organisations exists to help elderly people and also to promote the interests of elderly people. The best known of these groups are Age Concern and Help the Aged.

These organisations act as elderly pressure groups as well as voluntary agencies which look after the interests of older people. The money to run these voluntary groups comes mainly from donations, fundraising, charity shops and some grants.

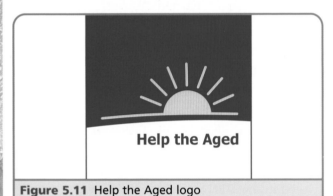

Figure 5.11 Help the Aged logo

Help the Aged

Help the Aged is Britain's leading charity working for older people. The main aim of the charity is to try and help elderly people to lead as happy and secure a life as possible.

The organisation has four main priorities:

◆ **to fight poverty**
◆ **to reduce loneliness**

Figure 5.12 Negative ideas about elderly people need to be challenged

214

◆ **to ensure older people receive good care**
◆ **to fight against negative ideas about elderly people.**

It works towards these goals by campaigning, carrying out or funding research and providing services, advice and information to support independent living.

Age Concern Scotland

Age Concern Scotland works throughout Scotland to help make the lives of older people more secure, comfortable, dignified and enjoyable.

Their aims are to ensure that older people in Scotland have:

◆ **their rights upheld**
◆ **their needs addressed**
◆ **their voices heard**
◆ **choice and control over all aspects of their lives.**

They support a wide network of older people and older people's groups, which in turn provide local services to older people in their own communities.

In addition, Age Concern Scotland offers a range of services directly itself. They work with members to develop locally-based services which draw on local needs, and volunteers as appropriate.

It provides information to meet the needs of older people living in the community, to publicise issues relevant to older people, and to inform them of their rights. Age Concern Scotland also campaigns with older people for:

◆ **an adequate retirement income**
◆ **improvement of older people's housing conditions**
◆ **better health and care services for older people**
◆ **an end to age discrimination.**

Activities

www.schools.helptheaged.org.uk

www.ageconcernscotland.org.uk

Use the websites above to write a report about the work of one of the voluntary organisations.

You should use the bullet points given as headings for your research.

Inequality in Retirement

A common misconception is that all elderly people are in the same financial situation. Not all pensioners are short of money.

Some may have savings of their own, an occupational pension, investments or even a part time job, as well as collecting their state pensions. This group of people has more money and a better lifestyle than people with only their state pension to rely on each week.

The most popular way of preparing for retirement is to contribute to an occupational pension. Employees pay money into their company pension scheme each week and when they retire they get money back each week in addition to their state pension. This means that they should be able to

buy necessities, pay bills and still have money left over for things that other pensioners may consider luxuries.

Membership of employer's pension schemes varies, depending on the type of jobs that people do.

The value of the pension also varies depending on how much is paid in by the employee and how much is paid by the employer. The more that is paid in, the higher the value of the pension on retirement. Pensioners who are relatively well off in retirement have been called many different names.

The most common nicknames are **Woopies** and **glams** or **SKIing** pensioners. Woopies stands for Well-Off Older People and Glams for Greying, Leisured, Affluent and Married.

The newer term SKIing stands for Spending the Kids Inheritance.

Members	Classification		
	Managerial	Intermediate	Manual
Men			
Occupational pension	69	62	40
Personal pension	25	14	21
Any pension	81	69	56
Women			
Occupational pension	73	58	33
Personal pension	15	11	10
Any pension	80	65	41

Figure 5.13 Percentages of people in different work groups with pensions
Source *Living in Britain* (2001)

Members	Wage					
	£100–200	£200–300	£300–400	£400–500	£500–600	£600+
Men						
Occupational pension	20	36	56	66	68	73
Personal pension	9	17	23	23	25	29
Any pension	29	48	71	79	85	86
Women						
Occupational pension	26	53	68	78	83	80
Personal pension	8	12	12	18	13	23
Any pension	33	61	73	86	88	89

Figure 5.14 Percentages of people in different earning groups with pensions
Source *Living in Britain* (2001)

Many firms actively pursue these older people as there are growing numbers in these groups who have money to spend. Figures show that the over-55s have over 43 per cent of the net wealth of the country.

Building firms and holiday companies are especially interested in this group and there is now a large market for retirement property and off-peak holidays for older people.

Activities

1 For what reasons do some elderly people enjoy a higher standard of living than others?

2 Examine Figure 5.13. What are the main factors in determining whether people have an occupational pension or not?

3 Explain the terms woopies, glams and SKIing pensioners.

4 Why would holiday companies and building firms be interested in these groups of people?

5 'Most elderly people often have to make a choice between eating or heating. The majority live in real poverty.' Help the Aged Spokesperson.

   Use the text box following to explain why this person could be accused of exaggeration.

'Party Pensioners' living it up in retirement

Six out of ten retired people say that they are having the time of their lives – collectively spending £1.5 billion a month on travel, meals out and hobbies. Around 83 per cent of people aged over 50 also say that they have no intention of holding back during retirement, even if this means spending their children's inheritance, according to Sainsbury's Bank.

The shift is part of a new trend emerging among well-off retirees dubbed SKIing, or Spending the Kids Inheritance, where people enjoy their hard earned cash themselves rather than leaving it to their children when they die.

Four out of ten people say they have fulfilled life-long ambitions or plans since they gave up work, with 28 per cent travelling, 18 per cent starting new hobbies and 3 per cent trying adventure activities such as white water rafting.

Retired people collectively spend an average of £535 million a month on travel, while splashing out £344 million on meals out, £332 million on presents for themselves or their loved ones and £310 million on their hobbies.

But Sainsbury's Bank warned that this trend means younger people would have to begin saving for retirement even earlier, as they not only faced the prospect of less generous company pensions, but they could also no longer rely on inheriting from their parents.

Mairi Hutchison, long-term saving's manager at Sainsbury's Bank, said 'It is clear that these 'party pensioners' are having the time of their lives, but the younger generation will generally have less generous company and state pensions to look forward to.'

Source: *Scotsman*, 28 October 2003

Ageing Europe

Britain is not the only European country to have an increasing number of elderly people. It is a matter which concerns other European nations. Italy, Belgium and Greece all have a higher proportion of people over 60 years of age than the UK, and the number of people over 60 is projected to increase in all the countries of the EU.

So Britain is not alone in having an increasing number of elderly people, but are all European pensioners treated the same? British pensioners do not think so.

They point to the fact that pensioners in other EU countries receive more money in their state pensions and very often receive extra benefits, which UK pensioners would like to have.

It is very difficult to compare pensions in the different EU member states as each country operates a different pension scheme, gives different benefits and has different costs of living.

In purely financial terms UK pensioners are the poor relations when it comes to direct comparisons. The UK government, however, would point to the fact that the cost of living is different in each of the EU countries.

The cost of living in Germany is 15 per cent higher than it is in the UK, and prices in France are 7 per cent higher than those in the UK.

(Source: Eurostat)

Another way to examine state pensions is to look at the amount that people get in their pensions compared with what they received when they were in work. In Scotland, a pensioner receives on average 46 per cent of their former wage as their state pension. In Germany a pensioner would receive 82 per cent of their former wage. In France a pensioner would receive 92 per cent of their former wage. (Source: Eurostat)

Indeed, the governments of large industrial countries of the EU such as France, Germany and Italy are facing the prospect of changing their pension regulations and have experienced a great deal of protest from pensioners and workers because of this.

Activities

1   'British pensioners consider themselves to be the poor relations of Europe.' Why do UK pensioners feel that this statement is justified?

2   How does the UK government explain the differing amounts of money that pensioners in EU countries receive?

Pensioners' Benefits in Selected EU States

British pensioners claim that it is not only in the amount of cash, which they receive, in their state pensions, which disadvantages them. Pensioner groups claim that other EU countries actually give their pensioners much more in the way of general benefits. A look at the range of benefits available in some EU countries should help you make up your own mind.

Activities

1   Make a list placing the countries in order of best for pensioners to the worst. You must also give reasons for your choices.

2   'British pensioners are easily the worst off in the whole of Europe.' (pensioner spokesperson) Using the information from the selected countries, how could the person making this statement be accused of exaggeration?

3   Could the UK learn any lessons from other EU countries in the way that pensioners are treated?

United Kingdom

Christmas bonus of £10
Winter fuel payment of £200
Cold weather payments
Free TV licences for over 75s
Travel reductions in regions they live in

France

Free telephone installation
Cheap telephone calls
Free TV licence for all pensioners
Cheap nationwide travel
Free travel on Paris Metro

Denmark

Half price TV licence for all pensioners
Half price nationwide travel
Reductions on telephone bills

Germany

Reduced TV licence fee
Reduced travel costs
Reduced telephone calls

Ireland

Free nationwide travel
Free electricity
Free telephone installation
Extra pension for living alone

Holland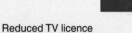

Reduced TV licence
Half-price nationwide travel
One week's free nationwide travel per year
An extra month's pension every year
Extra pension for holiday allowance

Belgium

Free TV licence
Half-price telephone charges
Half-price travel nationwide
Extra pensions for holidays
A extra month's pension per year

Figure 5.15 Benefits for the elderly in selected EU countries
Source Glaswegian Newspaper

Investigating on the Web

The following websites have been used in this book and are useful sources of further information.

UK Parliament and Government

www.parliament.uk
www.gov.uk
www.HM-treasury.gov.uk
www.royal.gov.uk
www.europa.eu.int

Political Parties and Voting

www.labour.org.uk
www.conservatives.org.uk
www.libdems.org.uk
www.snp.org.uk
www.scottishsocialistparty.org
www.greenparty.org.uk
www.obv.org.uk

MPs

www.barbara-follett.org.uk
www.sarwar.org.uk
www.nigelgriffiths.co.uk
www.peterduncan.org.uk

Scottish Parliament and Government

www.scottish.parliament.uk
www.scotland.gov.uk
www.gro-scotland.gov.uk

Local Government

www.glasgow.gov.uk
www.aberdeenshire.gov.uk
www.cosla.gov.uk
www.alba.org.uk

Participation – Pressure Groups

www.bma.org.uk
www.shelter.org.uk
www.ashscotland.org.uk
www.cnduk.org
www.mcspotlight.org
www.stopwar.org.uk
www.foe-scotland.org.uk
www.greenpeace.org.uk

Participation in the Workplace

www.amicustheunion.org.uk
www.eis.org.uk
www.fbu.org.uk
www.pcs.org.uk
www.rmt.org.uk
www.tgwu.org.uk
www.tuc.org.uk
www.unison-scotland.org.uk
www.bized.ac.uk

Employment/Unemployment

www.statistics.gov.uk
www.womenandequalityunit.gov.uk
www.scrol.gov.uk
www.dwp.gov.uk
www.dti.gov.uk
www.europa.eu.int/comm/eurostat

Elderly

www.gro-scotland.gov.uk
www.scotland.gov.uk/cru
www.helptheaged.org.uk
www.sunrisemedical.co.uk
www.aidcall-alarm.co.uk
www.ageconcernscotland.org.uk
www.thepensionservice.gov.uk

Family

www.scrol.gov.uk
www.nch.org.uk

Notes

Many of the websites above feature in more than one topic for instance the Scottish Executive website www.scotland.gov.uk is a useful portal to access the most up to date information on many issues affecting Scotland, not just on government and politics.

The UK government website www.gov.uk provides a similar function for 'reserved' matters and issues affecting England and Wales.

Pressure Group Issues

www.redpepper.org.uk The links section accessed through the homepage provides a comprehensive list of most UK (and some international) pressure groups and access to their websites.

Index

Figures in **Bold Blue** refer to 'Foundation/General' chapters.

Figures in **Bold Green** refer to 'General/Credit' chapters.

A

ACAS (Arbitration Conciliation and Advisory Service) **101**
Additional Member System (AMS) **24, 28, 68, 69**
adversarial politics **53**
age, and employment **128–9, 155–6**
Age Concern Scotland **196, 214**
agreements (union) **88, 96**
Alternative Voting System **24, 64**
amalgamated unions **95**
assisted areas **136, 164–5**
attendance allowance **193, 211**

B

Backbenchers **14**
ballot box **27**
ballot paper **27**
bed-blocking **189, 205**
benefits
    contributory pension **210**
    council tax **193, 194, 211, 212**
    elderly **193–5, 210–12**
    family **171–2, 179–80**
    lone parents **169–71, 178–9**
    means-tested **211–12**
    non-means tested **211**
    pensioners' in European Union (EU) **198, 217**
Best Value **76–7**
bills **3, 7, 48**
    legislative process **8–9, 48**
    Scottish Parliament **30–1, 68, 71–2**
budget **45**
by-elections **2**

C

Cabinet **4, 5, 46–7**
candidates **16**
Care in the Community **191–3, 207–10**
    criticisms **193, 208**
    services **191–2, 208–9**
care homes **209**
casting vote **35**
central government **33**
and local government **39–40, 76–80**
Chief Whip **14, 51**
child benefit **169, 178**
Child Support Agency **173, 180–2**
Child Tax Credit **171–2, 179**
childcare, and employment **170–1, 178–9**
civil service **4**
coalition government **29–30, 39**
cold weather payments **193, 211**
collective bargaining **88, 96**
community care **191–3, 207–10**
community nurses **189, 191, 205, 208**
Compulsory Competitive Tendering (CCT) **76–7**
computers, and work **118, 142**
Conservatives **19, 57**
    and unions **92, 106**
constituencies **3, 43**
    MPs' work in **16–17, 54–5**
constitutional monarchy **2–3, 43–4**
CoSLA (Convention of Scottish Local Authorities) **40, 76, 78, 80**
council tax **33**
    benefits **193, 194, 211, 212**
    and housing benefit **194, 212**
councillors **16**
    election of **33, 34–7**
    full-time **38–9, 74–6**
    profiles **37–8, 74**
    work of **36–7, 74–6**
councils **33, 73, 76**
    representativeness **78–9**
courts **5, 59**
craft unions **85, 87, 95**

D

day centres **192, 209**
debates, parliamentary **10, 49**
dementia (senile) **190, 206**
democracy **1–2, 43**
    local **79**
    and pressure groups **42, 83–4**
demonstrations **82–3**
devolution **27, 66**
    differences **72**
directives (EU) **109**
disability
and employment **130–1, 156–7**
    MPs with **13**
division lobbies **14**
divorce **168, 176–7**

E

education **170, 179**
elderly **183–98, 199–217**
    financial needs **193–5, 210–12**
    health care needs **189–93, 205–7**
    housing needs **188–9, 202–5**
    increase in **183–4, 199**
    personal care needs **209–10**
    in Scotland **184–6, 200–1**
elections **2, 6, 23**
    participation in **25–6**
    selection process **11**
electoral register **25**
electoral system
    British **21–3, 61–2**
    fairness **23–7, 62–6**
electorate **1, 24, 43**
employment **112–37, 138–65**
    age and **128–9, 155–6**
    by industry **123–4, 147–8**
    changes in **91–2, 114–15, 139**
    and childcare **170–1, 178–9**
    and disability **130–1, 156–7**
    and globalisation **144**
    and race **126–7, 152–4**
    women and **122–3, 124**
equality, at work **94, 122–3**
ethnic minorities
    employment **126–7, 152–4**
    in local councils **74**
    in Parliament **10, 12, 51**
    unemployment **127, 154–5**
    and unions **91–2**
    Europe
    ageing **197–8, 216–17**
    unemployment in **121–3, 145–7**
    and unions **94, 109**
European Regional Development Fund **147**
European Social Fund **147**
European Union (EU)
    action on unemployment **122, 146–7**
    age legislation **128–9, 155**
    directives **109**
    information and consultation

directive **94**
and Parliament **10**
pensioners' benefits **198, 217**
working time directive **94**
European Works Council Directive
109
executive **3, 4–5, 46–7**
extended family **166–7, 175**

F
families with children **166–74,
175–82**
family
benefits **171–2, 179–80**
types **166–9, 175–8**
Family Leave Directives (EU) **109**
finance, local government **33,
73**
First Past the Post **11, 21, 28, 34,
39, 43, 61, 68, 80**
advantages and disadvantages
22, 23, 24, 62–4
floating voters **22**
freedom of speech **40**
Front Benches **14**

G
general bills **48**
general election **2, 6, 61–3**
timing **23**
general unions **85, 87, 88, 96**
geriatric wards **189, 206**
globalisation, and jobs **144**
government
and the elderly **183–4, 199**
role of **44–5**
spending **45–6**
structure of British **3–7, 44–7**
use of pressure groups **41**
Government Bills **7, 48**
GPs (General Practitioners) **189,
206**
grassroots **89**
Green Paper **8, 48**
grey vote **195, 213**
group meetings **36**

H
health **170, 179**
elderly in Scotland **186, 201**
health care, needs of the elderly
189–93, 205–7
health centres **189, 206**
Help the Aged **195–6, 214**
home helps **191, 208**
House of Commons **3, 13–16,
44, 47, 51–3**
working hours **17**

House of Lords **4, 5, 20–1, 47,
58–60**
appeal court **10, 59**
functions **20, 58**
political parties in **20–1**
reform **59**
housing **170, 179**
needs of the elderly **186–8,
202–5**
housing benefit
and council tax **194, 212**
for the elderly **193, 211, 212**

I
income, family **169–70, 178**
income support **193**
industrial action **88–9, 97–9**
types of **88**
industrial conflict **85**
industrial dispute **88**
industrial unions **87, 96**
industries
employment by **114, 123–4,
147–8**
primary **147**
secondary **147**
tertiary **147**
inequality
in retirement **196–7, 215–16**
in the workplace **124–8,
148–52**
invalidity allowances **193**

J
job creation **120–1**
Job Seekers Allowance (JSA)
133–4, 160–1
contributions-based **133, 160**
income-based **133, 160**
Jobcentre Plus **134, 161**
judges **5, 59–60**
judiciary **3, 5–6, 59–60**

L
labour force **112, 138**
Scotland **116–17, 141**
Labour Force Survey **138**
Labour Party **19, 57–8**
and unions **92–3, 107**
see also New Labour
Labour-Liberal Democrat Coalition
29–30, 79–80
leader of the council **34**
legislation **7–9, 47–8, 49**
legislature **3–4**
legitimisation **48**
Liberal Democrats **19, 29–30,
79–80**

lobbying **41, 82**
local government **33–4, 73–80**
and central government
39–40, 76–80
elections **39–40**
finance **33, 73**
modernising **77–8**
services **33, 73**
lone parents **167, 170–1, 175**
benefits **169–71, 178–9**
and pressure groups **173–4,
182**
Lord Chancellor **5**
low pay **131–2, 158–9**

M
majority government **22**
manifesto **2, 3, 7, 34, 44**
manufacturing sector **91, 114**
Meals on Wheels **192, 208–9**
Member of the European
Parliament (MEP) **16, 43**
Member of Parliament (MP) **3, 43**
disabled **13**
work of **16–18, 53–5, 56**
Member of the Scottish
Parliament (MSP) **16**
constituency MSPs **31, 68–9**
independent MSPs **69**
regional list MSPs **31, 69, 83**
role of **31–2, 71**
minimum income guarantee **211**
ministers **4**
minority government **22**
monarch **4**

N
National Health Service (NHS) **189**
services for the elderly **189,
205–6, 207**
national minimum wage **93,
131–2, 158–9**
for and against **132, 159**
National Party List (NPL) **24, 65**
New Deal **134–5, 161**
50 plus **135, 163**
New Labour **19–20, 58**
new technology **117–20, 142–5**
for and against **119, 144–5**
and employment **120–1, 144**
and productivity **143**
nuclear family **166, 175**
nursing homes **188, 205**

O
OAPs (Old Age Pensioners) **184,
200**
opinion polls **23**

Opposition, Her Majesty's Official
6, 44
MPs 55–6
role of 15, 52–3
outsourcing 108–9

P
Parliament 3–4, 47
bicameral 47
and equality 10–13, 50–1
work of 9–10, 48–50
Part Time Work Directive (EU) 109
Partnership Agreement 29,
79–80
party line 14
peers 4, 47, 59
pension credits 193, 211
pensions 129, 156
contributions-based 193, 210
occupational 196, 215
state retirement 193, 210–11
petitions 72–3
PFI (Private Finance Initiative) 108
policy decisions 36
political levy 92
political participation 25–6
political parties 1–2, 18–20, 43,
44, 57–8
become government 6–7
list 18, 61
policies 61
polling cards 27
polling stations 27
population
ageing in Europe 197–8,
216–17
changes 183–5, 199, 200–1
positive action 11
pressure groups 40–2, 80–4
and democracy 42, 83–4
government use of 41
help for the elderly 195–6, 214
insider and outsider 81–2
and lone parents 173–4, 182
membership of 41
and Parliament 41
promotional 41, 81
sectional 40–1, 80–1
tactics 41, 81–2
trade unions as 95
primary care, for the elderly 189,
205
Prime Minister 4, 6, 46
Prime Minister's Question Time 9,
41, 49
private bills 8, 48
Private Member's Bills 7–8, 41,
48

professional unions 88
Proportional Representation 11,
24, 39, 68, 83
advantages and disadvantages
of 24–5
systems 24, 65–6
protests 82–3
provost 34
Public Bills 8, 48

Q
Queen 3, 43–4
quota formula 24

R
race, and employment 126–7,
152–4
rank and file 89, 99
referendum 27, 66
regional aid 136, 164–5
Regional Selective Assistance
(RSA) 136, 164–5
representative democracy 1–2, 43
representatives, pressures on
16–18, 53–7
residential homes 188, 204–5
respite care 189, 206
responsibilities, and rights 40, 89
restrictive practices 97–8
retirement 129, 156
inequality in 196–7, 215–16
rights, and responsibilities 40, 89
Royal Assent 3, 9, 31, 43, 48

S
Scottish Enterprise 135–6, 163–4
Scottish Executive 67, 76
Partnership Agreement 79–80
Scottish Parliament 27–32,
66–73
bills 30–1, 72
committees in 31
devolved matters 29, 30, 66,
71
elections to 27–8, 68
First Minister 29
legislation 30–1
and local government elections
39–40
mandatory committees 31, 71
Presiding Officer 32
and the public 72–3
reserved matters 29, 66
subject committees 31, 71
women in 11, 70–1
work of 29, 66–8
working hours 17
Scottish Trade Union Congress

(STUC) 90, 100
scrutiny 9, 49
seats
marginal 22, 62
safe 22, 62
secret ballot 27
separation of powers 3
service sector 91, 114, 116
Shadow Cabinet 14, 15, 52–3
sheltered housing 187, 202–3
shop stewards 89, 99–100
Single Transferable Vote (STV) 24,
40, 65–6, 80
Speaker of the House of
Commons 5, 14
sponsoring 41, 92
standards of living, Scotland 185,
201
Statute Book 9, 48
strikes 88, 97, 98
super unions 85
surgeries, councillors' 37, 74

T
technology, *see* new technology
trade unions *see* unions
Trades Union Congress (TUC)
89–90, 100, 102–3

U
unemployed, the 112–14, 138–9
claimant count 113, 138
helping 133–7, 159–65
intentionally 113
women 113
young 113
unemployment 91, 112–37,
138–65
cyclical 113, 139
in Europe 121–3, 145–7
male 123
North-South divide 115–16,
140–1
seasonal 113, 139
structural 113, 139
types 113, 139
unions 85–94, 95–111
Branch 89, 100
characteristics 103–4
common policy 90, 102
Conservatives and 92, 106
defined 85, 95
District/Regional Office 89, 100
and ethnic minorities 91–2
and Europe 94, 109
General Secretary 100
job security and pay 105–6
Labour Party and 92–3, 107

members **86, 89, 90, 99, 102, 103**
National Conference **89, 100**
National Executive **89, 100**
National Office **100**
negotiations **85, 88–9, 96–7**
organisation **89, 99–100**
reasons for joining or not **86–7, 96**
recruitment and retention **105**
reforms **93–4**
rights and responsibilities **89**
types of **85, 87–8, 95–6**
women and **91–2**

V
voluntary organisations, help for the elderly **195–6, 214**
voter apathy **2, 26, 62**
voter turnout **2, 62**
voting **25–6**

W
ward **33**
welfare state **133, 159**
Whip system **14–15, 51–2**
White Paper **8**
white-collar unions **85, 88, 91, 96**

winter fuel allowance **193, 194, 211, 212–13**
women
    equality at work **94, 123**
    inequality in the workplace **124–8, 148–52**
    in Parliament **10–11, 50, 70–1**
    unemployed **113**
    and unions **91–2**
    and work **122–3, 124**
Workers on Fixed Term Contracts Directives (EU) **109**
Working Tax Credit **172, 179–80**